Grade 4

TEA

Making Meaning®

SECOND EDITION

DEVELOPMENTAL STUDIES CENTER™

Strategies That Build
Comprehension and Community

Table of Contents

VOLUME 2

Unit 6 • Making Inferences: Fiction and Narrative Nonfiction 279
    Week 1 280
    Week 2 298
    Week 3 318
    Week 4 338

Unit 7 • Analyzing Text Structure: Expository Nonfiction 355
    Week 1 356
    Week 2 382
    Week 3 404
    Week 4 430

Unit 8 • Determining Important Ideas and Summarizing:
Narrative Nonfiction 445
    Week 1 446
    Week 2 468
    Week 3 484
    Week 4 506
    Week 5 525

Unit 9 • Revisiting the Reading Life 539
    Week 1 540

Texts in the Program 562

Bibliography 567

Blackline Masters (volume 2)

Unit 6

Making Inferences

FICTION AND NARRATIVE NONFICTION

During this unit, the students make inferences to understand characters and continue to use text structure to explore narrative text. They practice using schema to articulate all they think they know about a topic before they read, and they make inferences to understand causal relationships in nonfiction. During IDR, the students use comprehension strategies to make sense of their independent reading. Socially, they continue to practice the group skills of asking one another clarifying questions, including one another, and contributing to group work. They also have a check-in class meeting.

Week 1 *Amelia's Road* by Linda Jacobs Altman

Week 2 *Peppe the Lamplighter* by Elisa Bartone

Week 3 *Coming to America* by Betsy Maestro

Week 4 *A Picture Book of Harriet Tubman* by David A. Adler

Week 1

Overview

UNIT 6: MAKING INFERENCES
Fiction and Narrative Nonfiction

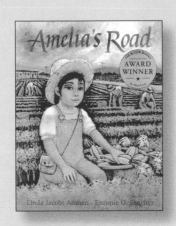

Amelia's Road
by Linda Jacobs Altman, illustrated by Enrique O. Sanchez
(Lee & Low, 1993)

Amelia Martinez, a child of migrant workers, fulfills her dream of finding a place to call her own.

ALTERNATIVE BOOKS

Virgie Goes to School with Us Boys
by Elizabeth Fitzgerald Howard

Flossie & the Fox by Patricia C. McKissack

Comprehension Focus

- Students *make inferences* to understand characters.

- Students continue to *use text structure* to explore narrative text.

- Students read independently.

Social Development Focus

- Students analyze the effect of their behavior on others and on the group work.

- Students develop the group skills of asking clarifying questions, including one another, and contributing to group work.

DO AHEAD

- Prior to Day 1, decide how you will randomly assign partners to work together during the unit.

- Prepare the "Clues to Inferences in *Amelia's Road*" chart (see Day 2, Step 2 on page 286).

- Make transparencies of the "Excerpt from *Amelia's Road*" (BLM19–BLM20).

- Prepare the directions chart for Guided Strategy Practice (See Day 3, Step 2 on page 291).

- Prepare the chart for Independent Strategy Practice (see Day 4, Step 3 on page 295).

- (Optional) Prepare to model making inferences about characters in independent reading (see Day 4, Step 4 on page 296).

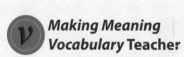

Making Meaning Vocabulary Teacher

If you are teaching Developmental Studies Center's *Making Meaning Vocabulary* program, teach Vocabulary Week 15 this week. For more information, see the *Making Meaning Vocabulary Teacher's Manual*.

Day 1

Read-aloud

In this lesson, the students:

- Begin working with new partners
- Hear and discuss a story
- Discuss setting and plot
- Read independently for up to 30 minutes
- Include one another
- Contribute to group work

Materials

- *Amelia's Road*
- "Self-monitoring Questions" chart

Being a Writer™ **Teacher**

You can either have the students work with their *Being a Writer* partner or assign them a different partner for the *Making Meaning* lessons.

1 ▶ **Pair/Group Students and Review "Heads Together"**

Randomly assign partners; then assign pairs to groups of four and have them sit together. Explain that for the next four weeks they will work with these assigned partners and groups.

Remind the students that they learned to use "Heads Together" the previous week. Ask:

 Q *What did you learn in your last group that might help your new group work together well? Put your heads together and talk about your ideas.*

Have a few groups share what they talked about, and explain that this week you would like them to continue to focus on contributing to the group discussion and including everyone in the discussion. Point out that it is every student's responsibility to participate in the discussion, and it is every group's responsibility to make sure all the members feel welcome to participate. Tell them that you will check in on how they did at the end of the lesson.

2 ▶ **Introduce *Amelia's Road***

Remind the students that they have been making inferences to better understand stories they hear and read. Explain that this week they will continue to explore inference and revisit story elements—character, setting, conflict, and plot.

Show the cover of *Amelia's Road* and read the title and the names of the author and illustrator. Explain that the main character in the story is Amelia Martinez, who is the daughter of migrant farm workers. Explain that migrant farm workers move from farm to farm throughout the harvest season to find work gathering crops. Often, children like Amelia work in the fields alongside their parents.

 Read *Amelia's Road* Aloud

Read the book aloud, showing the illustrations.

Suggested Vocabulary

grim: gloomy, unpleasant (p. 5)

shanties: small, poorly built cabins (p. 5)

bruise the fruit: handle the fruit roughly, causing a dark spot to form on the skin (p. 12)

wondrous: amazing (p. 18)

permanent: meant to last a long time (p. 18)

ELL Vocabulary

English Language Learners may benefit from discussing additional vocabulary, including:

tidy: neat and clean (p. 7)

settle down: live in one place (p. 8)

harvest: the gathering of crops that are ripe (p. 11)

shortcut: quicker way of reaching a place (p. 16)

freshly turned ground: ground where someone has recently been digging (p. 27)

 Discuss the Story in Groups and as a Class

First in groups, and then as a whole class, discuss:

Q *What happens in this story (or what is the plot)?*

Q *Is the setting (time and place) an important part of this story? Why do you think so?*

ELL Note

You might preview the text and illustrations with the students prior to reading the book aloud to the class. During the reading, you might stop periodically to have the students briefly discuss what is happening in the story. Possible stops are at the bottom of pages 7, 14, and 23.

Teacher Note

As groups talk, circulate among them and note both groups in which all members are participating well and groups in which only some members are participating. Be ready to share your observations at the end of the lesson.

Students might say:

"The setting is important because the story takes place where migrant workers work, maybe California or Texas."

"I think the setting is important because the story is about migrant workers and how they move from farm to farm to work. It wouldn't make sense for the story to happen in a city or in a desert."

Facilitate interaction among groups and students during the whole-class discussion using questions such as:

Q *Who will confirm [Travis's] thinking by repeating back what you heard [him] say?*

 Q *Put your heads together in your group and discuss whether you agree or disagree with what [Travis] just said.*

Explain that the students will explore inferences they make in *Amelia's Road* tomorrow.

5▶ Discuss "Heads Together"

Facilitate a brief discussion about how the students did contributing and including one another during "Heads Together." Ask:

Q *Was it easy or difficult for you to contribute to your group's discussion? Why?*

Q *What might make it difficult for a group member to contribute? What can groups do to make sure everyone feels comfortable contributing?*

Share examples of successes or problems you observed as the students worked in their groups of four.

INDIVIDUALIZED DAILY READING

 ## Review and Practice Self-monitoring

Refer to the "Self-monitoring Questions" chart and review the questions. Remind the students that it is important to stop to think about what they are reading and use the questions to help them track when they are understanding their reading, and when they are not. When they are not understanding, they may need to reread, use a comprehension strategy, or get a different book.

Have the students read books at their appropriate reading levels independently for up to 30 minutes. Stop them at 10-minute intervals and have them monitor their comprehension by thinking about the charted questions.

Circulate among the students and ask individuals to read a passage to you and tell you what it is about.

At the end of the reading time, have a brief whole-class discussion about using the self-monitoring questions to track their reading comprehension. Ask and briefly discuss questions such as:

Q *How does noticing if you don't understand what you are reading help you when you read?*

Q *Why does rereading help you make sense of text?*

Q *Which comprehension strategy do you find the most helpful? Why?*

> ### Self-monitoring Questions
>
> - Do I know what is happening in my text right now?

 Note

To support your English Language Learners, consider modeling reading a text and stopping periodcally to ask yourself the self-monitoring questions listed on the chart. Discuss each question with your students to make sure they understand the process.

Day 2

Materials

- *Amelia's Road*
- "Clues to Inferences in *Amelia's Road*" chart, prepared ahead (see Step 2)
- "Reading Comprehension Strategies" chart

Guided Strategy Practice

In this lesson, the students:

- *Make inferences* about a character as they hear a story
- Discuss character and conflict
- Read independently for up to 30 minutes
- Ask clarifying questions
- Contribute to group work

▶1 Review Confirming One Another's Thinking and Asking Clarifying Questions

Briefly review that several weeks ago the students learned to ask their partners clarifying questions. Explain that you would like them to practice this in their group today.

Briefly discuss the kinds of questions and statements the students have used to clarify what others said.

▶2 Highlight Clues to Inferences in *Amelia's Road*

Remind the students that they heard *Amelia's Road* yesterday. Direct their attention to the "Clues to Inferences in *Amelia's Road*" chart, on which you have written:

> "Amelia sighed. Other fathers remembered days and dates. Hers remembered crops."

> "There, where the accidental road ended, stood a most wondrous tree. It was old beyond knowing, and quite the sturdiest, most permanent thing Amelia had ever seen."

> "For the first time in her life, she didn't cry when her father took out the road map."

Explain that these are sentences in the story from which a reader can infer how Amelia feels. Read the sentences aloud. Then explain that you will read the story aloud again, and that you will stop after each of these lines and have the students put their heads together to talk about Amelia's feelings.

◀ **Teacher Note**

You may want to remind the students that when they *infer*, or *make inferences*, they use clues from the story to figure out something that is not stated directly.

3 ▶ Reread *Amelia's Road* and Use "Heads Together" to Discuss Inferences

Reread the story, slowly and clearly. After each passage on the chart (on pages 11, 18, and 31), stop, reread the passage, and then have the groups use "Heads Together" to discuss:

Q *What can you infer (figure out) about how Amelia is feeling from this passage?*

Students might say:

"We think that Amelia is probably angry at her dad because he can't remember her birthday. All he does is think about the crops and his work."

"We think that Amelia is amazed by the tree, which is big and old. And it's the kind of tree she'd like to have in front of her dream house."

"We inferred that Amelia is feeling okay about her life now. She may not like it much, but now she has the tree and the road and the treasure box to come back to."

Have one or two groups report their inference for each passage and the clues in the passage or story that helped them to make the inference. Then reread the passage and continue reading to the next stop. Do not spend too long at any one stop.

◀ **Teacher Note**

Hearing from only one or two groups at each stop will keep the lesson moving.

If groups disagree significantly on inferences that make sense for any of the three "clues to inferences," discuss this before continuing with the lesson. Ask the students to refer to the text to support their opinions. Ask question such as:

Q *What do you think Amelia is thinking at that moment? Why does that make sense?*

Q *Why is Amelia so excited about the tree? What in the book makes you think that?*

FACILITATION TIP

During this unit, we encourage you to **avoid repeating or paraphrasing** students' responses. Repeating what students say when they speak too softly or paraphrasing them when they don't speak clearly teaches the students to listen to you but not to one another. Help the students learn to take responsibility by asking one another to speak up or by asking a question if they don't understand what a classmate has said.

4 ▶ Discuss Character and Conflict in the Story as a Class

Facilitate a whole-class discussion, using the following questions:

Q *What problem, or conflict, does Amelia face in* Amelia's Road? *Does she resolve (work out) the problem? How?*

Students might say:

"Amelia is frustrated because she moves all the time. When she finds the tree, she feels better because now she has a place to come back to—sort of a home."

"I agree with [Loren]. I don't think Amelia feels like she belongs anywhere until she buries the treasure box. The box is a record of her life."

Q *How does Amelia change in the story? What in the story makes you think that?*

Have one or two students respond to each question. As volunteers share their ideas, prompt the students to confirm one another's thinking and ask clarifying questions by asking:

Q *What did you hear [Sandeep] say? Did [Mattie] get it right, [Sandeep]?*

Q *What questions do you want to ask [Sandeep] about what he said?*

As the students discuss the conflict and the change in Amelia's personality, point out that they are using inference to make sense of these important elements of the story. Explain that in the next lesson they will continue to make inferences about *Amelia's Road,* and remind them that one of the goals of studying inferences is for them to become more aware of when they are making inferences as they read independently.

5 ▶ Reflect on Confirming and Clarifying Thinking During "Heads Together"

Briefly discuss how the students did with "Heads Together" by sharing examples you observed of students clarifying one another's thinking and by asking groups to share examples. Ask:

Q *What do you think we can do better the next time we use "Heads Together"?*

INDIVIDUALIZED DAILY READING

 6 ▶ **Document IDR Conferences/Review the Reading Comprehension Strategies**

Direct the students' attention to the "Reading Comprehension Strategies" chart and remind them that these are the strategies they have learned so far this year. Ask them to notice which strategies they use and where they use them during their reading today. At the end of IDR, they will share with their groups.

Have the students read independently for up to 30 minutes.

Use the "IDR Conference Notes" record sheet to conduct and document individual conferences.

 At the end of independent reading, have the students share their reading and a strategy they used—the name of the strategy and where they used it—with their group. Have students who cannot think of a comprehension strategy they used talk about what they read.

Reading Comprehension
Strategies

- recognizing text
features

Day 3

Materials

- *Amelia's Road*
- *Student Response Book* page 33
- Charted directions, prepared ahead (see Step 2)
- *Assessment Resource Book*
- Transparencies of the "Excerpt from *Amelia's Road*" (BLM19–BLM20)
- *Student Response Book,* IDR Journal section

Guided Strategy Practice

In this lesson, the students:

- *Make inferences* to understand a character
- Read independently for up to 30 minutes
- Ask clarifying questions
- Include one another
- Contribute to group work

▶ 1 Review Working in Groups of Four

Explain that the students will work in their groups of four again today and that you would like them to continue to focus on both making sure everyone is participating and confirming and clarifying one another's thinking during group discussion.

▶ 2 Use "Heads Together" to Explore Inferences About Amelia's Actions

Remind the students that in the previous lesson they heard parts of *Amelia's Road* again and made inferences about Amelia's feelings. Explain that today they will read a key part of the story and use inference to think about Amelia's actions.

Read pages 24–27 in *Amelia's Road* aloud. Have the students think quietly about the following questions:

Q *Why is Amelia making a treasure box?*

Q *Why does she bury the box near the tree?*

Without discussing the questions, have the students turn to the excerpt from *Amelia's Road* on *Student Response Book* page 33. Explain that this is the part of the story you just read aloud. Explain the following directions, which you have written where everyone can see them:

1. Reread the excerpt quietly to yourself.

2. Underline passages that help you answer these questions:

   - Why is Amelia making a treasure box?

   - Why does she bury the box near the tree?

3. Put your heads together to talk about the passages you underlined and what you inferred about Amelia's actions.

Before the students begin, briefly discuss:

Q *If you finish before others in your group are ready to talk, what can you do?*

 As the students work individually and in their groups of four, circulate and ask them the following questions to help them think about the inferences they are making:

Q *You underlined ["She set to work at once, filling it with 'Amelia-things.' "] What did you infer from that sentence about why Amelia is making the treasure box? Why does that inference make sense based on other things you know about her?*

Q *Do other group members agree or disagree with [Leslie Ann] that this sentence helps to explain why she made the treasure box? What other sentences help you understand her reasons for making the box? Explain your thinking.*

Q *What question do you want to ask [Leslie Ann] to better understand what [she's] thinking?*

 Note

English Language Learners may benefit from extra support to make sense of the excerpt. Show and discuss the illustrations on pages 24–27 again, and then read the excerpt aloud as they follow along, stopping intermittently to talk about what is happening. The students may benefit from explanations of:

- "Amelia-things"
- "accidental road"
- "freshly turned ground"

3 ▶ Infer the Reasons for Amelia's Actions as a Class

When most groups have finished, place the transparency of the excerpt on the overhead projector. Review the two questions you asked the students to think about, and have a few groups share the passages they underlined and what they inferred. Facilitate a discussion among the students by asking questions such as:

Q *Do you agree or disagree with what [Jamil] and [his] group shared? Why?*

Point out that preparing and burying the treasure box is an important turning point in the story because afterwards Amelia's feelings about her migrant life change. Ask:

Q *How does making and burying the treasure box help Amelia to feel differently about her life?*

Students might say:

"I think the box is like a record of her life. If someone finds it someday, they'll know there was this kid named Amelia and she had a family."

"In addition to what [Paul] said, we inferred yesterday that Amelia was sad because she didn't have a home. Burying the box near the tree makes that spot her own."

"I agree with [Hannah]. It's like she left a part of herself near the tree."

Point out that characters in stories behave as they do for reasons, and that sometimes readers must infer the reasons. Explain that tomorrow the students will practice making inferences about characters in their own books.

Reflect on Taking Responsibility During Group Work

Give the students an opportunity to think about how they did today with making sure everyone was participating and clarifying one another's thinking. Ask:

Q *What did you personally contribute to your group's discussion today? How do you think that helped your group?*

INDIVIDUALIZED DAILY READING

Read Independently/Write About Strategies They Used

Have the students read independently for up to 30 minutes.

As the students read, circulate among them. Observe their reading behavior and engagement with the text. Ask individual students questions such as:

Q *What is your book about?*

Q *What made you decide to read this book?*

Q *(Nonfiction book) What do you already know about [planets]? How does knowing this information about [planets] help you understand this book?*

Q *(Fiction book) Who is the main character in your book? How would you describe him or her?*

Q *What comprehension strategies are you using to help you understand the character and what is happening?*

ELL Note

If your English Language Learners are struggling to write, have them draw to express their thoughts about their reading.

At the end of independent reading, have the students write in their IDR Journals about their reading and a strategy they used—the name of the strategy and where they used it. Have students who cannot think of a strategy they used write about their reading. Have a few students share their writing with the class.

Day 4

Independent Strategy Practice

In this lesson, the students:

- *Make inferences* to understand characters as they read independently
- Ask clarifying questions

1 Review the Week

Tell the students that they will work in pairs today.

Remind them that this week they heard *Amelia's Road* and explored the story and Amelia's feelings and actions by making inferences. Explain that today they will practice making inferences about characters in their independent reading, and that they should be reading books that are about characters or real people.

Tell the students that they will read for 15 minutes, then reread while thinking about inferences they might be making about characters.

2 Read Independently Without Stopping

Ask the students to use self-stick notes to mark the place they begin reading today. Have them read independently for 15 minutes.

3 Prepare to Look for Inferences About a Character

After 15 minutes, stop the students and direct their attention to the following questions, which you have written where everyone can see them:

- What do you know about the main character, or one of the main characters, in your story?

- Is that stated directly in the text? How?

- If not, what clue(s) tell you what you know?

Materials

- Narrative fiction texts at appropriate levels for independent reading
- Small self-stick note for each student
- Charted questions, prepared ahead (see Step 3)
- (Optional) Narrative text for modeling making inferences in independent reading (see Step 4)

 Note

You might want to model this activity for your English Language Learners.

Explain that the students will reread, starting again at their self-stick notes, and ask them to think about the questions as they read. Tell them that you will stop them every few minutes to think about the questions and talk to their partners.

Save the charted questions for Week 2.

4 ▶ Reread Independently and Talk to a Partner

Have the students begin rereading. Stop them at 5-minute intervals. At each stop, ask one question at a time, and pause after each question to give the students time to think. After they have thought about all three questions, have them use "Turn to Your Partner" to discuss their thinking. Remind them to clarify each other's thinking.

As partners talk, circulate among them and notice whether they recognize both directly stated and inferred meanings in their books. Ask individual students questions such as:

Q *What do you know about this character? How do you know? Are those things stated directly or are you inferring them from clues? What clues?*

Teacher Note ▶

If you notice that many students are having difficulty making inferences about characters or distinguishing between directly stated and inferred meanings, you might bring the class together and model the process again using a text of your own.

5 ▶ Discuss Inferences as a Whole Class

At the end of the rereading time, have several students share with the class what they read and inferred about the characters. Remind each student to give the title and author of the book and briefly tell what it is about. Prompt the students by asking:

Q *What is one thing that you know about a character in your book?*

Q *Was that stated directly or indirectly in the text? Read us the passage where it is stated directly or where you had a clue to help you infer.*

Q *What did you hear [Alma] say about [her] book?*

Q *What do you want to ask [Alma] about [her] book or what [she] shared?*

6 ▶ Reflect on Partner Work

Facilitate a brief discussion about how partners worked together. Ask:

Q *What did you do today to make sure you understood your partner's thinking?*

Q *What would you like to do [the same way/differently] the next time you work with your partner? Why?*

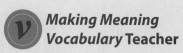

Making Meaning Vocabulary **Teacher**

Next week you will revisit this week's reading to teach Vocabulary Week 16.

Week 2

Overview

UNIT 6: MAKING INFERENCES

Fiction and Narrative Nonfiction

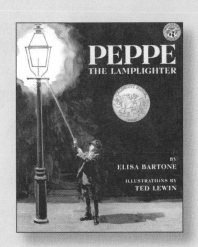

Peppe the Lamplighter
by Elisa Bartone, illustrated by Ted Lewin
(Mulberry, 1993)

Peppe finds a job lighting street lamps in New York City to help support his large family.

ALTERNATIVE BOOKS

When Jessie Came Across the Sea by Amy Hest

Just a Dream by Chris Van Allsburg

Comprehension Focus

- Students *make inferences* to understand a character.

- Students continue to *use text structure* to explore narrative text.

- Students read independently.

Social Development Focus

- Students take responsibility for their learning and behavior.

- Students develop the group skills of asking clarifying questions, including one another, and contributing to group work.

- Students have a check-in class meeting to discuss how they are doing working with different partners.

DO AHEAD

- Prepare the "Clues to Inferences in *Peppe the Lamplighter*" chart (see Day 2, Step 2 on page 304).

- Prepare the directions chart for Guided Strategy Practice (see Day 3, Step 3 on page 310).

- Make transparencies of the "Excerpt from *Peppe the Lamplighter*" (BLM21–BLM22).

- (Optional) Prepare to model making inferences about a character in independent reading (see Day 4, Step 4 on page 314).

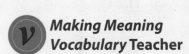

***Making Meaning Vocabulary* Teacher**

If you are teaching Developmental Studies Center's *Making Meaning Vocabulary* program, teach Vocabulary Week 16 this week. For more information, see the *Making Meaning Vocabulary Teacher's Manual*.

Day 1

Materials

- *Peppe the Lamplighter*

Read-aloud

In this lesson, the students:

- Hear and discuss a story
- Discuss setting and plot
- Read independently for up to 30 minutes
- Include one another
- Contribute to group work

1 Review "Heads Together"

Remind the students that they have been using "Heads Together" to discuss their thinking, and that they are focusing on contributing to the group work and including one another in the discussion. Ask:

Q *What happens when some group members contribute to the group while others don't? Why is it important for each group member to contribute [her] thinking to the discussion?*

Q *If you realize that only some members are contributing to the discussion in your group, what can you do?*

Tell the students that you will check in with them at the end of the lesson to see how they did working in their group.

2 Review Making Inferences and Introduce *Peppe the Lamplighter*

Remind the students that last week they focused on making inferences to understand the character Amelia in *Amelia's Road*. Explain that this week they will continue to explore making inferences to understand characters and also to explore the story setting and plot.

Show the cover of *Peppe the Lamplighter* and read the title and the names of the author and illustrator aloud. Explain that this story takes place in New York City in the late 1800s. At that time, many families moved from countries like Italy to the United States, hoping for better living conditions. For many immigrants, life in the United States continued to be difficult. First in groups, and then as a class, have the students discuss:

Q *What challenges do you think families might face when they move from one country to another?*

Students might say:

"They might not understand the language that is spoken there."

"It could be hard to find a job."

"People wouldn't know anyone in the new country and would have a hard time understanding what to do."

Show the cover of *Peppe the Lamplighter* again and explain that most neighborhoods did not have electricity at the time of the story, so streets were often lighted by gas lamps that were lit each night by lamplighters.

3 Read Aloud

Read the book aloud, showing the accompanying illustrations.

Suggested Vocabulary

tenement: run-down, low-rent apartment building (p. 3)

piecework: work paid for by the number of items made (p. 14)

embroider: sew designs onto cloth (p. 16)

Dov' è mia bambina?: (Italian) Where is my little girl? (p. 22)

ELL Vocabulary

English Language Learners may benefit from discussing additional vocabulary, including:

orphans: children whose parents have died (p. 3)

business has been slow: people have not been buying meat (p. 4)

anxious: very eager (p. 11)

Don't mind him: Don't pay attention to him (p. 12)

twilight: sunset (p. 14)

You'll never amount to anything: You won't have a good job when you grow up or be a man I can be proud of (p. 19)

stubborn: unwilling to change (p. 22)

collected his things: picked up his lamplighter's stick (p. 24)

 Note

You may want to explain that *challenges* are *things that are difficult*. People often have to work hard to overcome challenges.

 Note

You might preview the text and illustrations with your English Language Learners prior to reading the book aloud to the class. During the reading, you might stop periodically to have the students briefly discuss what is happening in the story. Possible stops are at the bottom of pages 9, 19, and 24.

4 ▶ Discuss the Story in Groups and as a Class

 First in groups using "Heads Together," and then as a whole class, discuss:

Q *What happens in this story (what is the plot)?*

Q *Is the setting (time and place) an important part of this story? Why do you think so?*

Students might say:

"In this story, Peppe has to support his family because his mom is dead and his dad is sick. He gets a job lighting lamps but his father is ashamed of him."

"The setting is important because it takes place long ago, during a time when there was no electricity."

Teacher Note ▶

As groups talk, circulate among them and note groups in which all members are participating and groups in which only some members are participating. Be ready to share your observations at the end of the lesson.

Facilitate interaction among groups and students during the whole-class discussion using questions such as:

 Q *Put your heads together and discuss whether you agree or disagree with what [Wilson] just said.*

Explain that the students will explore inferences in *Peppe the Lamplighter* tomorrow.

Teacher Note ▶

During the whole-class discussion, be ready to reread passages from the text and show illustrations again to help the students recall what they heard.

5 ▶ Reflect on "Heads Together"

Facilitate a brief discussion of how the students did contributing and including one another during "Heads Together." Share examples of successes or problems you observed as the students worked in their groups of four.

INDIVIDUALIZED DAILY READING

 **Review Previewing a Text Before Reading/
Read Independently**

Remind the students that readers often look over a book before
reading it. A reader might look at the cover, read the information
on the back of the book, and preview the book by looking through
the pages. Previewing a book is particularly helpful when reading
expository text. Ask the students to take the time to do this today
before starting to read, even if they are part way through their books.

Have the students read independently for up to 30 minutes.

Circulate as the students read, stopping to ask individual students
questions such as:

Q *What did you notice about your book when looking it over before
reading? How is this helpful to you?*

Q (Expository text) *What are some features in your book? How
might these features help you understand the text?*

Q *Do you think you will enjoy this book? Why do you think that?*

 At the end of independent reading, have the students share their
reading with their groups.

 Note

You may want to remind the
students that *features* are things
such as photographs, captions,
charts, and maps that help
readers better understand the
topic of an expository text.

Day 2

Materials

- *Peppe the Lamplighter*
- "Clues to Inferences in *Peppe the Lamplighter*" chart, prepared ahead (see Step 2)

Guided Strategy Practice

In this lesson, the students:

- *Make inferences* about a character as they hear a story
- Read independently for up to 30 minutes
- Confirm one another's thinking by repeating back what they heard
- Ask clarifying questions
- Contribute to group work

1 ▶ Review Working in Groups of Four

Briefly review that the students have been focusing on asking clarifying questions, including one another, and contributing to the group work. Explain that you would like them to continue to practice these skills in their groups today.

2 ▶ Highlight Clues to Inferences in *Peppe the Lamplighter*

Remind the students that they heard *Peppe the Lamplighter* yesterday. Direct the students' attention to the "Clues to Inferences in *Peppe the Lamplighter*" chart, on which you have written the following sentences from the story:

> "Peppe tugged gently on Assunta's hair and smiled at them. But he did not really feel like smiling."

> "Peppe just lowered his eyes and didn't answer. And from then on he rushed through the lighting of the lamps, sometimes forgetting which was which."

> "As Peppe walked, he held his head up, and his eyes were bright again."

Explain that these are sentences in the story from which a reader can infer how Peppe feels. Read the sentences aloud, and explain that you will read the story again, stop at each of the lines, and have them put their heads together to talk about what they can infer about Peppe's feelings from the sentences.

3 Reread *Peppe the Lamplighter* and Use "Heads Together" to Discuss Inferences

Reread the story, slowly and clearly. Stop after each passage on the chart (on pages 12, 20, and 29), reread the passage, and have the groups use "Heads Together" to discuss:

Q *What can you infer about how Peppe feels in this passage?*

Have one or two groups report their inference for each passage and the clues in the passage that helped them to make the inference. Then reread the passage and continue reading to the next stop. Do not spend too long at any one stop.

> **Students might say:**
>
> "We inferred that Peppe is worried that his father doesn't like Peppe's job. It says that Peppe did not feel like smiling."
>
> "In addition to what [Jolene's] group said, we noticed that Peppe lowered his eyes and didn't answer his father. From that, we figured out that he is ashamed of his job. It also says he rushed through the job, which he wouldn't do if he was feeling proud about it."
>
> "When Peppe held his head up, we knew that he felt better. We inferred that he was proud of his job and finding his sister."

If groups disagree significantly on inferences that make sense for any of the "clues to inferences," discuss this before continuing with the lesson. Ask the students to refer to the text to support their opinions, and ask probing questions such as:

Q *What do you think [Peppe] is thinking at that moment? Why does that make sense?*

Q *What do Peppe's actions tell you about how he feels? Explain your thinking.*

ELL Note

You might prompt the students to begin their response by saying, "I can infer…."

4 ▶ Discuss Character Change as a Class

Facilitate a whole-class discussion, using the following questions:

Q *How do Peppe's feelings about his job change during the story? Explain your thinking.*

Q *How do the father's feelings about Peppe's job change? What in the story helps you infer that?*

As the students share their ideas, encourage them to confirm one another's thinking and ask clarifying questions by asking:

Q *What did you hear [Renata] say? Did [Mark] get it right, [Renata]?*

Q *Do you agree or disagree with what [Renata] said? Explain your thinking.*

Q *What questions do you want to ask [Renata] about what [she] said?*

After the discussion, point out that both Peppe's and his father's feelings must be inferred. Point out that many of the students naturally made these inferences, and that they are learning to become more aware of when they are making inferences as they read. Being aware of making inferences will help them better understand and think about what they read.

5 ▶ Briefly Reflect on Using "Heads Together"

Briefly discuss how the students did with "Heads Together" by asking:

Q *How did you personally contribute to your group's work today?*

INDIVIDUALIZED DAILY READING

 Read Independently/Discuss the Students' Reading

Have the students read independently for up to 30 minutes.

As they read, circulate among the students and talk to individuals about whether they are understanding and enjoying their books. Ask questions such as:

Q *What is your book about? What do you think will happen next?*

Q *Are you enjoying your book? Why do you enjoy it?*

Q *Have you read other books by this author? If so, how are they similar? How are they different?*

Ask any student who is not enjoying her book why this is so, and explain that readers sometimes need to read a good portion of a book before they get into it. At other times, readers decide to get a different book. Ask the student whether she wants to read on or choose a new book.

 Note

Before the students begin to read independently, preview the questions you plan to ask them as they are reading.

Day 3

Materials

- *Peppe the Lamplighter*
- Chart paper and marker
- *Student Response Book* page 34
- Charted directions, prepared ahead (see Step 3)
- *Assessment Resource Book*
- Transparencies of the "Excerpt from *Peppe the Lamplighter*" (BLM21–BLM22)
- *Student Response Book,* IDR Journal section

Guided Strategy Practice

In this lesson, the students:

- *Make inferences* to understand characters
- Read independently for up to 30 minutes
- Ask clarifying questions
- Include one another
- Contribute to group work

1 ▶ Discuss Ways to Work More Effectively in Groups

Explain that the students will work in their group of four again today, and ask them to continue to focus on making sure everyone is participating and on clarifying one another's thinking during group discussions. Ask:

Q *What is one way you think your group can work more effectively? Put your heads together and briefly discuss this.*

Q *How do you think that will help your group?*

Q *What will each group member need to do to make that happen?*

> ***Students might say:***
>
> "We can go around the group and everyone can say one thing. That way we hear from everyone."
>
> "We can make sure we all have our pencils sharpened before we start so we don't have to wait for anyone."
>
> "We can start talking about the question right away, rather than talking about other things first."

If the students do not have ideas for ways to work together more effectively, briefly offer some yourself, like the ones listed in the "Students might say" note or those based on your recent observations of problems the groups are having.

Explain that you would like each group to try their idea and that you will check in with them at the end of the lesson to see how they did.

2 Brainstorm About Peppe's Character

Remind the students that last week they used inference to help them understand Amelia's feelings and actions in *Amelia's Road*. Explain that today they will continue to practice using inference to help them understand characters.

Explain that authors rarely list a character's personality traits. Instead, readers must infer what a character is like from what he thinks, says, and does. Ask:

Q *How would you describe Peppe?*

Q *Would you want Peppe for a friend? Why or why not?*

As the students report, record their ideas on a sheet of chart paper entitled "Peppe's Personality."

> **Students might say:**
>
> Peppe is:
>
> "serious"
>
> "worried about his father"
>
> "responsible"
>
> "sad"
>
> "a hard worker"
>
> "a caring brother"
>
> "nice"

Review the brainstormed list, and ask:

Q *Which of these descriptions do you think are inferred, and which do you think are stated directly?*

◀ **Teacher Note**

If necessary, review *Peppe the Lamplighter* by having a student summarize the story, showing the illustrations again, or reading various sentences from the story and having volunteers say what they remember about that part of the story.

Teacher Note

Have students who are unable to read the excerpt on their own read it quietly aloud with a partner, or you might read it aloud yourself as the students follow along. Then have them go back and underline the clues in the passage.

 Note

English Language Learners may benefit from extra support to make sense of the excerpt. Show and discuss the illustrations on pages 18–21 again; then read the excerpt aloud as they follow along, stopping intermittently to talk about what is happening.

3 ▶ Explore Inferences About Peppe

Have the students turn to the excerpt from *Peppe the Lamplighter* on *Student Response Book* page 34, and explain that the excerpt contains information about the kind of person Peppe is. Explain the following directions, which you have written where everyone can see them:

1. Read the excerpt quietly to yourself.

2. Reread the excerpt, underlining passages that reveal something about Peppe.

 3. Put your heads together to talk about the passages you underlined and what you inferred about Peppe.

As the students work individually and in their groups of four, circulate and ask them the following questions to help them think about the inferences they are making:

Q *You underlined ["And from then on he rushed through the lighting of the lamps, sometimes forgetting which was which"]. What did you infer about Peppe from that line? Why does that inference make sense based on other things you know about him?*

Q *Do other group members agree or disagree with [Asim] that this sentence shows he doesn't want to do the job anymore? What else might you infer about Peppe from that line? Why?*

Q *What question do you want to ask [Asim] to better understand what [he's] thinking?*

CLASS COMPREHENSION
ASSESSMENT

As you circulate among the groups, notice which passages
they underline, and ask yourself:

Q *Are the students underlining passages that give clues about
Peppe's character?*

Q *Do their inferences about Peppe make sense?*

Record your observations on page 20 of the *Assessment
Resource Book.*

4 ▶ Discuss Inferences About Peppe as a Class

When most groups have finished, place the transparency of the
excerpt from *Peppe the Lamplighter* on the overhead projector. Ask
groups to share passages they underlined and what they inferred
about Peppe. Facilitate a discussion among the students using
questions such as:

Q *Do you agree or disagree with what [Sakura and her group]
shared? Why?*

Q *Some of you said that the passage "Soon he would not show
his face outside the tenement" reveals that Peppe is ashamed of
himself. Others inferred that he wants to quit lighting the lamps.
What do you think? What evidence in the text supports your
opinion?*

Students might say:

"Peppe wants to quit because it says that he rushes through
lighting the lamps, and he forgets which ones he's lit. I think he
just doesn't like doing it anymore."

"I disagree with [Ramón]. I think Peppe has become more and
more ashamed because his father doesn't want him to light
the lamps."

5 ▶ **Reflect on Ideas for Working Together More Effectively**

Give the students an opportunity to think about how they did today implementing their idea for working together more effectively. Ask:

Q *How did your group's ideas for working together turn out?*

Q *If it helped, how did it help? If it didn't help, why do you think it didn't help? What might you want to try next time?*

INDIVIDUALIZED DAILY READING

6 ▶ **Document IDR Conferences/Have the Students Write in Their IDR Journals**

Have the students read independently for up to 30 minutes.

Use the "IDR Conference Notes" record sheet to conduct and document individual conferences.

At the end of independent reading, have the students write in their IDR Journals about their books. Have each student write whether or not he would recommend it to another fourth grader to read. Remind the students to give reasons for their thinking. As a class, discuss questions such as:

Q *What might you say to another fourth grader about your book?*

Q *Would you recommend the book? Why or why not?*

Have several students share what they wrote. Remind the students that they can read another student's book when that person is finished with it.

Day 4

Independent Strategy Practice

In this lesson, the students:

- *Make inferences* to understand characters as they read independently
- Ask clarifying questions
- Have a class meeting to check in on working with a partner

1 ▶ Review the Week and Get Ready to Read Independently

Tell the students that they will work in pairs today.

Remind them that this week they heard *Peppe the Lamplighter* and explored the story and the character of Peppe by making inferences. Explain that today they will practice making inferences about characters in their independent reading, and that they should be reading books that are about characters or real people.

Tell the students that they will read for 15 minutes, and then read the same section again while thinking about inferences they might be making about characters.

2 ▶ Read Independently Without Stopping

Ask the students to use self-stick notes to mark the place they begin reading today, and have them read independently for 15 minutes.

Materials

- Narrative texts at appropriate levels for independent reading
- Small self-stick notes for each student
- Charted questions (from Week 1, Day 4)
- "Class Meeting Ground Rules" chart
- "Ways to Work with Any Partner" chart (from the class meeting in Unit 5, Week 1)

Prepare to Look for Inferences About Characters

After 15 minutes, stop the students and direct their attention to the charted questions:

Teacher Note ▶

The same questions were used in Week 1.

- *What do you know about the main character, or one of the main characters, in your story?*

- *Is that stated directly in the text? How?*

- *If not, what clue(s) tell you what you know?*

Explain that the students will reread, starting again at their self-stick notes, and think about these questions as they read. Tell them that you will stop them every few minutes to think about the questions and talk to their partners.

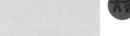 **Read Independently and Talk to a Partner**

Have the students begin rereading. Stop them at 5-minute intervals. At each stop, ask one question at a time, and pause after each question to give the students time to think. After they have thought about all three questions, have them use "Turn to Your Partner" to discuss their thinking. Remind them to ask clarifying questions if they are not sure they understand each other's thinking.

Teacher Note ▶

As you did in Week 1, model making inferences about a character in your own reading if many students are having difficulty.

As the students talk in pairs, circulate among them and notice whether they recognize both directly stated and inferred meanings. Ask individual students questions such as:

Q *What do you know about this character? How do you know? Are those things stated directly, or are you inferring them from clues? What clues?*

5 ▶ Discuss Inferences as a Class

At the end of the rereading time, have several students share what they read and inferred with the class. Remind each student to tell the title and author of the book and briefly what it is about. Prompt the students by asking:

Q *What is one thing that you know about a character in your book?*

Q *Was that stated directly or indirectly? Read us the passage where it is stated directly or where you had a clue to help you infer.*

Q *What do you want to ask [Teresa] about [her] book or what [she] shared?*

6 ▶ Reflect on Partner Work

Facilitate a brief discussion about how partners worked together. Ask:

Q *What did you do today to confirm or clarify your partner's thinking? How did that work?*

7 ▶ Have a Brief Check-in Class Meeting

Have the students move into a circle for a class meeting and review the class meeting ground rules. Remind them that in the last class meeting they talked about the challenges of working with a good friend or with a person they would not choose as a friend. Refer to the "Ways to Work with Any Partner" chart and remind them that they came up with positive ideas for working with any partner. First in pairs, and then as a class, discuss:

Q *What were some of the challenges we discussed about being partners with a close friend? With someone we would not choose as a friend?*

Teacher Note

In Unit 6, Week 3, the students will focus on inferring about causes. If you feel they need more practice making inferences about characters before going on, repeat this week with an alternative book. Alternative titles are listed on this week's Overview page.

Ways to Work with Any Partner

- *If we have a problem, we can try to talk it out.*

Q *What ideas on the "Ways to Work with Any Partner" chart have you tried? How did that work? If it didn't work well, what happened? What might you try instead?*

Q *What have you personally done to be a responsible partner, regardless of who your partners or group members were?*

State your ongoing expectation that each student will be responsible for learning to work in a productive way with her partner, and that sometimes this will be easier than other times.

Briefly discuss how the students did following the ground rules during the class meeting. Review the procedure for returning to their desks, and adjourn the meeting.

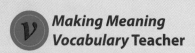

Making Meaning
Vocabulary Teacher

Next week you will revisit this week's reading to teach Vocabulary Week 17.

Week 3

Overview

UNIT 6: MAKING INFERENCES
Fiction and Narrative Nonfiction

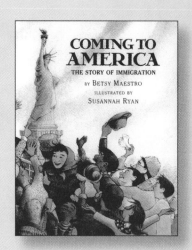

Coming to America
by Betsy Maestro, illustrated by Susannah Ryan
(Scholastic, 1996)

This is a history of immigration to the United States, from the first arrivals more than 20,000 years ago to the present day.

ALTERNATIVE BOOKS

"A Longer Look: Interview with Dyli" in **The Colors of Freedom** by Janet Bode

The Real McCoy by Wendy Towle

Comprehension Focus

- Students *make inferences* to understand causal relationships in nonfiction.

- Students *use schema* to articulate all they think they know about a topic before they read.

- Students read independently.

Social Development Focus

- Students take responsibility for their learning and behavior.

- Students develop the group skills of asking clarifying questions, including one another, and contributing to group work.

DO AHEAD

- Prepare the "Clues to Inferences in *Coming to America*" chart (see Day 2, Step 1 on page 326).

- Make transparencies of the "Excerpt from *Coming to America*" (BLM23–BLM24).

- Prepare the directions chart for Guided Strategy Practice (see Day 3, Step 3 on page 331).

- Prepare to model asking *why* questions in independent reading (see Day 4, Step 3 on page 334).

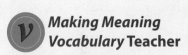

Making Meaning Vocabulary Teacher

If you are teaching Developmental Studies Center's *Making Meaning Vocabulary* program, teach Vocabulary Week 17 this week. For more information, see the *Making Meaning Vocabulary Teacher's Manual.*

Day 1

Materials

- *Coming to America* (pages 3–12 and 20–29)
- Chart paper and a marker
- "Reading Comprehension Strategies" chart

Teacher Note

If your students are already familiar with "Group Brainstorming," you may not need to teach it. Briefly review the procedure and go on with the rest of the lesson.

Teacher Note

The 30-second limit for choosing a group recorder encourages them to pick a recorder quickly without getting stuck in a selection process.

Read-aloud

In this lesson, the students:

- *Make inferences* as they hear a nonfiction text
- Learn "Group Brainstorming"
- Read independently for up to 30 minutes
- Include one another
- Contribute to group work

1 ▶ Introduce "Group Brainstorming"

Review that in previous lessons the students learned to work in groups of four and to use "Heads Together" to discuss their ideas. Ask:

Q *What are some things that are helpful to keep in mind to make your work go smoothly in a group of four?*

Explain that today they will learn a cooperative structure called "Group Brainstorming," in which group members generate and record as many ideas as they can in a short period of time. Group members will state their ideas briefly and these will be written down quickly by the group recorder, without discussion. Tell the students that all ideas should be recorded, and that the ideas do not have to be written as complete sentences.

Choose a topic (for example, "fiction characters I like" or "topics I enjoy reading about") and model quickly jotting down a few of your own brainstormed ideas.

Explain that the students will use "Group Brainstorming" to think about what they know about the topic of today's book before they hear it. Give the groups 30 seconds to determine who will be their group recorder today.

Introduce *Coming to America* and Brainstorm About Immigration

Remind the students that they heard *Peppe the Lamplighter,* which told the story of one immigrant family. Tell them that this week you will read aloud from the book *Coming to America.* Show the cover and read the author's and illustrator's names aloud. Explain that this nonfiction book focuses on how people came from other lands to live in this country.

 Have the students use "Group Brainstorming" to respond to this question:

Q *What do you think you know about how and why people from many different countries came to live in America?*

Students might say:

"Some people came here looking for a better life, because they were poor in their own country, or there was a war."

"I know blacks came from Africa as slaves."

"I think the Native Americans were always here. I don't know where they first came from."

Give groups 3–4 minutes to brainstorm and record their ideas, then stop them and have them review their list and select one idea to share with the whole class. Ask them to select a backup idea in case their first idea is shared by another group.

Have all the groups report their ideas; then ask if there are any additional ideas the groups generated that have not been reported.

Ask the students to keep these ideas in mind as they listen to the reading today.

 Read *Coming to America* Aloud with Brief Section Introductions

Explain that you will read two sections of the book aloud today (pages 3–12 and pages 20–29), and that you will stop periodically to have groups put their heads together to discuss their thinking about the book.

 ELL Note

Many of your English Language Learners will have personal stories about coming to America from another country. You might want to take extra time for volunteers to tell their stories of moving to the United States.

◀ **Teacher Note**

Limiting the brainstorming time encourages the students to be brief and to get out many ideas without getting stuck on any particular idea.

Asking the groups to select a backup idea encourages them to listen to one another and to avoid repeating what others have said.

Teacher Note

This week's read-aloud contains a lot of factual information that the students might have difficulty following. To support them, you will briefly introduce each section before you read it. This will help to focus the students' listening on the main ideas discussed in that section.

▶ Tell the students that the first section you will read is about the first people to arrive in America. Read pages 3–12, showing the illustrations and stopping as described below.

Stop after:

p. 6 "By the time Christopher Columbus 'discovered' America in 1492, millions of people lived in the great civilizations of the Americas."

Teacher Note ▶ 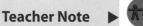 Have the students use "Heads Together" to discuss:

During the stops, listen for evidence that the students are discussing the book and understanding it. If necessary, reread parts of the text to help them recall what they heard. Also, look for examples of groups working together well and groups having difficulty, and be ready to share your observations at the end of the lesson.

Q *What did you learn about the first immigrants to America?*

After a minute or two, explain that the next section you will read tells about the immigrants who came to America in the centuries after Columbus's arrival in 1492. Reread the last sentence before the stop; then continue reading. Stop after:

p. 12 "Stormy seas made shipboard life even more miserable."

Have the students use "Heads Together" to discuss:

Q *What did you learn about immigrants in the section you just heard?*

After a minute or two, explain that during the 1800s immigrants continued to arrive in America in growing numbers from countries around the world. Tell the students that the next section you will read tells what the government did to control immigration. Read pages 20–29, stopping as described below.

Stop after:

p. 22 "The travelers were relieved that their journey was over, but they worried about what awaited them on Ellis Island."

 Have the students use "Heads Together" to discuss:

Q *How did the government regulate, or control, immigration?*

After a minute or two, explain that the last part you will read tells what happened to immigrants at Ellis Island. Reread the last sentence before the stop; then continue reading. Stop after:

p. 29 "When they received their entry cards, at last, the immigrants could officially enter their new country."

 Have the students use "Heads Together" to discuss:

Q *What happened to the immigrants at Ellis Island?*

 Discuss the Reading as a Class

Facilitate a discussion of the reading, using the following questions. Be ready to reread passages from the text to help the students recall what they heard.

Q *What were some of the reasons immigrants came to America?*

Q *What were some of the difficulties immigrants faced in America?*

Teacher Note

Facilitate interaction among students during the whole-class discussion by:

- Probing their thinking by asking follow-up questions, such as: *Can you say more about that? What in the book makes you think that? Why does that make sense?*

- Using "Turn to Your Partner" or "Heads Together" to engage everyone in thinking about the important questions.

- Asking them to agree or disagree with their classmates and explain their thinking.

Grade Four | 323

Students might say:

"The book said people on the ships were scared because they didn't know what to expect at Ellis Island."

"Sometimes families got separated, like if someone was sick."

"Some immigrants, like the Native Americans, were driven off their land by the other immigrants."

"In addition to what [Dion] said, Africans were brought here against their will as slaves."

Q *What do you think the author means by "All Americans are related to immigrants or are immigrants themselves"?*

5 Reflect on "Group Brainstorming"

Facilitate a brief discussion about "Group Brainstorming" using questions such as:

Q *How did you take responsibility in your group today?*

Q *What went well in your "Group Brainstorming"? What do you want to do differently the next time your group does "Group Brainstorming"?*

INDIVIDUALIZED DAILY READING

6 Document IDR Conferences/Review Reading Comprehension Strategies

Direct the students' attention to the "Reading Comprehension Strategies" chart and ask them to notice which strategies they use and when they use them during their reading today. At the end of IDR, they will share with their groups.

Have the students read independently for up to 30 minutes.

At the end of independent reading, have the students share their reading with their groups and ask one another questions about their books. Ask:

Q *What questions might you ask about a classmate's book?*

Reading Comprehension Strategies

- recognizing text features

EXTENSION

Discuss Family Backgrounds

Have the students explore their immigrant roots by interviewing the adults in their home to find out how their family came to America. Explain that some families do not know the countries their ancestors came from, although they may be able to guess their continent of origin. Other families are recent immigrants, who may be able to contribute personal experiences to the discussion.

Give the students an opportunity to share what they learned with the class, and to ask one another questions. You might have them mark their families' countries or continents of origin on a world map.

Day 2

Materials

- *Coming to America* (pages 3–12 and 20–29)
- "Clues to Inferences in *Coming to America*" chart, prepared ahead (see Step 1)

Guided Strategy Practice

In this lesson, the students:

- *Make inferences* as they hear a nonfiction text
- Explore ethical issues in the text
- Read independently for up to 30 minutes
- Include one another
- Contribute to group work
- Ask clarifying questions

1 Highlight Clues to Inferences in *Coming to America*

Remind the students that they heard parts of *Coming to America* yesterday. Direct their attention to the "Clues to Inferences in *Coming to America*" chart, on which you have written the following sentences from the book:

> "By the time Christopher Columbus 'discovered' America in 1492, millions of people lived in the great civilizations of the Americas."
>
> "Instead of finding freedom, these Africans lost theirs, and most never returned to their homelands, so very far away."
>
> "A number of years later, the government began to limit immigration by saying that people from some countries could not come to the United States at all."
>
> "Wealthy passengers traveling first class were usually allowed to leave the ship right away."

Explain that these are sentences in the book from which a reader can infer meanings that are not stated directly. Read the sentences aloud, and explain that you will reread the parts of the book you read yesterday, and that you will stop at each of the lines and have the students put their heads together to talk about what they infer from the sentences.

2 ▶ Reread *Coming to America*

Reread pages 3–12 and 20–29, slowly and clearly. Stop after each of the charted sentences (pages 6, 11, 20, and 24), reread the sentence, and have groups use "Heads Together" to discuss what they infer.

Have one or two groups report their inference for each passage; then reread the passage and continue reading to the next stop. Do not spend too long at any one stop.

> *Students might say:*
>
> "The book says that there were millions of people in America when Columbus came, so we inferred that Columbus didn't really discover America."
>
> "We inferred that for Africans, life in America was not better than life in Africa."
>
> "It doesn't say it in the book, but we think they passed laws to keep some people out because they didn't like the countries they came from."
>
> "Based on what we heard in the book, rich people coming to the United States got better treatment."

If groups disagree significantly about inferences that make sense for any of the "clues to inferences," discuss this before continuing with the lesson. Ask the students to refer to the text to support their opinions, and ask probing questions such as:

Q *Why do you think the author put quotation marks around the word "discovered" in this sentence?*

Q *Why do you think wealthy people were allowed to leave the boat before the others?*

3 ▶ Discuss *Coming to America* as a Class

Read the following passage on page 19: "Although life was hard for new immigrants, it still was better than the perils and poverty they faced in their native countries. So immigrants continued to come to the United States."

◀ **Teacher Note**

You can use "Heads Together" as needed during this discussion to increase participation.

Ask:

Q *Was this true for all immigrants? Who was it true for? Who was it not true for? Explain your thinking.*

Reread the passage on pages 10–11, beginning "As the population grew, the Europeans competed with the Indians for land and food" and ending "Instead of finding freedom, these Africans lost theirs, and most never returned to their homelands, so very far away." Ask:

Q *What does this passage tell you about the immigrant experience for some groups of people?*

Students might say:

"The white immigrants' lives got better, but for Native Americans and Africans, their lives got worse."

Explain that the students made inferences to understand that the immigrant experience was quite different depending on the country people came from and the color of their skin. Point out that many of them naturally made these inferences, and that they are learning to become more aware of when they are making inferences as they read. Being aware of making inferences will help them better understand what they read.

 4 ▶ Reflect on Group Work

Facilitate a brief discussion of how the students contributed to their group discussions and included one another.

INDIVIDUALIZED DAILY READING

5 ▶ Read Independently/Think About Inferences

Ask the students to think about inferences they make as they read.

Have the students read independently for up to 30 minutes.

As the students read, circulate among them and talk to individuals to monitor whether they are making sense of their reading and are aware of making inferences. Ask questions such as:

Q *What is your book about? What do you think will happen next? Why do you think that?*

Q *What are you learning about the character(s) in your book? What parts of the text reveal those things about that character?*

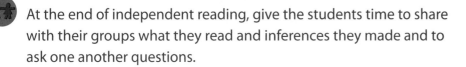 At the end of independent reading, give the students time to share with their groups what they read and inferences they made and to ask one another questions.

EXTENSION

Read the Rest of *Coming to America*

If the students are interested, you might read the rest of *Coming to America* aloud. Facilitate a class discussion comparing immigration before and after Ellis Island closed, including the lives immigrants led in their new country. In addition, you may want to read the sections labeled "Immigration Today" and "Other Interesting Facts About Immigration" on page 39.

Day 3

Materials

- *Coming to America*
- *Student Response Book* pages 35–36
- Charted directions, prepared ahead (see Step 3)
- *Assessment Resource Book*
- Transparencies of the "Excerpt from *Coming to America*" (BLM23–BLM24)
- *Student Response Book*, IDR Journal section

Guided Strategy Practice

In this lesson, the students:

- Explore causes of events in a nonfiction text
- Read independently for up to 30 minutes
- Include one another
- Contribute to group work
- Ask clarifying questions

1▶ Review Working in Groups of Four

Explain that the students will work in their groups again today and ask them to continue to focus on including one another and contributing to the group work.

2▶ Introduce Exploring Causes

Remind the students that they have been making inferences to help them understand what happens in stories like *Peppe the Lamplighter* and *Amelia's Road*. Point out that they can also use the strategy to help them figure out why something happens—what causes an event to happen—the way it does.

Explain that today they will explore why some of the things described in *Coming to America* happened as they did.

3▶ Explore Causes in *Coming to America*

Remind the students that at Ellis Island, immigrants endured numerous health examinations and questioning by doctors and inspectors. Recall that the author calls the experience at Ellis Island an "ordeal."

Teacher Note ▶

If necessary, explain that an *ordeal* is a *very difficult or painful experience.*

Have the students talk briefly in their groups about the following question:

Q *Why did the immigrants have to go through so much examination and questioning at Ellis Island?*

Direct the students' attention to the excerpt from *Coming to America* on *Student Response Book* pages 35–36, and explain that the excerpt describes what the immigrants had to do to enter the United States at Ellis Island. Explain the following directions, which you have written where everyone can see them:

1. Read the excerpt quietly to yourself.

2. Reread the excerpt, and underline sentences that help to answer this question: Why were immigrants examined and questioned at Ellis Island?

 3. Talk with your group about the sentences you underlined and the inferences you made.

As the students work individually and in groups, circulate and ask the following questions to help them think about the inferences they are making and clarify their thinking:

Q *You underlined ["signs of contagious disease"]. What did you infer from that sentence about why the immigrants were examined and questioned?*

Q *Can you confirm [Martine's] thinking by repeating back what you heard [her] say?*

Q *Do you agree or disagree with [Martine]? Why?*

Q *What question do you want to ask [Martine] to better understand what [she's] thinking?*

Teacher Note

Have students who are unable to read the excerpt on their own read it quietly aloud with a partner, or you might read it aloud yourself as the students follow along. Then have them go back and underline the clues in the passage.

 Note

English Language Learners may benefit from extra support to make sense of the excerpt. Show and discuss the illustrations on pages 24–29 again; then read the excerpt aloud as they follow along, stopping periodically to talk about what is happening. The students might benefit from explanations of the following words and passages:

• "Those with health problems were marked with colored chalk."

• "kept on the island for observation"

• "permanent health problems"

• "native country"

• "translators"

Circulate among the students and ask yourself:

Q *Are the students identifying clues about why immigrants were examined and questioned at Ellis Island?*

Record your observations on page 21 of the *Assessment Resource Book*.

 Discuss Causes as a Whole Class

When most groups have finished, place the transparency of the excerpt from *Coming to America* on the overhead projector, and ask a few students to share the sentences they underlined and the inferences they made. Facilitate a discussion among the students using questions such as:

Q *Do you agree or disagree with what [Juanita and her group] shared? Why?*

Students might say:

"I underlined the sentences 'Sometimes immigrants had permanent health problems that would make it hard for them to work. This often meant that they would be sent back to their native country.' It seems like if you couldn't work, you weren't welcome in America."

"In addition to what [Bryan] said, I think the line 'The inspectors looked for signs of contagious disease' shows that they wanted to make sure that sick people didn't spread their disease to other immigrants."

"I underlined 'The immigrants had to show that they would work hard and stay out of trouble.' I think this explains one reason they had to answer so many questions."

Point out that the author does not directly explain why the immigrants had to go through so much examination and questioning in order to enter the U.S., but that the students inferred this information from the clues. Explain that writers often don't directly explain why events happen the way they do. Instead, readers have to make inferences to understand the reasons.

Explain that in the next lesson the students will practice making inferences about why things happen in books they read independently.

INDIVIDUALIZED DAILY READING

 ## Document IDR Conferences/Have the Students Write in Their IDR Journals

Encourage the students to continue to think about inferences they make as they read.

Have the students read nonfiction books independently for up to 30 minutes.

Use the "IDR Conference Notes" record sheet to conduct and document individual conferences.

At the end of independent reading, have the students write in their IDR Journals about what they read and any inferences they made about characters in their books. Have a few volunteers share their writing with the class. Ask:

Q *What question do you have for [Sonja] about [the main character of her book]?*

Q *What question do you have for [Henry] about the inferences [he] made?*

Day 4

Materials

- Texts at appropriate levels for independent reading
- Small self-stick notes for each student
- Book for modeling *why* questions (see Step 3)

Independent Strategy Practice

In this lesson, the students:

- Explore causes of events as they read independently
- Ask clarifying questions

1 ▶ Review the Week

Have partners sit together. Remind them that this week they heard *Coming to America,* made inferences, and explored causes of events in the book. Explain that today they will use *why* questions to explore causes in the books they are reading independently.

2 ▶ Read Independently Without Stopping

Ask the students to use self-stick notes to mark the place they begin reading today, and have them read independently for 15 minutes.

3 ▶ Model Asking *Why* Questions

Stop the students after 15 minutes. Explain that you would like them to reread and use "Stop and Ask Questions" to identify places they can ask *why* questions about what is in the book. They will use additional self-stick notes to mark the places where questions come to mind, and they will write the questions on the notes.

Teacher Note ▶

To prepare for the modeling, have the *why* questions you will ask in mind ahead of time. (For example, using the book *Slinky Scaly Slithery Snakes,* you might open to page 14 and ask "Why do snakes have different kinds of markings on their skin?")

Model the procedure by briefly introducing the text you selected. Read several sentences aloud, and think aloud about a *why* question that comes to mind. Jot the question on a self-stick note, and place the note in the margin where you stopped reading.

Reread Independently and Ask *Why* Questions

Have the students reread independently for 15 minutes, stopping to mark places in their reading where *why* questions arise and record the questions on the notes. Circulate and look for evidence that the students are able to write *why* questions.

Some students may have difficulty generating questions. To help these students, you might ask them questions such as:

Q *What is happening in this part of the book? What question that begins with* why *can you ask about this part of the book?*

 ## Have Partners Discuss Their Questions

After 15 minutes, stop the students. Ask them to choose one *why* question they marked, and use "Think, Pair, Share" to discuss whether the question was answered, and how. Remind each student to tell his partner the title and author of the book and, briefly, what it is about.

 ## Discuss Questions as a Class

Have a few volunteers share their *why* questions with the class. Remind them to tell the title and author of their book. Probe the students' thinking by asking:

Q *What was happening in the text when your question came to mind?*

Q *Is the question answered? If so, is it answered directly, or did you figure out the answer by making an inference? Read us the passage in which it is answered.*

Q *What do you want to ask [Nadine] about [her] book or what [she] shared?*

ELL Note

You might need to provide additional support for your English Language Learners. Consider having these students dictate *why* sentences as you write them.

Reflect on This Week's Partner and Group Work

Facilitate a brief discussion about how the students worked with their partners and groups over the week. Ask:

Q *What did you enjoy about working with your partner or group this week?*

Q *What is one way your partner or group work is improving? What is one thing you want to keep working on as you continue to work together?*

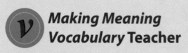 **Making Meaning Vocabulary Teacher**

Next week you will revisit this week's reading to teach Vocabulary Week 18.

Week 4

Overview

UNIT 6: MAKING INFERENCES
Fiction and Narrative Nonfiction

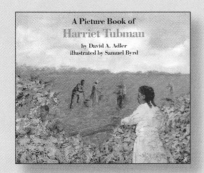

A Picture Book of Harriet Tubman
by David A. Adler, illustrated by Samuel Byrd
(Holiday House, 1992)

This biography of Harriet Tubman traces her life as a slave, escape from slavery, and exploits as a conductor on the Underground Railroad.

ALTERNATIVE BOOKS

More Than Anything Else by Marie Bradby

A Picture Book of Frederick Douglass by David A. Adler

Comprehension Focus

- Students *make inferences* to understand causal relationships in nonfiction.

- Students read independently.

Social Development Focus

- Students take responsibility for their learning and behavior.

- Students develop the group skills of confirming and clarifying another person's thinking.

DO AHEAD

- Prepare the "Clues to Inferences in *A Picture Book of Harriet Tubman*" chart (see Day 2, Step 1 on page 344).

- Make transparencies of the "Excerpt from *A Picture Book of Harriet Tubman*" (BLM25–BLM26).

- Prepare the directions chart for Guided Strategy Practice (see Day 3, Step 3 on page 349).

- (Optional) Prepare to model asking *why* questions in independent reading (see Day 4, Step 3 on page 352).

- Make copies of the Unit 6 Parent Letter (BLM15) to send home with the students on the last day of the unit.

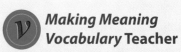

Making Meaning Vocabulary Teacher

If you are teaching Developmental Studies Center's *Making Meaning Vocabulary* program, teach Vocabulary Week 18 this week. For more information, see the *Making Meaning Vocabulary Teacher's Manual.*

Day 1

Materials

- *A Picture Book of Harriet Tubman*

Read-aloud

In this lesson, the students:

- *Make inferences* as they hear a biography
- Explore social and ethical issues in the text
- Read independently for up to 30 minutes
- Confirm one another's thinking by repeating back what they heard
- Ask clarifying questions

 ## Get Ready to Work Together

Have partners sit together. Review that in previous lessons the students learned to use prompts to add to their partner conversations. (These are "I agree with you, because…," "I disagree with you, because…," and "In addition to what you said, I think….") They also learned how to confirm that they understood their partners' thinking by repeating back what they heard and asking clarifying questions. Tell the students that you would like them to use these skills as needed in their conversations this week.

Introduce *A Picture Book of Harriet Tubman*

Teacher Note

If necessary, build background knowledge about the Underground Railroad before reading. Explain that it was not a physical railroad, but rather a secret network of people who helped slaves escape from the South to the Northern states and Canada in the years before the Civil War. Slaves hid during the day and traveled at night, stopping at hiding places or "stations" along the way.

Review that in the previous week the students heard *Coming to America* and used the strategy of *making inferences* to make sense of the book. Explain that this week they will hear another book and make inferences to help them understand it.

Tell the students that the book you will read aloud is *A Picture Book of Harriet Tubman*. Show the cover of the book and read the author's and illustrator's names aloud. Explain that the book is a biography of Harriet Tubman, and that a *biography* is a story of someone's life. Tell them that Harriet Tubman was born a slave in the 1800s. She later escaped from slavery and led hundreds of other slaves to freedom by means of the Underground Railroad.

3 **Read Aloud with Brief Section Introductions**

Explain that you will stop periodically during the reading to have partners talk about what they have learned about Harriet Tubman.

Tell the students that the first part of the book is about Harriet's early life as a slave. Read aloud, showing the illustrations, and stopping as described below.

ELL Note

You might preview the book with your English Language Learners by showing the pictures and reading or summarizing the text prior to the whole-class read-aloud.

Suggested Vocabulary

plantation: large farm (p. 4)
protest: show they disagreed with slavery (p. 9)
Moses: an ancient Jewish leader who led his people out of slavery (p. 10)
rebellion: armed fight against people in power (p. 10)
patrollers: guards who tried to catch runaway slaves (p. 13)
liberty: freedom (p. 15)
amendment: change to laws of the U.S. Constitution (p. 27)

ELL Vocabulary

English Language Learners may benefit from discussing additional vocabulary, including:

in chains: with chains on their feet and hands to prevent escape (p. 8)
sleeping spells: falling asleep unexpectedly (p. 12)
conductor: person who works on a train collecting fares (p. 20)
used songs as a secret code: used songs to send secret messages (p. 21)
spy: person who watches others secretly to get information about them (p. 26)

Stop after:

p. 12   "After the accident she often prayed."

Have the students use "Turn to Your Partner" to discuss:

Q *What did you learn about Harriet's life as a slave?*

After a minute or two, explain that the next part of the book describes Harriet's escape from slavery. Reread the last sentence on page 12 and continue reading to the next stopping point:

p. 18   "She said later, 'The sun came like gold through the trees and over the fields, and I felt like I was in heaven.'"

◀ **Teacher Note**

During the stops, listen for evidence that the students are discussing the book and understanding it. If necessary, reread parts of the text to help the students recall what they heard. Also, look for examples of pairs working together well and pairs having difficulty, and be ready to share your observations at the end of the lesson.

Have the students use "Turn to Your Partner" to discuss:

Q *What did you learn about Harriet's escape from slavery?*

After a minute or two, explain that the next part of the book tells about Harriet's adventures on the Underground Railroad. Reread the last sentence on page 18 and continue reading to the next stopping point:

> **p. 24** "He called her 'General Tubman.'"

 Have the students use "Turn to Your Partner" to discuss:

Q *What did you learn about Harriet's years as a conductor on the Underground Railroad?*

After a minute or two, explain that the last part of the book describes Harriet's later years. Reread the last sentence on page 24 and continue reading to the end of the book.

▶ 4 Discuss the Book in Pairs and as a Class

 First in pairs, and then as a class, discuss the following questions. Remind the students to use the prompts in their partner conversations and to confirm and clarify their partners' thinking. Ask:

Q *What do you think were important events in Harriet Tubman's life? Explain your thinking.*

Students might say:

"When she was little, she was whipped for taking a piece of sugar. That probably made her hate being a slave even more."

"Harriet saw her sisters get sold. She didn't want that to happen to her."

"She escaped on the Underground Railroad and decided to help other slaves escape. That's why she's famous today."

Q *After Harriet escaped, she said, "I had a right to liberty or death. If I could not have one, I would have the other." What do you think she meant?*

Teacher Note

These questions help the students explore the social and ethical themes and make personal connections to the text.

Q *What do you admire about Harriet Tubman? What can we learn from her life that might help us in our own lives?*

During the whole-class discussion, be ready to reread passages from the text and show illustrations again to help the students recall what they heard. As the students make inferences about Harriet Tubman, point them out. (You might say, "The author does not say directly that Harriet was strong-willed and determined, but you inferred that, or figured it out, using clues in the story.")

Explain that in the next lesson the students will continue to explore making inferences in the book.

5 ▶ Reflect on Partner Work

Briefly discuss how partners did using prompts and confirming and clarifying one another's thinking. Share your own observations.

INDIVIDUALIZED DAILY READING

6 ▶ Document IDR Conferences

Ask the students to continue to think about the inferences they are making as they read and when they are making them.

Have the students read independently for up to 30 minutes.

Use the "IDR Conference Notes" record sheet to conduct and document individual conferences.

At the end of independent reading, have the students share their reading in pairs. Ask each student to show her partner the cover of her book, read the title, and briefly tell what the book is about. Remind the students to ask clarifying questions to help them understand their classmates' thinking.

If time allows, have one or two students each share an inference they made during independent reading and read the passage that helped them infer.

◀ **Teacher Note**

Facilitate interaction among the students during the whole-class discussion with questions such as:

Q *Who will confirm [Yuri's] thinking by repeating back what you heard [him] say?*

Q *Turn to your partner and discuss whether you agree or disagree with what [Yuri] just said.*

Q *Did you agree or disagree? Explain your thinking.*

Day 2

Materials

- *A Picture Book of Harriet Tubman*
- "Clues to Inferences in *A Picture Book of Harriet Tubman*" chart, prepared ahead (see Step 1)

Guided Strategy Practice

In this lesson, the students:

- *Make inferences* as they hear a biography
- Read independently for up to 30 minutes
- Confirm one another's thinking by repeating back what they heard
- Ask clarifying questions

 Highlight Clues to Inferences in *A Picture Book of Harriet Tubman*

Remind the students that they heard *A Picture Book of Harriet Tubman* yesterday. Direct their attention to the "Clues to Inferences in *A Picture Book of Harriet Tubman*" chart, on which you have written the following sentences from the book:

> "He said that if she ran off he would tell her master and soon the patrollers and their dogs would be after her."

> "'The sun came like gold through the trees and over the fields, and I felt like I was in heaven.'"

> "Years later Harriet said proudly, 'I never ran my train off the track. I never lost a passenger.'"

> "She supported the suffragist movement, the fight for the right of women to vote in the United States."

Explain that these are sentences in the book from which a reader can infer meanings that are not stated directly. Read the sentences aloud, and explain that you will read the book aloud again, and that you will stop at each of the lines and have partners talk about what they infer from the sentences.

2 ▶ Reread *A Picture Book of Harriet Tubman*

Reread the book. Stop after each of the charted passages (on pages 13, 18, 23, and 29), reread the sentence, and have the students use "Think, Pair, Share" to discuss what they infer.

Have one or two pairs report their inferences at each stopping point; then reread the passage and continue reading to the next stop. Do not spend too long at any one stop.

> *Students might say:*
>
> "We inferred that maybe her husband didn't really care about her because he would turn her in if she escaped."
>
> "When she arrived in Pennsylvania, she felt like she was finally safe."
>
> "Harriet meant that she never lost any slaves that she was leading to freedom on the Underground Railroad."
>
> "From this sentence we can infer that Harriet didn't just care about equality and freedom for slaves, but for everyone."

If the students disagree significantly about inferences that make sense for any of the "clues to inferences," discuss this before continuing with the lesson. Ask the students to refer to the text to support their opinions, and ask probing questions such as:

Q *Why do you think Harriet's husband would have turned her in if she tried to escape?*

Q *What does this sentence tell you about how Harriet felt about being free?*

3 ▶ Discuss Inferences in Pairs and as a Class

Facilitate a discussion using the questions that follow. Use "Turn to Your Partner" during this discussion to increase participation.

Reread the following passage on page 22: "Once slaves began their journey north with Harriet, she wouldn't let them turn back. When slaves were too scared to go on, Harriet pointed a gun at their heads and said, 'You'll go on, or you'll die.'"

Q *What does this passage tell us about Harriet? Why do you think she was so determined not to let them turn back?*

Students might say:

"Harriet felt like she would rather be dead than a slave. Maybe she felt the same way about other slaves."

"I think this tells us that she was determined not to fail. She did it for their own good."

"I disagree with [Kit]. If slaves turned back, they might have talked about the Underground Railroad and made it unsafe for everyone else. She had to make sure they didn't turn back."

Point out that there are many clues in the book to help the reader infer what kind of person Harriet Tubman was. Many of the students naturally made these inferences, and they are learning to become more aware of making inferences as they read. Being aware of making inferences will help them better understand what they read.

 ## 4 Reflect on Partner Work

Facilitate a brief discussion of how partners worked together. Share examples you noticed of ways partners confirmed and clarified each other's thinking and used the discussion prompts to add to each other's thinking and to agree and disagree.

INDIVIDUALIZED DAILY READING

 ## 5 Document IDR Conferences

Ask the students to continue to think about and be aware of when they are making inferences as they read.

Have the students read independently for up to 30 minutes.

Use the "IDR Conference Notes" record sheet to conduct and document individual conferences.

 At the end of independent reading, have the students share their reading in pairs. Have each student tell his partner the title of the book and what the book is about. Ask the students to share any inferences they made as they read today and read the passage to each other that helped them infer. Remind them to ask clarifying questions to help them understand their partners' thinking.

EXTENSION

Read More About the Underground Railroad

Read other books about the Underground Railroad with the class. Stop occasionally as you read and ask the students to share their thoughts about each book in pairs or groups, or as a class. As the students make inferences about events and characters, point them out. Some books you might read are: *Aunt Harriet's Underground Railroad in the Sky* by Faith Ringgold, *A Freedom River* by Doreen Rappaport, and *Journey to Freedom: A Story of the Underground Railroad* by Courtni C. Wright.

Day 3

Materials

- *A Picture Book of Harriet Tubman*
- *Student Response Book* page 37
- Charted directions, prepared ahead (see Step 3)
- *Assessment Resource Book*
- Transparencies of the "Excerpt from *A Picture Book of Harriet Tubman*" (BLM25–BLM26)
- "Reading Comprehension Strategies" chart
- *Student Response Book,* IDR Journal section

Guided Strategy Practice

In this lesson, the students:

- Explore causes of events in a biography
- Read independently for up to 30 minutes
- Confirm one another's thinking by repeating back what they heard
- Ask clarifying questions

1 ▶ Review Working with a Partner

Explain that the students will work with their partners again today and ask them to continue to focus on confirming one another's thinking and asking clarifying questions.

2 ▶ Review Exploring Causes

Remind the students that they have been making inferences to help them understand what is happening in texts. Point out that they can also use the strategy to help them figure out why something happens—what causes an event to happen as it does.

Explain that today they will explore why some things happened as they did in *A Picture Book of Harriet Tubman.*

3 ▶ Explore Causes in *A Picture Book of Harriet Tubman*

Teacher Note

Explain that a general is the highest-ranking officer in the army. A general is a leader and is responsible for the lives of all the people who are under his or her command.

Reread page 24 of the book and show the illustration again. Point out that even though Harriet Tubman was not a soldier in any army, John Brown called her "General Tubman."

Have partners talk briefly about the following question:

Q *What qualities do you think a real general needs to have to be a good leader?*

Direct the students' attention to *Student Response Book* page 37, and explain that this is an excerpt from the book. The excerpt tells about Harriet's life in the years between 1850 and 1860. Explain the following directions, which you have written where everyone can see them:

1. Read the excerpt quietly to yourself.

2. Reread the excerpt, and underline sentences that explain why John Brown called Harriet "General Tubman."

3. Talk to your partner about the sentences you underlined and the inferences you made about why he called her "General Tubman."

As the students work individually and in pairs, circulate and ask them the following questions to help them think about the inferences they are making and confirm and clarify one another's thinking:

Q *You underlined ["She used much of the money she earned to make nineteen trips south to lead about three hundred slaves to freedom"]. What did you infer from that sentence about why John Brown called Harriet "General Tubman"?*

Q *Can you confirm [Sadao's] thinking by repeating back what you heard [him] say?*

Q *Do you agree or disagree with [Sadao]? Why?*

Q *What question do you want to ask [Sadao] to better understand what [he's] thinking?*

CLASS COMPREHENSION ASSESSMENT

Circulate among the students and notice which sentences they underline. Ask yourself:

Q *Are the students underlining sentences that give clues about why John Brown called Harriet "General Tubman"?*

Q *Can they support their inferences using evidence from the text?*

Record your observations on page 22 of the *Assessment Resource Book*.

Teacher Note

Have students who are unable to read the excerpt on their own read it quietly aloud with a partner, or you might read it aloud yourself as the students follow along. Then have them go back and underline the clues in the passage.

ELL Note

English Language Learners may benefit from extra support to make sense of the excerpt. Show and discuss the illustrations on pages 19–23 again; then read the excerpt aloud as the students follow along, stopping intermittently to talk about what is happening. Ensure that the students know the meaning of the word *general*.

4 ▶ **Discuss Inferences About Causes as a Class**

When most pairs have finished, place the transparencies of the excerpt from *A Picture Book of Harriet Tubman* on the overhead projector, and ask a few pairs to share the sentences they underlined and the inferences they made. Facilitate a discussion among the students using questions such as:

Q *Do you agree or disagree with what [Kara and her partner] shared? Why?*

Point out that the author does not directly say why John Brown calls Harriet "General Tubman," but that the students can infer this using information from the story. Explain that writers often don't explain why things happen or why characters behave as they do. Instead, readers have to make inferences to figure out why. Figuring out why characters behave as they do can help readers better understand what they read.

Explain that in the next lesson the students will again practice making inferences about why things happen in their independent reading.

INDIVIDUALIZED DAILY READING

5 ▶ **Document IDR Conferences/Have the Students Write in Their IDR Journals**

Refer to the "Reading Comprehension Strategies" chart and review the strategies. Encourage the students to use the strategies to make sense of their reading today.

Have the students read independently for up to 30 minutes.

Use the "IDR Conference Notes" record sheet to conduct and document individual conferences.

At the end of independent reading, have the students write in their IDR Journals about a comprehension strategy they used today—the name of the strategy and where they used it. Have students who cannot think of a comprehension strategy they used write about their reading.

Reading Comprehension Strategies

- recognizing text features

Day 4

Independent Strategy Practice

In this lesson, the students:

- Explore causes of events as they read independently
- Confirm one another's thinking by repeating back what they heard
- Ask clarifying questions

Materials

- Texts at appropriate levels for independent reading
- Small self-stick notes for each student
- (Optional) Text for modeling asking *why* questions in independent reading (see Step 3)
- *Assessment Resource Book*
- Unit 6 Parent Letter (BLM15)

1 ▶ Review the Week

Have partners sit together. Remind them that this week they heard *A Picture Book of Harriet Tubman* and made inferences as they thought about what happened in the book and why. Explain that today they will explore *why* questions in the books they are reading independently.

2 ▶ Read Independently Without Stopping

Ask the students to use self-stick notes to mark the place they begin reading today, and have them read independently for 15 minutes.

3 ▶ Reread Independently and Ask *Why* Questions

Stop the students after 15 minutes. Explain that you would like them to reread and use "Stop and Ask Questions" to identify places they can ask *why* questions about events or characters in their books. They will use additional self-stick notes to mark the places questions come to mind, and they will write the questions on the notes.

Have the students reread independently for 15 minutes, stopping to mark places in their reading where *why* questions arise and recording the questions on the notes.

◀ **Teacher Note**

The students used "Stop and Ask Questions" to ask *why* questions about their independent reading in Week 3.

Teacher Note ▶

If many students are having difficulty generating *why* questions, you might bring the class together and again model the process using your own book. (See page 334 for an example of how to model asking *why* questions.)

Circulate and look for evidence that the students are able to write *why* questions. Some students may have difficulty generating questions. To help these students, you might ask questions such as:

Q *What is happening in this part of the story? What question that begins with* why *can you ask about what is happening?*

Q *What question that begins with* why *can you ask about the person you're reading about?*

4 ▸ Have Partners Discuss Their Questions

After 15 minutes, stop the students. Ask them to choose one *why* question they marked, and have them use "Think, Pair, Share" to discuss whether the question was answered, and if it was, how. Remind each student to tell her partner the title and author of the book she is reading and a few sentences about its topic.

5 ▸ Discuss *Why* Questions as a Class

Have a few volunteers share their *why* questions with the class. Remind them to say the title and author of their book. Probe the students' thinking by asking:

Q *What was happening in the text when your question came to mind?*

Q *Is the question answered? If so, is it answered directly, or did you figure out the answer by making an inference? Read us the passage where it is answered.*

Q *What do you want to ask [Lea] about her book or what she shared?*

Teacher Note

This is the last week in Unit 6. In Unit 7, the students will explore expository text structures such as compare and contrast and chronological order in both books and articles. If you feel your students need more experience with inference, you may want to repeat this week's lessons with an alternative book. Alternative books are listed on this week's Overview page.

You will reassign partners for Unit 7.

6 ▸ Reflect on Partner Work

Facilitate a brief discussion about how partners worked together. Ask:

Q *What did you enjoy about working with your partner this week?*

Q *What is one way your partner work is improving? What is one thing you want to keep working on as you continue to work together? Talk to your partner about your thinking.*

INDIVIDUAL COMPREHENSION ASSESSMENT

Before continuing with Unit 7, take this opportunity to assess individual students' progress in inferring causes to understand text. Please refer to pages 42–43 in the *Assessment Resource Book* for instructions.

Parent Letter

Send home with each student the Parent Letter for this unit (see "Do Ahead," page 339). Periodically, have a few students share with the class what they are reading at home.

Making Meaning Vocabulary **Teacher**

Next week you will revisit this week's reading to teach Vocabulary Week 19.

Unit 7

Analyzing Text Structure

EXPOSITORY NONFICTION

During this unit, the students explore how articles can inform by highlighting pros and cons and by investigating one side of an issue. They examine how functional texts such as maps and directions are organized to inform readers. They also look at textbooks and think about how chronological and compare and contrast relationships are used to organize information. During IDR, the students monitor their own reading and use comprehension strategies to help them read textbooks. Socially, they take responsibility for their own learning during group work and develop the group skills of including one another and contributing to group work.

Week 1 "Virtual Worlds: Community in a Computer"
"School Uniforms: The Way to Go"

Week 2 "How to Make Ooblek"
"Simon's Sandwich Shop"
"City of Lawrence Street Map"

Weeks 3 & 4
Farm Workers Unite: The Great Grape Boycott

Week 1

Overview

UNIT 7: ANALYZING TEXT STRUCTURE

Expository Nonfiction

"Virtual Worlds: Community in a Computer"

This article explores the pros and cons of playing video games.

"School Uniforms: The Way to Go"

This article discusses the benefits of students wearing school uniforms.

ALTERNATIVE RESOURCES

Scholastic News, teacher.scholastic.com/activities/scholasticnews

PBS NewsHour Extra, pbs.org/newshour/extra/speakout

Comprehension Focus

• Students *use text structure* to explore expository text.

• Students explore how articles can inform by highlighting pros and cons and by investigating one side of an issue.

• Students read independently.

Social Development Focus

• Students take responsibility for their own learning during group work.

• Students include one another and contribute to group work.

DO AHEAD

• Prior to Day 1, decide how you will randomly assign partners to work together during the unit.

• Collect magazine and newspaper articles and a variety of functional texts for the students to examine and read independently throughout the unit. If possible, include examples of articles that inform by highlighting pros and cons and by investigating one side of an issue in depth.

• Prior to Day 4, make a transparency of the excerpt from "School Uniforms: The Way to Go" (BLM27).

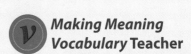

Making Meaning Vocabulary Teacher

If you are teaching Developmental Studies Center's *Making Meaning Vocabulary* program, teach Vocabulary Week 19 this week. For more information, see the *Making Meaning Vocabulary Teacher's Manual*.

Day 1

Materials

- "Virtual Worlds" (see pages 368–369)
- "Self-monitoring Questions" chart

Being a Writer™ **Teacher**

You can either have the students work with their *Being a Writer* partner or assign them a different partner for the *Making Meaning* lessons.

Read-aloud

In this lesson, the students:

- *Use text structure* to explore expository text
- Identify what they learn from an article
- Read independently for up to 30 minutes
- Practice "Heads Together"

About Expository Text Structures

The purpose of this unit is to help the students make sense of expository texts, including articles and functional texts, and to introduce the students to expository text structures found in many school textbooks, such as chronology and compare and contrast. In addition, the students explore different text structures used by authors when writing articles, such as highlighting pros and cons and investigating one side of an issue. The students have opportunities to examine such functional texts as directions, maps, schedules, and tables. The unit's primary goal is for the students to have an opportunity to explore these structures in order to help them make sense of what they are reading and set the groundwork for exploration of these structures in later years. Mastery of these structures is not expected in this exploratory unit.

1 Pair Students and Get Ready to Work Together

Randomly assign partners and have pairs sit in groups of four. Explain that in the coming weeks the students will work in pairs and groups to read various kinds of expository texts and analyze how they are organized and written.

Explain that today the students will hear a text read aloud and use "Heads Together" to help them talk and think about the reading.

Ask and discuss as a whole class:

Q *What have you learned about including one another in your work that can help you as you work with your new group?*

Encourage the students to keep these things in mind as they work with their new groups today.

2 ▶ Review Expository Texts

Remind the students that the purpose of expository nonfiction is to give the reader factual information about a topic. Review that they have heard and read a variety of expository texts already this year. Show and briefly review some of the expository texts they have heard, including *Digging Up Tyrannosaurus Rex* and *Italian Americans* from Unit 2 and *Coming to America* from Unit 6. Ask:

Q *What have you learned so far this year about expository nonfiction?*

3 ▶ Introduce "Virtual Worlds"

Explain that today the students will hear and discuss a news article called "Virtual Worlds: Community in a Computer" about the effects of playing video games on the people who play them.

Explain that as you read the article you will stop to have the students use "Heads Together" to discuss what they are hearing.

4 ▶ Read "Virtual Worlds" Aloud

Read the two introductory paragraphs of the article aloud and then reread them, asking the students to listen for any information they might have missed. Continue reading, stopping as described on the next page.

ELL Note

Prior to reading the article aloud, summarize the article for your English Language Learners. Then read the article aloud to them, stopping frequently to check for understanding. If necessary, reread sections of the article and discuss them with your students.

Suggested Vocabulary

virtual: computerized; not real (p. 368)

controversial: causing argument (p. 368)

cooperating: working together (p. 368)

ELL Vocabulary

English Language Learners may benefit from discussing additional vocabulary, including:

interact: work or play (p. 368)

confident: feeling good about yourself (p. 368)

mentally challenging: hard for your brain to do (p. 368)

historical event: something that happened a long time ago (p. 368)

physical inactivity: not moving your body (p. 369)

Stop after:

> **p. 368** "…the more confident and better they become using them in real life."

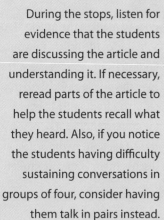

Teacher Note

During the stops, listen for evidence that the students are discussing the article and understanding it. If necessary, reread parts of the article to help the students recall what they heard. Also, if you notice the students having difficulty sustaining conversations in groups of four, consider having them talk in pairs instead.

 Have the students use "Heads Together" to discuss what they have heard. After a minute or two, signal for their attention and ask:

Q *What have you learned so far about playing video games?*

Have a couple of volunteers share, and then continue reading to the next stopping point:

> **p. 368** "…students could put themselves in the place of soldiers to understand them better."

 Have the students use "Heads Together" to discuss what they have heard. Without sharing as a class, continue reading. Follow the same procedure at the next stopping point:

> **p. 369** "…they might feel encouraged to take dangerous risks in real life."

Have students use After giving groups time to discuss, reread the last sentence before the stop and continue to the end of the article.

Discuss the Article

Facilitate a whole-class discussion using the questions that follow. As the students respond, be ready to reread from the article to help them recall what they heard:

Q *What did you learn about playing video games from this article?*

Q *According to this article, what are some of the benefits of playing video games?*

Q *According to this article, what are some of the reasons playing video games might be bad for the people who play them?*

> **Students might say:**
>
> "I learned that police and fire fighters can train for their jobs by playing video games."
>
> "In addition to what [Paula] said, playing video games is a good thing because the games can make kids smarter."
>
> "The article also says that kids who play a lot of violent video games might try to solve problems by using violence in real life."

Explain that the students will reread the article tomorrow and discuss how the author wrote the article.

 Reflect on Working in New Groups

 Ask and have the students use "Heads Together" to discuss:

Q *What went well working with your new group today?*

Q *What did you do to be sure everyone was included?*

Have several groups report what they discussed.

Self-monitoring Questions

- *What is happening in my story right now?*
- *Does the reading make sense?*

INDIVIDUALIZED DAILY READING

7 ▶ Review and Practice Self-monitoring with Articles and Other Expository Texts

Refer to the "Self-monitoring Questions" chart and review the questions. Remind the students that it is important to stop to think about what they are reading and to use the questions to help them track whether they are understanding their reading. When they are not understanding, they may need to reread, use a comprehension strategy, or get a different text.

Have the students independently read articles and other expository texts at their appropriate reading levels for up to 30 minutes. Stop them at 10-minute intervals and have them monitor their comprehension by thinking about the questions on the chart.

Circulate among the students and ask individual students to read a passage to you and tell you what it is about.

At the end of the reading time, have a whole-class discussion about how the students used the self-monitoring questions to track their reading comprehension. Ask questions such as:

Q *Which self-monitoring question did you find the most helpful? Why?*

Q *What do you want to continue to be aware of when you read to make sure you understand what you are reading?*

Day 2

Strategy Lesson

In this lesson, the students:

- *Use text structure* to explore expository text
- Explore how articles can inform by highlighting pros and cons
- Read independently for up to 30 minutes
- Include one another and contribute to group work

 Review "Virtual Worlds"

Have pairs sit in their groups of four. Review that in the previous lesson the students heard and discussed the article "Virtual Worlds: Community in a Computer." Ask and briefly discuss as a class:

Q *What did you find out about the pros and cons of playing video games from this article?*

Have a few volunteers share what they remember.

 Introduce Highlighting Pros and Cons

Remind the students that in this article we are being informed about the reasons playing video games might or might not be good for kids. Explain that authors organize articles and other kinds of expository nonfiction texts deliberately to inform their readers in a particular way.

Explain that it is common for articles to be written in a way that highlights the pros and cons of—or arguments for and against—something. This technique helps readers to consider both sides of an issue and deepen their understanding of it.

Materials

- "Virtual Worlds" (see pages 368–369)
- *Student Response Book,* pages 38–39
- "Reading Comprehension Strategies" chart

Explain that today the students will think and talk about how "Virtual Worlds: Community in a Computer" is organized to highlight pros and cons.

▶3 Reread "Virtual Worlds" and Discuss in Groups

Have the students turn to *Student Response Book* pages 38–39 and explain that they will read along silently as you reread the article. Have them consider the following questions while you reread the article aloud without stopping:

Q *What are some of the benefits of playing video games?*

Q *What are some reasons playing video games might be bad for kids?*

When you finish reading the article, have the students use "Heads Together" to discuss the pros and cons of playing video games.

Teacher Note ▶

Circulate among the groups and notice whether group members are contributing to and including each other in the discussion. Note examples of what is working well in the groups to bring to the students' attention later.

▶4 Discuss Pros and Cons as a Class

When most of the students have had time to talk in their groups, facilitate a whole-class discussion about the pros and cons of playing video games by asking questions such as:

Q *According to the article, how might playing video games help kids? What did you read that makes you think that?*

Q *According to the article, what are some problems that can come from playing video games?*

Q *Are you more persuaded by the arguments for or against playing video games? Explain your thinking.*

Teacher Note ▶

Remind the students to connect their comments to comments made by others using the discussion prompts:

- *I agree with _____ because…*
- *I disagree with _____ because…*
- *In addition to what _____ said, I think…*

Students might say:

"I think that playing video games can help shy kids learn how to interact with others. The article said that for kids to be successful playing MMOGs they have to cooperate and play with other kids."

"I disagree with [Juan] because the article also says that interacting with other people while playing video games is different than interacting with people in real life. A kid might be social on the computer and not have learned how to be social with kids in real life."

"I am more against playing video games because for kids to be good at them, they have to play a lot. If kids play too much they could get hurt or not get enough exercise, or not have enough time to do other stuff, like homework."

Explain that tomorrow the students will hear and discuss another news article.

5 Reflect on Working in Groups

Share any observations you made about how the students worked together during "Heads Together." Ask and briefly discuss:

Q *How did your group do with making sure everyone was included in the conversation? If everyone was not included, what can you do next time to make sure everyone is included?*

INDIVIDUALIZED DAILY READING

6 Have the Students Read Articles and Other Expository Texts/Document IDR Conferences

Direct the students' attention to the "Reading Comprehension Strategies" chart. Review each strategy with the students and remind them that these are the strategies they have learned so far this year. Ask them to notice which strategies they use and where they use them during their reading today. At the end of IDR, they will share with their groups.

Have the students read articles and other expository texts independently for up to 30 minutes.

▶ **Teacher Note**

If the students have difficulty answering the questions, suggest some ideas like those in the "Students might say" note.

Reading Comprehension Strategies

- *recognizing text features*

Use the "IDR Conference Notes" record sheet to conduct and document individual conferences.

 At the end of independent reading, have each student share her reading and a strategy she used—the name of the strategy and where she used it—with her group. Have students who cannot think of a comprehension strategy they used discuss what they read. Ask questions, such as:

Q *How did making inferences about [the effect of global warming on the polar bear population] help you make sense of the text?*

Q *[Jackie] said [she] was able to visualize [the hardships a gold miner faced as he panned for gold during the gold rush]. How did visualizing help you make sense of your text?*

Q *How did recognizing the pros and cons of [receiving a weekly allowance] help you understand the article you read?*

EXTENSION

Read More Articles About Video Games

You might have the students read and discuss other articles about the pros and cons of playing video games. You can find articles on websites such as timeforkids.com and newsweek.com; search these sites or elsewhere on the Internet using keywords such as "pros and cons of playing video games."

VIRTUAL WORLDS
COMMUNITY IN A COMPUTER

These days, you don't have to leave your home to have fun or to play with other people. Within the world of a video game, a person can kick a virtual soccer ball, defeat a virtual army, or build a virtual city. Two players from opposite sides of the world can team up, create plans, and work together.

There are video games in one out of three households in the United States. These games have never been more popular—or controversial. Some people say video games can help players learn skills such as quick thinking and problem solving, but there is evidence that gaming can be harmful to players' health.

PRO

Teamwork and Community

For people who are shy, video gaming is a way to learn how to interact with others. Video games called Massively Multiplayer Online Games, or MMOGs, allow thousands of players around the world to play the same video game at one time. Each MMOG player creates a virtual character that interacts with other players' characters in the virtual world. Players work together to accomplish goals, for example, building cities or defeating an army. In order to be successful in a MMOG game, players have to spend a lot of time playing with and cooperating with other players.

Improved Motor Skills

There is evidence that video gaming may improve motor skills, the ability to use your muscles to do things. Gaming may also improve your hand-eye coordination, or how well your eyes and hands work together. Video games may also help increase players' ability to respond quickly to a situation. This can help with all kinds of real-world activities. Some video game programs even simulate, or imitate, certain activities to help people practice skills they will need in their careers. Using video games called simulation programs, airplane pilots, fire fighters, or police officers can all practice skills needed for their jobs. The more that people can practice these skills, the more confident and better they become using them in real life.

Problem Solving

In the United States, intelligence test scores are rising faster than ever before. Some researchers say that one reason could be video gaming. Virtual games present a series of problems that players must solve to succeed in the game. Like anything else mentally challenging, this could make people smarter. In the fast-paced modern world where decisions often need to be made quickly, young people could be learning skills that will help them to succeed in the future.

Playing to Learn

If video games could be used in the classroom, perhaps students would be able to pay more attention to what they are learning. For example, when learning about a historical event such as a battle, students could put themselves in the place of soldiers to understand the situation better.

A pilot using a simulation program can practice skills, such as crash landing, without being hurt.

REAL-WORLD ISOLATION

Video game critics worry that young people who spend too much time playing video games don't learn important social skills needed to make friends and succeed in the real world. Interacting with a person in an online video game is very different from interacting with a person face-to-face. The etiquette, or social rules, is different within each setting. So while a person might feel confident and make friends easily within the virtual world, outside of that world, he or she might feel increasingly shy and have trouble talking to people.

HEALTH RISKS

Apart from exercising the hands and wrists, video gaming isn't a physical activity. Young people who spend hours gaming each day could develop weight problems due to physical inactivity. Doctors have also found that some gamers complain of eyestrain, headaches, and wrist pain. People who spend hours playing these games can develop problems such as RSI (Repetitive Strain Injury), which occurs when a person repeats the same action over and over for hours. Additionally, some people argue that since gamers can engage in dangerous behavior while playing—such as racing cars at fast speeds—without worrying about hurting themselves or others, they might feel encouraged to take dangerous risks in real life.

VIOLENT TENDENCIES

Critics argue that violent video games encourage players to solve problems using violence. One 2005 study found that when people play violent video games, their brains react in the same way as if they were confronted with violence in the real world. In other words, their brains aren't able to tell the difference between virtual danger and real-life danger. Because of this, video game opponents say that players become used to reacting to problems violently, rather than trying peaceful solutions. They say that players of violent video games therefore become more likely to fight when faced with a problem in the real world.

BEHIND ON THE BOOKS

Teachers worry that those students who spend hours playing video games fall behind on schoolwork. There is also a risk that using video games as learning tools would keep students from learning the importance of reading and using their imaginations. Reading helps people learn and think about information independently. Through reading, a person uses his or her imagination to understand ideas. Video games in classrooms might discourage students from learning how to think imaginatively.

It's easy to lose track of time during an intense video gaming session—which means that schoolwork can suffer.

Day 3

Materials

- "School Uniforms" (see pages 380–381)
- *Student Response Book* pages 40–41
- *Student Response Book*, IDR Journal section

Read-aloud

In this lesson, the students:

- *Use text structure* to explore articles
- Identify what they learn from an article
- Read headings to skim a text
- Read independently for up to 30 minutes
- Practice "Heads Together"

1 ▸ Get Ready to Work Together

Have pairs sit in their groups of four and remind them that they have been working on including one another and contributing to group discussions. Have partners discuss the following question. Ask:

Q *Why is it important for all the members of your group to share their ideas?*

Have a few students share with the class. Encourage them to continue working on including one another and contributing ideas to the group discussions.

2 ▸ Review Highlighting Pros and Cons

Remind the students that they read the article "Virtual Worlds: Community in a Computer" and noticed how the article was written to inform the reader by highlighting the pros and cons of the effects of playing video games on kids. Ask:

Q *Which side of the issue did you find the most convincing? Why was it the most convincing to you?*

Explain that today the students will hear and discuss another article.

3 **Introduce and Preview "School Uniforms"**

Introduce "School Uniforms: The Way to Go," another news article written for young people. Have the students turn to *Student Response Book* pages 40–41, where the article is reproduced, and ask the students to read the title, subtitle, and section headings. If necessary, take time to explain the purpose of the title, subtitle, and section headings in an article. Then ask and briefly discuss:

Q *Based on the title, subtitle, and section headings, what do you think this article is about?*

Students might say:

"I think it's about wearing school uniforms being good because the title and subtitle is 'School Uniforms: The Way to Go.'"

"One section heading says 'Self-Expression.' That may mean that wearing school uniforms keeps kids from expressing themselves."

Explain that skimming articles by reading the title and section headings will give the students some idea of what the article is about before they read the article. Encourage the students to follow this procedure before reading articles and other expository texts.

4 **Read "School Uniforms" Aloud**

Explain that you will stop during the reading to have the students use "Heads Together" to discuss what they are learning. Read the article aloud to the class, using the procedure described on the next page.

> **Suggested Vocabulary**
>
> **express themselves:** show who they are (p. 380)
> **'in' or 'out':** in style or out of style (p. 380)
> **costly designer labels:** expensive clothes (p. 380)
> **mode:** way of feeling (p. 381)

ELL Note

Prior to this activity, read the title, subtitle, and section headings to your English Language Learners. Then summarize the article for them.

ELL Vocabulary

English Language Learners may benefit from discussing additional vocabulary, including:

identify: connect; associate (p. 380)

judge me: think I am either good or bad (p. 380)

advantage: something that helps (p. 380)

pressure: feeling like you have to do something (p. 380)

belong: are a member of a group; fit in (p. 381)

pride: feeling good (p. 381)

limit: give fewer choices about (p. 381)

creative: fun and different (p. 381)

their appearance: how they look (p. 381)

Read the first two paragraphs of the article aloud and then reread them, asking the students to listen for any information they might have missed. Continue reading, stopping as described below.

Stop after:

> **p. 380** "…and there's no pressure to wear costly designer labels to school."

 Have the students use "Heads Together" to discuss what they have heard. After a minute or two, signal for their attention and ask:

Q *What have you heard about wearing school uniforms so far?*

Have a couple of volunteers share, and then continue reading to the next stopping point:

> **p. 381** "…so the intruders are more likely to stay away."

 Have the students use "Heads Together" to discuss what they have heard. Without sharing as a class, reread the last sentence before the stop and continue reading to the end of the article.

5   Discuss the Reading

Facilitate a whole-class discussion using the questions that follow. As the students respond, be ready to reread sections of the article to help them recall what they heard.

Q   *According to the article, what are some of the reasons wearing a school uniform is a good idea?*

Q   *What do you think about wearing school uniforms? Explain your thinking.*

6   Reflect on Working in New Groups

Ask and have the students use "Heads Together" to discuss:

Q   *How did your group work go today?*

Q   *What problems did you have? What might you do the next time to avoid those problems?*

Have several groups report what they discussed.

INDIVIDUALIZED DAILY READING

7   Read Independently/Have the Students Write in Their IDR Journals

Have the students read articles and other expository texts independently for up to 30 minutes.

As the students read, circulate among them. Observe their reading behavior and their engagement with the text. Ask individual students questions such as:

Q   *What is your [article/book] about?*

Q   *What do you already know about this topic? What new information are you learning?*

Teacher Note

Today's discussion focuses on surface-level comprehension of the article. Tomorrow, the students will look more closely at the article to discuss what the author's purpose might be and why the article was written the way it was.

Q *What comprehension strategies are you using to help you understand what you're reading?*

At the end of independent reading, have each student write in his IDR Journal about his reading and a strategy he used—the name of the strategy and where he used it. Have students who cannot think of a strategy write about their reading. Have a few students share their writing with the class.

Day 4

Strategy Lesson

In this lesson, the students:

- *Use text structure* to explore expository text
- Learn how articles can inform by investigating one side of an issue
- Read independently for up to 30 minutes
- Include one another and contribute to group work

 ### Review "School Uniforms"

Have pairs sit in their groups of four. Review that in the previous lesson the students heard and discussed an article called "School Uniforms: The Way to Go." Ask and briefly discuss:

Q *What do you remember about why the article said wearing school uniforms is a good idea?*

Remind the students that news articles and other kinds of expository text inform the reader; in this article the reader is informed about the benefits of students wearing school uniforms. In order to help us understand why wearing school uniforms is a good idea, the author made a number of choices about how the article was written.

Have the students turn to *Student Response Book* pages 40–41, where the article is reproduced. Ask them to read along as you reread the first four paragraphs of the article.

Point out that the first two paragraphs introduce the subject of the article by telling a little about school uniforms and that the rest of the article gives reasons why wearing school uniforms is good for students. Ask:

Q *After reading the article, do you agree with the author? What in the article makes you [agree/disagree] with the author?*

Materials

- "School Uniforms" (see pages 380–381)
- *Student Response Book* pages 40–41
- Transparency of the excerpt from "School Uniforms" (BLM27)
- *Assessment Resource Book*

Teacher Note

Other evidence that supports this idea includes:

- "Some studies have also shown that wearing a uniform does even more than that: it could help you to focus on your schoolwork."

- "Uniforms help keep students safer by showing who does—and doesn't—belong in the school."

- "School uniforms encourage us to get to know people's personalities rather than judging them by what they wear."

Highlight and Discuss Evidence in the Article

Explain to the students that authors often have a point of view or an opinion that they want the reader to understand. Explain that in this article, the author gives many examples to support the opinion that school uniforms are a good idea.

Put the transparency of the excerpt from "School Uniforms: The Way to Go" (BLM27) on the projector and read and underline the sentence "Wearing a uniform helps you to feel more confident because everyone else at school will be wearing the same outfit." Explain that this is one example that supports the point of view that wearing school uniforms is good for students. Tell the students that they will read the article in pairs and underline other examples that support this point of view.

▶ In their *Student Response Books,* have the students work in pairs to find and underline examples that the author uses to support the benefits of wearing school uniforms.

> ### CLASS COMPREHENSION ASSESSMENT
>
> Circulate among the students and ask yourself:
>
> **Q** *Do the students understand the article?*
>
> **Q** *Are they able to identify examples that support the point of view expressed in the article?*
>
> Record your observations on page 23 of the *Assessment Resource Book.*

Teacher Note

If you notice students who are not participating with their group, ask the students questions such as:

Q *How are you making sure that everyone is included in your group's discussion?*

Q *What can you do if everyone is not included?*

Discuss the Author's Point of View

▶ After sufficient time, have pairs share the examples that they underlined in their groups of four. Remind the students to be sure that everyone is included in the group conversation.

Facilitate a whole-class discussion using questions such as those that follow.

Q *What did you and your partner underline in the article that supports the point of view that wearing school uniforms is a good idea?*

Q *How does [there's no pressure to wear costly designer labels to school] support the point of view that wearing school uniforms is good for students?*

Q *What questions can we ask [Kiara] about [her] thinking?*

Q *After reading "School Uniforms," do you agree that wearing school uniforms is a good idea? Why? Why not?*

Explain to the students that many articles in newspapers and magazines and on the Internet are written from one side of an issue or one point of view. It is important to be aware of the author's purpose as you read so that you can think about whether you have enough information to form an opinion.

Explain that next week the students will continue to explore other kinds of expository text.

4 ▸ Reflect on Group Work

Help the students reflect on how they worked together during "Heads Together."

Q *What did you do to contribute to the group conversation during "Heads Together"?*

Q *What might you do the next time you work with a group to help the group work well?*

INDIVIDUALIZED DAILY READING

5 ▸ Think About How Authors Write Articles and Other Expository Texts

Remind the students that they have been thinking about different ways that articles inform readers about topics and issues. Encourage the students to think about the author's purpose, or what the author is trying to tell you, in the articles and other expository texts they read today.

Have the students independently read articles or other expository texts for up to 30 minutes.

As the students read, circulate among them. Ask individual students questions such as:

Q *What is your text about?*

Q *What do you notice about how the author chose to write this piece?*

At the end of independent reading, have a few volunteers share what they read and how their texts are written.

EXTENSION

Read More Articles and Discuss Author's Point of View

Have the students bring in articles from newspapers and magazines that highlight either one side of an issue or the pros and cons of an issue. As a class, discuss several of the articles. Have the students decide if the articles give them enough information to form an opinion.

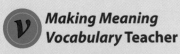

Making Meaning Vocabulary Teacher

Next week you will revisit this week's reading to teach Vocabulary Week 20.

School Uniforms

The Way to Go

Jackets, ties, and dress pants, knee socks, skirts, and blouses—in schools around the world, students prepare for the school day by putting on a uniform. Love it or hate it, the school uniform is the most common kind of uniform in the world. School uniforms make students look neat and clean, and identify them as students at a certain school.

Many students say that uniforms look boring or that they don't allow kids to express themselves with the clothes they choose to wear. On the surface, school uniforms might not seem cool, but wearing one has some big benefits.

Students at about 23 percent of public elementary schools in the United States wear uniforms, and the trend is growing.

An End to Indecision

Many young people worry about how they look: "Will people judge me by what I'm wearing?" "Is green 'in' or 'out' this season?" Wearing a uniform helps you to feel more confident because everyone else at school will be wearing the same outfit. Nobody will judge you by what clothing you wear.

Because you don't need to decide what to wear, a uniform also helps you to save time in the morning. There is another advantage to wearing a uniform: it will help you to save money, because usually, you'll only need to buy one or two at the start of the year—and there's no pressure to wear costly designer labels to school.

Judging people by how they look is human nature, but we need to find other ways of learning about one another, too.

Identity and Belonging

It's good to feel that you belong! A school uniform gives you a sense of identity and a sense of pride in your school. Some studies have also shown that wearing a uniform does even more than that: it could help you to focus on your schoolwork. It's similar to how a business person dresses in a suit when he or she goes to work. Dressing in more formal clothes helps you to shift from "play mode" into "work mode." After all, the main reason you go to school is to study and learn.

Teachers and parents like school uniforms for another reason. Uniforms help keep students safer by showing who does—and doesn't—belong in the school. Intruders realize that if they enter a school where the students are all in uniform, they will stand out—so the intruders are more likely to stay away.

Self-Expression

Belonging is good—but what about expressing yourself? It's true that school uniforms limit the ways you can look. However, a uniform doesn't limit who you are, the way you speak, and how you behave. In fact, it helps you to learn to express yourself in more creative ways. Knowing how to talk about your opinions, ideas, and beliefs is a great life skill, and wearing a school uniform encourages you to practice that skill.

Have you ever heard the expression "judging a book by its cover"? It means to judge something by how it looks before you've taken the time to understand it. We all judge people a little by how they look—for example, we can guess that someone with spiky blue hair likes punk music or that someone who wears red from head to toe likes to stand out. But you can't know what a person is really like if you don't get past their appearance.

School uniforms encourage us to get to know people's personalities rather than judging them by what they wear. That's one of the most valuable things we can learn from wearing school uniforms. Who knows what friendships, conversations, and ideas we miss out on by judging people only by their clothes?

Week 2

Overview

UNIT 7: ANALYZING TEXT STRUCTURE

Expository Nonfiction

Functional Texts

"How to Make Ooblek"

This functional text provides step-by-step instructions for making ooblek.

"Simon's Sandwich Shop"

This functional text is an example of a menu from a sandwich shop.

"City of Lawrence Street Map"

This functional text is a sample street map and street index for a small town.

ALTERNATIVE RESOURCE

As an alternative resource for these lessons, you might use the functional texts from *Student Response Book* pages 42–43.

Comprehension Focus

• Students explore functional texts.

• Students *use text structure* to explore expository text.

• Students read independently.

Social Development Focus

• Students take responsibility for their own learning and behavior.

• Students include one another and contribute to group work.

DO AHEAD

• Prior to Day 1, prepare a sheet of chart paper with the title "Functional Texts at Our School."

• (Optional) Collect a variety of functional texts for the students to examine and read on Day 1.

• Prior to Day 3, make a transparency of the "City of Lawrence Street Map" (BLM28).

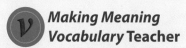

Making Meaning Vocabulary Teacher

If you are teaching Developmental Studies Center's *Making Meaning Vocabulary* program, teach Vocabulary Week 20 this week. For more information, see the *Making Meaning Vocabulary Teacher's Manual.*

Day 1

Strategy Lesson

In this lesson, the students:

- Look for and read functional texts inside and outside the classroom
- Identify what they learn from functional texts
- Read independently for up to 30 minutes
- Act responsibly during a school walk

1 ▸ Get Ready to Work Together

Gather the class together and have pairs sit in their groups of four. Remind the students that they have been working on taking responsibility for their own learning and on including one another during group work. Encourage the students to continue to practice these skills this week.

2 ▸ Review Articles and Introduce Functional Texts

Review that last week the students heard and read articles about playing video games and about the benefits of wearing school uniforms. They thought about how articles are written and organized to help readers understand the articles. Explain that today the students will explore another kind of expository nonfiction called functional texts.

Explain that functional texts help readers make decisions and function in their everyday lives. Some examples of functional texts are street signs, labels, posters, recipes, instructions, and schedules.

Point out one or two functional texts in the classroom, and then have the students use "Turn to Your Partner" to discuss:

Q *What other functional texts do you see in our classroom?*

Materials

- Scratch paper and pencil
- "Functional Texts at Our School" chart, prepared ahead, and a marker
- (Optional) A variety of functional texts that students can examine and read independently
- (Optional) *Student Response Book* pages 42–43
- *Student Response Book,* IDR Journal section

Teacher Note

Other examples of functional texts are tickets, bills, menus, receipts, calendars, and nutritional labels on food wrappers. ▶

Teacher Note

If the students have difficulty answering the question, offer some suggestions like those in the "Students might say" note. Then ask them to name other examples of functional text they notice in the classroom. ▶

Have several volunteers point out the functional texts they noticed. As they share, briefly discuss how each functional text is helpful.

Students might say:

"I see the 'Reading Comprehension Strategies' chart. Having the comprehension strategies posted reminds us to use them while we are reading."

"In addition to what [Rita] said, the class computer sign-up sheet helps us figure out whose turn it is to use the computer."

"The instructions on the fire extinguisher tell us how to use it."

3 Introduce the School Walk

Explain that today the class will take a walk around the school to look for other functional texts. Explain that during the walk you will stop a few times so the students can look around and talk about the functional texts they see. Remind the students how you expect them to behave on the walk. (For example, you might say, "I expect you to walk with your partner. I expect you to watch me for signals about when to stop, listen, and talk. When you talk to your partner, I expect you to whisper.")

Ask and briefly discuss:

Q *Who do we want to be considerate of when we walk around outside the classroom? Why do we want to be considerate of them?*

Q *What can we do so we don't disturb other classes when we walk around?*

Students might say:

"It's important to be considerate of teachers and students in other classrooms so they don't get interrupted from their work."

"We can walk quietly in the halls and not look for our friends as we pass other classrooms."

"If we pass the principal in the hall, we can smile at her."

Ask the students to keep in mind what they talked about, and tell them that you will check in with them after the walk to see how they did.

◀ **Teacher Note**

You might take the students to the office, library, nurse's office, or another public space in the school. If a walk around the school is not possible, provide a variety of functional texts that the students can examine or use the sample functional texts on *Student Response Book* pages 42–43.

4 ▶ Take a Class Walk Around the School

Lead the students on a walk around the school. Bring paper and a pencil with you to jot down their observations. At the first stop, ask:

Q *What functional texts do you see? Turn and whisper to your partner.*

Signal for the students' attention and have a couple of students quietly share their observations. If necessary, share one or two functional texts you notice (for example, "I notice the lunch schedule and the exit sign"). Jot down functional texts the students mention. After a few students have shared, continue the walk, stopping to notice functional texts in other areas of the school.

5 ▶ List Functional Texts as a Class

When you return to the classroom, have pairs sit together in their groups of four. Use "Heads Together" to have them discuss:

Q *What functional texts did you see on our walk?*

Have a few volunteers share with the class, and as they share, record functional texts they mention on the "Functional Texts at Our School" chart. Help the students think about the purposes of functional texts by asking follow-up questions, such as:

Q *What information does [the lunch menu] give you?*

Q *How does the [in case of emergency poster] help us?*

Explain that tomorrow the students will look at more functional texts and talk about why they are helpful.

6 ▶ Reflect on Acting Responsibly

Ask and briefly discuss:

Q *What did you do to act in a responsible way during the walk? How do you think that helped the people around us?*

Q *What problems, if any, did we have? What can we do next time to avoid those problems?*

INDIVIDUALIZED DAILY READING

 Read Independently/Write About Strategies in Their IDR Journals

Have the students read articles and other expository texts independently for up to 30 minutes.

As the students read, circulate among them. Observe their reading behavior and engagement with the text. Ask individual students questions such as:

Q *What is your [article/book] about?*

Q *What do you already know about this topic? What new information are you learning?*

Q *What comprehension strategies are you using to help you understand what you're reading?*

At the end of independent reading, have each student write in his IDR Journal about his reading and a strategy he used—the name of the strategy and where he used it. Have students who cannot think of a strategy write about their reading. Have a few students share their writing with the class.

EXTENSION

Share Examples of Expository Text

Have the students bring in examples of functional text from their daily life. Have them point out the features in the examples and explain how the features help readers. Have pairs glue their examples to a large sheet of construction paper and label each example with its features and uses (for example, a weather graph from the newspaper might be labeled "newspaper weather graph— gives weather predictions for the next five days").

Day 2

Materials

- "How to Make Ooblek" (see page 393)
- "Simon's Sandwich Shop" (see page 394)
- "Functional Texts at Our School" chart
- *Student Response Book* pages 44–45
- *Assessment Resource Book*
- "Reading Comprehension Strategies" chart

Read-aloud/Guided Strategy Practice

In this lesson, the students:

- Identify what they learn from functional texts
- Explore the organization of functional texts
- Read independently for up to 30 minutes
- Include one another and contribute to group work
- Take responsibility for their learning and behavior

▶ 1 Review Functional Texts

Have pairs sit in their groups of four. Refer to the "Functional Texts at Our School" chart and remind the students that yesterday they explored functional texts in the classroom and around the school. Review that functional texts are a type of expository nonfiction that help readers do things and make decisions.

Explain that today the students will look closely at two functional texts and discuss how they help readers.

▶ 2 Introduce and Read Aloud "How to Make Ooblek"

Have the students turn to *Student Response Book* page 44. Read the title aloud and explain that these are directions for making a substance called ooblek. Explain that directions are examples of functional texts.

Ask the students to follow along as you read "How to Make Ooblek" slowly and clearly.

Ask and briefly discuss:

Q *What makes these directions easy to use?*

Students might say:

"There is a list of materials so you know what you need before you begin."

"In addition to what [Matthew] said, each thing you have to do is numbered, so you know what to do first."

"Step number four has a note to help the reader if the ooblek is too thick."

Point out that the author includes the materials list and the numbered steps to make this functional text easy for readers to use.

 ### Introduce and Read Aloud "Simon's Sandwich Shop"

Explain that the students will look at another kind of functional text, and have them turn to *Student Response Book* page 45. Read the title aloud and explain that this is an example of a menu from a sandwich shop.

Ask the students to read the menu to themselves.

After sufficient time, facilitate a whole-class discussion using the following questions:

Q   *What are the bread choices at Simon's Sandwich Shop? Where did you find that information?*

Q   *How much does a bottle of water cost? How do you know?*

Q   *How much does a 12-inch ham sandwich and a barbecue tofu burger cost? How did you figure that out?*

 ### Introduce the Sandwich Shop Activity

 Have the students look at the menu and work in pairs to order lunch for both of them. Explain that they have $20.00 to spend on the two lunches. They don't have to spend all of the $20.00, but they can't spend more than $20.00. Tell the students that they should be ready to explain to the other pair in their group of four what they ordered, how much both lunches cost, and how much money from the $20.00 they have left over.

 Note

Prior to today's lesson, read the menu to your English Language Learners and help them with unfamiliar vocabulary.

CLASS COMPREHENSION ASSESSMENT

Circulate among the students as they work. Randomly select students to observe and ask yourself:

Q *Are the students able to read and use the functional text?*

Q *Are students taking responsibility for their own learning?*

Record your observations on page 24 of the *Assessment Resource Book*.

5 ▶ Discuss Lunch Orders

Have pairs discuss in their groups of four what they ordered for lunch and how much they spent.

Then signal for the students' attention and discuss the following questions as a whole class:

Q *What did you and your partner order?*

Q *How much of the $20.00 did you spend?*

Q *How did you make sure that you didn't spend more than $20.00?*

Q *How is the menu organized to help the customer decide what to buy?*

Students might say:

"It has different sections so you can easily see everything that they sell."

"There are two columns that have two different sandwich sizes, 6 inches and 12 inches. It also tells you the prices for every sandwich at both sizes."

"The bread choices and dressing choices are in boxes, which makes them easy to find."

Explain that the sandwich shop menu and the directions for making ooblek are organized differently because they have different purposes. Both are organized in a way that helps the reader get and make sense of information easily and quickly. Tell the students that reading functional texts carefully and noticing how they are organized helps readers understand and use them more easily. Encourage the students to continue to notice functional texts in their everyday lives.

 ## Reflect on Working in Groups

Ask and briefly discuss:

Q *What did your group do to make sure everyone was included in the conversation?*

Q *How did you contribute to your group's conversation?*

INDIVIDUALIZED DAILY READING

 ## Read Independently/Conduct IDR Conferences/Share Strategies

Refer to the "Reading Comprehension Strategies" chart and review the strategies with the students. Explain that at the end of IDR partners will each share a strategy they used that helped them make sense of their reading.

Have the students read articles and other expository texts for up to 30 minutes while you conduct reading conferences with individual students. Use the "IDR Conference Notes" record sheet to note individual student progress.

 At the end of the IDR, have partners share with one another the strategies they used to help them make sense of what they read today. Have a few volunteers share the strategies they used and how those strategies help them make sense of their reading.

> *Reading Comprehension Strategies*
>
> - *recognizing text features*

EXTENSION

Make Ooblek

Provide the students with the materials to make ooblek and have them follow the directions in the functional text to make it. After the students have had time to explore ooblek, have them share their observations about how it feels, what it looks like, and how it moves. If time permits, have the students write a short piece describing ooblek. Encourage the students to use descriptive language to describe how it feels, looks, and moves.

HOW TO MAKE OOBLEK

Materials needed:

- Newspapers to cover work area
- Paper towels for cleanup
- 1 box cornstarch
- 1 1/2 cups water (more if your ooblek is too firm)
- Green food coloring (or another color)
- Mixing bowl

1 Measure water and pour into bowl.

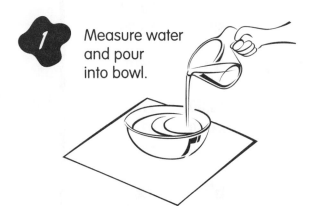

2 Add 15 drops of food coloring to water.

3 Add cornstarch.

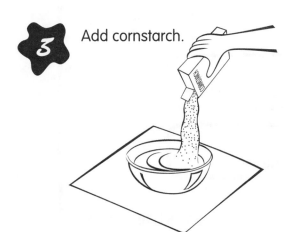

4 Mix by hand.

Note: You may have to add more water if the ooblek is too thick to flow when the bowl is tilted.

It won't take long before you realize you've made ooblek. It's sticky goo that flows like a syrup but holds together like a solid.

Simon's Sandwich Shop

All sandwiches come with your choice of bread and dressing.
(See below)

Favorites	6"	12"
Tuna	$3.50	$6.50
Roast Beef	$3.50	$6.50
Ham	$3.50	$6.50
Meatball	$3.50	$6.50
Turkey Breast	$3.50	$6.50

Speciality Sandwiches	6"	12"
Organic Free-Range Chicken and Cranberry Sauce	$4.50	$7.50
Grilled Veggies and Cheese	$4.50	$7.50
Barbecue Tofu Burger	$4.50	$7.50

Extras	6"	12"
Cheese	$ .25	$ .50
Lettuce	$ .25	$ .50
Tomato	$ .25	$ .50

Breads
White, Whole Wheat, Honey Bran, Italian Herb

Dressings
Mayonnaise, Mustard, Oil and Vinegar

Drinks
Lemonade	$1.25	$1.50	$2.00
Milk, Juice, and Water	$1.00		

Sides
Green Salad	$2.50
Pickle	$ .50

Day 3

Guided Strategy Practice

In this lesson, the students:

- Identify what they learn from a functional text
- Explore the organization of a functional text
- Read independently for up to 30 minutes
- Take responsibility for their learning and behavior

1 ▶ Review Functional Texts

Have partners sit together. Remind the students that yesterday they read two functional texts and thought about how they are organized to help readers understand them.

Explain that today the students will look closely at another functional text and discuss how it helps readers.

2 ▶ Introduce "City of Lawrence Street Map" and Model Finding a Location on the Map Using the Index

Remind the students that maps are another kind of functional text. Ask and briefly discuss:

Q *What are some reasons people use maps?*

Explain that today the students will work in pairs to find locations on a street map.

Show the transparency of "City of Lawrence Street Map" (BLM28), and tell the students that this is a street map of an imaginary city called Lawrence. Draw the students' attention to the letters down the side of the map and the numbers across the top of the map. Explain that using the letters and numbers on the map helps readers find specific locations on the map. Model for the students how to locate Lawrence Elementary School on the map. (For example, point to the letter D along the side of the map and the number 2 along

Materials

- "City of Lawrence Street Map" (see page 399)
- Transparency of "City of Lawrence Street Map" (BLM28)
- *Student Response Book* page 46
- "Self-monitoring Questions" chart

the top of the map, and then model moving your fingers to D2 to show the students that Lawrence Elementary School is on the map where row D and column 2 intersect, or meet.) Explain that Lawrence Elementary School is located at D2 on the map.

Explain that most street maps include an index to help readers find different streets and locations on the map. Ask the students to turn to *Student Response Book* page 46, where the map is reproduced, and find the index.

Ask the students to find the Lawrence Shopping Center in the index and read the letter and number that indicate where the Lawrence Shopping Center is located on the map. On the transparency of the map, model for the students how to locate the shopping center. (For example, point to the letter C along the side of the map and the number 4 along the top of the map, and then model moving your fingers to C4 to show the students that the Lawrence Shopping Center is located at C4 on the map.) Explain to the students that the letters along the side of the map and the numbers along the top of the map are called *coordinates*.

3 ▶ Have Pairs Find Locations on the Map

Explain that partners will use the "City of Lawrence Street Map" index to help them find five locations on the map. Ask pairs to circle five locations in the index, and then, using the coordinates listed in the index for those locations, find and circle the five different locations on the map. Ask the students to write the coordinates beside each circled location on the map.

4 ▶ Discuss Partner Work

Signal for the students' attention and ask a few students to share their work on the transparency of the "City of Lawrence Street Map."

Ask and briefly discuss:

Q *In addition to the index, what makes this map easy to use?*

Students might say:

"The coordinates are easy to find and use because they're on the top and side of the map."

"There is a key that gives you symbols so you can find important places like the hospital."

"In addition to what [Kendra] said, the streets and places on the map are labeled."

Point out to the students that maps are organized so that readers can find information quickly and easily. Remind the students that reading functional texts carefully and noticing how they are organized will help them understand and use them more easily. Encourage them to continue to notice functional texts in their everyday lives and how those texts are organized to give information.

 ## Reflect on Taking Responsibility

Ask and briefly discuss:

Q *How did you take responsibility for your own learning today?*

INDIVIDUALIZED DAILY READING

 ## Review Self-monitoring

Refer to the "Self-monitoring Questions" chart and review the questions. Remind the students that it is important to check their reading comprehension as they read. Explain that today you will stop them periodically to have them monitor their own comprehension.

Have the students read articles and other expository texts independently for up to 30 minutes. As the students read, circulate and ask individual students questions such as:

Q *What is your [article] about?*

Q *What do you do if the [book] you are reading has too many words you do not know?*

> ### Self-monitoring Questions
>
> - What is happening in my story right now?
> - Does the reading make sense?

Q *If you don't understand what you are reading, what should you do? How might that be helpful?*

Stop the students at 10-minute intervals and have them monitor their comprehension by thinking about the questions on the "Self-monitoring Questions" chart.

At the end of independent reading, have the students discuss how they did monitoring their own comprehension. Ask questions such as:

Q *Which question on the chart helped you the most today?*

Q *If you realized the text was not making sense to you, what did you do?*

Q *What do you want to do to monitor your comprehension the next time you read?*

EXTENSION

Find Locations on Local Street Maps

Repeat this lesson using a variety of street maps. Your students might enjoy collecting a variety of street maps to use in this extension activity. Interested students might want to find additional street maps on the Internet. They might be interested in locating their homes, school, or other places in their community on these street maps.

CITY OF LAWRENCE STREET MAP

Index	Reference/Location on Map
Alamo Park	C2
Centennial Dr.	D1–D4
Cherry Tree Ln	D1
City Hall	A2
City Park	B1
Columbus Ave	A3
Dayton St	A4–C4
East Jackson St.	A1–A4
Glenview Dr	A2–D2
Harmony Rd	C1–C4
Jefferson St.	A3
Lambert Science Museum	D4
Lawrence Elementary	D2
Lawrence Shopping Center	C4
Liberty Boulevard	A1–C4
Mayflower St.	D3
McCabe Alley	D2
North Juniper St	C1–C4
Oak Terrace Playground	A1
Ohio Rd.	B1–B4
Police Station	A3
President Ave	A2–D2
Spring Park	B3
St. Francis Hospital	A4
Texas Ave	D4
Washington Pl	A1

KEY

🚉 Train Station 🅿 Police Station ▣ Park ✚ Hospital

Map labels:
1 2 3 4
A B C D

St. Francis Hospital ✚
Columbus Ave
Dayton St
Jefferson St
President Ave
Police Station 🅿
Spring Park
Lawrence Shopping Center
Liberty Boulevard
Liberty Train Station
Texas Ave
Mayflower St.
Lambert Science Museum
City Hall
East Jackson St
Oak Terrace Playground
Ohio Rd
City Park
North Juniper St
Harmony Rd
Alamo Park
Glenview Dr
Centennial Dr
Cherry Tree Ln
McCabe Alley
Lawrence Elementary
Washington Pl

Day 4

Materials

- "Class Meeting Ground Rules" chart
- "Self-monitoring Questions" chart

Class Meeting Ground Rules

- one person talks at a time
- listen to one another

Class Meeting

In this lesson, the students:

- Have a class meeting to discuss working in groups of four
- Read independently for up to 30 minutes
- Take responsibility for their learning and behavior

1 Gather for a Class Meeting

Post the "Class Meeting Ground Rules" chart where everyone can see it. Explain to the students that they are going to have a check-in class meeting. Review the procedure for coming to a class meeting.

Have the students move to their places for the meeting, with partners sitting together. Ask the students to make sure they can see all their classmates.

2 Discuss the Challenges of Working in Groups of Four

Briefly review the class meeting ground rules. Explain that the purpose of this class meeting is to talk about working in groups of four.

Ask and discuss the following questions one at a time. Remind the students to avoid using names during the discussion. Use "Turn to Your Partner" as needed during this discussion to increase participation, especially if you are hearing from only a few students. You can also use "Turn to Your Partner" if many students want to speak at the same time.

Q *What has gone well for you working in your group of four?*

Q *What has been challenging about working in a group of four?*

Q *[Rajeed] said that it's challenging to make sure everyone is included in the discussions. What might be challenging about including one another in your group discussions?*

Q *[May Chin] said that [she] finds it challenging to contribute ideas to the discussion. What might be challenging about contributing ideas to the group discussions?*

Students might say:

"It is challenging to know when to speak in a group of four people. Sometimes more than one person wants to share at one time."

"Since there are so many people in a group, if one person speaks for a long time the other kids in the group might not get a chance to share."

"In addition to what [Ansel] said, you might have a different idea than the group and you're not sure how they will feel if you share it."

If the students have difficulty discussing these questions, stimulate their thinking using examples like those in the "Students might say" note, and then repeat the questions.

◀ **Teacher Note**

Remind the students to connect their comments to comments made by others by using the discussion prompts they learned in previous lessons:

- *I agree with _____ because…*
- *I disagree with _____ because…*
- *In addition to what _____ said, I think…*

3 ▶ **Discuss Solutions**

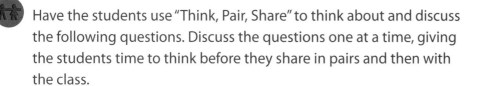

Have the students use "Think, Pair, Share" to think about and discuss the following questions. Discuss the questions one at a time, giving the students time to think before they share in pairs and then with the class.

Q *What are some ways that you can try to make sure everyone is included and that you contribute your ideas during group work?*

Q *Why is it important for all the members in the group to share their thinking?*

Students might say:

"You can ask anyone who hasn't shared if they have anything to share."

"If one person shares too much, we can nicely tell them that we are almost out of time and group members haven't had a chance to share."

FACILITATION TIP

Continue to focus on **responding neutrally** with interest during class discussions by refraining from overtly praising or criticizing the students' responses. Instead, build the students' intrinsic motivation by responding with genuine curiosity and interest; for example:

- *Interesting—say more about that.*
- *What you said makes me curious. I wonder…*
- *You have a point of view that is [similar/different] from what [Paula] just said. How is it [similar/different]?*

> "I agree with [Freddy]. And we can ask each other questions about what we are sharing. That way we'll feel more comfortable contributing ideas because we'll know that people are interested in what we have to say."

> "It is important to have everyone share because then we hear more ideas and that way we will learn more."

Explain that you would like the students to use some of their suggestions the next time they work in groups of four. Remind them that you will be checking in with them to see how they are doing.

▶ 4 Reflect on the Ground Rules and Adjourn the Meeting

Briefly discuss how the students felt they did following the ground rules during the class meeting. Review the procedure for returning to their desks and adjourn the meeting.

INDIVIDUALIZED DAILY READING

▶ 5 Use Self-monitoring Questions

Remind the students that they have been monitoring their comprehension as they read. Explain that the students will continue to monitor their reading today. Refer to the "Self-monitoring Questions" chart and briefly discuss which questions they have found the most helpful and why.

Have the students read nonfiction texts independently for 15 minutes; then stop them and ask them to think about the questions on the "Self-monitoring Questions" chart. After a moment, have the students read for another 15 minutes.

At the end of IDR, briefly discuss questions such as:

Q *Did you make sense of what you were reading today? How do you know?*

Q *If you were having difficulties making sense of the text, what might you do the next time you read independently?*

Self-monitoring Questions

- What is happening in my story right now?
- Does the reading make sense?

(v) *Making Meaning* Vocabulary Teacher

Next week you will revisit this week's reading to teach Vocabulary Week 21.

UNIT 7: ANALYZING
TEXT STRUCTURE
Expository Nonfiction

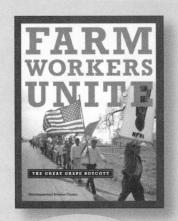

*Farm Workers Unite: The Great Grape Boycott**
(Developmental Studies Center, 2008)

The Great Delano Grape Strike and the Great Grape Boycott, masterminded by union activists César Chávez and Dolores Huerta, raised public awareness of the plight of farm workers and led to lasting improvements in migrant workers' living and working conditions.

* This book will also be used in Week 4.

ALTERNATIVE BOOKS

Japanese American Internment Camps by Gail Sakurai

Living at Ellis Island by Dale Anderson

Not in the Kit

Comprehension Focus

- Students hear and discuss expository nonfiction.

- Students identify what they learn from expository nonfiction.

- Students read independently.

Social Development Focus

- Students develop the group skills of including one another, contributing to group work, and using prompts in small group discussions.

- Students explain their thinking.

DO AHEAD

- Prior to Day 1, decide which of the students' social studies textbooks you would like them to read this week during IDR. If the textbooks are challenging for your students, plan to read the textbooks aloud with the students before having them read the textbooks independently.

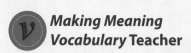

***Making Meaning Vocabulary* Teacher**

If you are teaching Developmental Studies Center's *Making Meaning Vocabulary* program, teach Vocabulary Week 21 this week. For more information, see the *Making Meaning Vocabulary Teacher's Manual.*

Day 1

Materials

- *Farm Workers Unite* (pages 1–10)
- Wall map of the United States
- *Student Response Book* page 47
- Textbooks for students to read during IDR
- Small self-stick notes, one per student

Read-aloud

In this lesson, the students:

- Hear expository nonfiction read aloud
- Identify what they learn from expository text
- Read independently for up to 30 minutes
- Explain their thinking
- Use discussion prompts in small group discussions

About Reading Textbooks

The students have spent the first two weeks of this unit analyzing text structure to help them make sense of articles and functional texts, two kinds of expository nonfiction. The focus of the final two weeks is on analyzing text structure in textbooks. The students hear and read a book written to resemble textbooks the students might read in school. This week the students hear the book read aloud and identify and discuss what they learn from the text. Next week the students analyze parts of the book in depth and explore several text structures commonly used to organize the information in textbooks: compare and contrast and chronology. This week's and next week's lessons on exploring how expository texts are organized lay the foundation for work that the students will do in middle school and high school. Mastery of these concepts is not expected at this point. The goal, as with all the reading comprehension strategies, is for the students to be able to use the strategy to help make sense of their independent reading.

Discuss Reading Textbooks

Have pairs sit in their groups of four. Remind the students that they have been reading articles and functional texts and thinking about how expository nonfiction can inform readers. Explain that in the coming weeks they will look at another kind of expository nonfiction—textbooks—and work in groups and as a class to explore how textbooks are written.

Point out that textbooks are a kind of expository text that the students read often in school. Ask:

Q *What kinds of textbooks have you been reading this year?*

Q *What can be hard about reading textbooks?*

Explain that this week the students will hear a book written in the style of a textbook. They will think about and discuss how textbooks can be organized to give readers information and use what they learn to help them make sense of their own textbooks. They will also have opportunities to explain their thinking and use discussion prompts in their groups.

 Introduce *Farm Workers Unite*

Tell the students that the book you will read aloud over the next few days is titled *Farm Workers Unite: The Great Grape Boycott.* Show the cover and explain that this book is written like many social studies textbooks.

Explain that *Farm Workers Unite* is about how two Mexican American leaders, César Chávez and Dolores Huerta, helped migrant farm workers in California and other states improve their living and working conditions. Ask and briefly discuss:

Q *What do you know, or think you know, about how produce (or fruits and vegetables) is grown in the United States?*

Locate California's Central Valley on a map of the United States. If the Central Valley is not labeled on your map, tell the students that it is roughly located between Redding and Bakersfield, California.

Provide historical background by explaining that since the early 1900s, produce growers in California, where most of the country's fruit and vegetables come from, have hired mostly temporary workers to do the planting and harvesting on their farms. These "migrant workers," many of whom are Mexican American, move from farm to farm looking for work. Up until the late 1960s, migrant workers often lived and worked in terrible conditions. To this day, some still do. César Chávez and Dolores Huerta helped farm workers stand up for themselves and their rights. Also explain that the Great Grape Boycott of 1967, which Chávez and Huerta helped organize, helped people all over the United States learn about the lives of farm workers.

ELL Note

Prior to each read-aloud lesson this week, show your English Language Learners the sections you will be reading. Point out the text features and summarize the information in the text, making sure your students have at least a surface-level understanding of the information.

3 ▶ **Introduce the Reading and Read the Introduction**

Show the table of contents of *Farm Workers Unite* and ask the students to turn to their own copy of it on *Student Response Book* page 47. Read the chapter headings and subheadings aloud, then ask:

Q *What topics do you think you will hear about in this book?*

Have one or two volunteers share their thinking.

Explain that today the students will hear the introduction and the first two chapters of the book. Explain that you will stop periodically during the reading and have them discuss what they have learned from the book up to that point.

4 ▶ **Read Aloud with Brief Section Introductions**

Read the Introduction and Chapters 1 and 2 (pages 1–10) as described below, clarifying vocabulary as you read.

Suggested Vocabulary

produce: fruits and vegetables (p. 1)

deportation: being sent back to their home countries (p. 6)

exposure to: being close to (p. 8)

ELL Vocabulary

English Language Learners may benefit from discussing additional vocabulary, including:

permanent staff: people who work there all the time (p. 1)

make a bigger profit: keep more money for themselves (p. 6)

crossing the border illegally: coming from other countries even though they were not allowed to (p. 6)

bad conditions: ways that were not safe (p. 7)

thin out crops: cut down some of the plants so they're not growing too closely together (p. 7)

permanently stooped: bent over for their whole lives (p. 7)

cause headaches, dizziness, and nausea: make them very sick (p. 8)

shack: very small, poorly built house (p. 9)

bathing facilities: bathrooms (p. 9)

participate: talk to their teachers or to other students (p. 10)

Read the first three paragraphs of the Introduction aloud, and then reread them, asking the students to listen for information they might have missed the first time. Ask and briefly discuss:

Q *What did you hear on the second reading that you missed the first time?*

Continue reading to the end of the Introduction, showing the photographs and reading the captions.

Read the title of Chapter 1, "Competition for Work," and explain that this chapter tells about how starting in the mid-1900s there weren't as many jobs for farm workers. Read Chapter 1 aloud. Show the accompanying photograph and read the caption. Ask the students to listen for what they find out about why it became harder for farm workers to find jobs.

Ask:

Q *What are some reasons it became harder for farm workers to find jobs?*

Have a couple of students share what they found out. Tell the students that the next chapter, Chapter 2 (pages 7–10), is titled "The Life of a Migrant Worker." This chapter talks about what life was like for many migrant farm workers. The first section, "Working Conditions," describes what it was like to work in the fields.

Read "Working Conditions" aloud, showing the accompanying photographs. Ask:

Q *What did you find out about what it was like to work in the fields?*

Have a few volunteers share what they found out. Tell the students that the next section in Chapter 2 is called "Living Conditions." Explain that this section discusses where and how many migrant workers lived.

Read the section "Living Conditions" aloud, showing the photograph on page 9.

Teacher Note

This week's read-aloud contains a lot of factual information that the students might have difficulty following. To support them, you will briefly introduce each section before you read it. This will help to focus the students' listening on the main ideas discussed in that section.

Teacher Note

As you read aloud this week, show the illustrations to the students and read the captions, subheadings, and information in the sidebars.

Ask:

Q *What did you find out about how some migrant workers lived from this reading?*

Have a few volunteers share what they found out.

Explain that the next section, "Education," discusses some of the challenges faced by the children of migrant workers when they tried to go to school. Read the section aloud, showing the accompanying photo. Ask:

Q *What made going to school difficult for the children of migrant workers?*

Have a few volunteers share what they found out.

5 ▶ Discuss the Reading

Facilitate a discussion about Chapter 2 by asking the following questions and having the students use "Heads Together" to discuss their thinking in groups of four. Encourage the students to use the discussion prompts they have learned to respond to one another. Ask:

Q *What are some important things we've learned from Chapter 2 about what life was like for many migrant farm workers?*

After sufficient time for groups to discuss the question, signal for attention and have a few volunteers share with the class. Be ready to reread from the text to help the students support their thinking.

> **Students might say:**
>
> "We learned that a lot of times their working conditions were not safe."
>
> "I agree with [Sadie], because the book said that workers had to use dangerous tools."
>
> "We learned that it was hard for the children of migrant workers to go to school because their families moved around so much."
>
> "In addition to what [Sterling] said, we learned that it was hard for the kids because they couldn't speak English."

Teacher Note ▶

If necessary, review the following discussion prompts:

- *I agree with _____ because…*
- *I disagree with _____ because…*
- *In addition to what _____ said, I think…*

Explain that tomorrow the students will hear and discuss Chapter 3, "Time for a Change."

6 Reflect on Group Work

Ask and briefly discuss:

Q *How did you do with explaining your thinking in your group?*

Q *How did the discussion prompts help you participate in your group discussion?*

INDIVIDUALIZED DAILY READING

7 Practice Self-monitoring and Rereading Textbooks

Tell the students that for the next two weeks they will read their social studies textbook during IDR. Explain that they will focus on how they are making sense of the information in the textbook.

Remind the students that they have been practicing checking their comprehension as they are reading. Review with the students that one of the best techniques for helping them comprehend what they are reading is to go back and reread. Explain that this is especially true when they are reading textbooks. Tell them that rereading a textbook helps them understand more deeply and clarify misunderstandings. Explain that today they will practice rereading their social studies textbook and partners will share what they read with each other.

Distribute a self-stick note to each student. Ask the students to open their textbooks to a chapter that looks interesting to them and to place a self-stick note on that page. Have the students read independently for 10 minutes.

Stop the students after 10 minutes and have them use "Turn to Your Partner" to talk in pairs about what they have learned in the part of the text that they just read.

 Note

Consider modeling this activity for your English Language Learners.

As the students read, circulate and help them with vocabulary as needed.

After a few minutes, signal for the students' attention. Ask them to turn back to the page with the self-stick note and reread the part they just read.

 Stop the students after 10 minutes and have them use "Turn to Your Partner" to talk in pairs about any new details they learned from the rereading.

At the end of independent reading, have the students share their experience of how rereading helped them understand. Ask and briefly discuss the following questions as a class:

Q *What information did you learn when you reread that you missed during the first reading?*

Q *How might rereading help you understand textbooks and other expository nonfiction?*

EXTENSION

Learn More About Migrant Workers

Interested students may want to do further research about the history of migrant labor in California or in the United States. You can find information on websites such as pbs.org and farmworkers.org, or elsewhere on the Internet by conducting searches using keywords such as "migrant workers," "migrant labor," and "farm workers."

Day 2

Read-aloud

In this lesson, the students:

* Hear expository text read aloud
* Identify what they learn from expository text
* Read independently for up to 30 minutes
* Include others in group work
* Use discussion prompts in small group discussions

1 ▶ Review and Introduce the Reading

Have groups of four sit together. Show the cover of *Farm Workers Unite* and remind the students that they heard the first two chapters, "Competition for Work" and "The Life of a Migrant Worker," yesterday. Ask and briefly discuss:

Q *What have we learned so far about migrant workers?*

Explain that today you will read Chapter 3, "Time for a Change" (pages 11–14). Explain that this chapter talks about how things changed when farm workers began to fight for their rights as workers. Explain that you will stop periodically during the reading and have groups discuss what they have learned from the reading up to that point.

2 ▶ Read Aloud with Brief Section Introductions

Read Chapter 3 aloud to the class, following the procedure described on the next page.

> **Suggested Vocabulary**
>
> **on behalf of:** speaking for (p. 11)
> **injustices:** unfair treatment (p. 12)
> **government officials:** people who work for the government (p. 14)

Materials

* *Farm Workers Unite* (pages 11–14)
* "Reading Comprehension Strategies" chart
* Textbooks for students to read during IDR

ELL Vocabulary

English Language Learners may benefit from discussing additional vocabulary, including:

improve: make better (p. 11)

organize: get people together to make something happen (p. 11)

bullied: made to feel afraid (p. 11)

determined: very sure he wanted (p. 12)

stood up for: protected; defended (p. 12)

enrolling: signing up (p. 13)

bold and outgoing: brave and good at talking to people (p. 14)

Explain that the first section of Chapter 3, "Unionization," talks about why it was difficult for migrant workers to change their living and working conditions. Read "Unionization" aloud. Ask the students to listen for why it was difficult for workers to improve their living and working conditions.

Ask:

Q *Why was it difficult for farm workers to improve their living and working conditions?*

Have a few volunteers share their thinking.

Point out the text box on page 12 entitled "Unions and Contracts" and explain that it gives readers useful information about unions. Read "Unions and Contracts" aloud. Ask:

Q *What information did you find out about unions?*

Explain that the next section, "César Chávez and Dolores Huerta," discusses how César Chávez and Dolores Huerta got involved in trying to organize farm workers. Read the first three paragraphs of "César Chávez and Dolores Huerta" aloud. Stop after:

> **p. 13** "…he got to know a woman named Dolores Huerta."

Ask and have the students use "Heads Together" to discuss:

Q *What do you think made César Chávez decide to fight for the rights of farm workers?*

◄ Teacher Note

As groups talk, listen for evidence that the students are discussing the book and understanding it. If necessary, reread parts of the text to help the students recall what they heard.

Without discussing the question as a class, continue reading. Read the next paragraph aloud, showing the photographs of César Chávez's family and Dolores Huerta. Stop after:

> **p. 13**   "'…than by trying to teach their hungry children.'"

 Ask and have the students use "Heads Together" to discuss:

Q *What do you think made Dolores Huerta decide to fight for the rights of farm workers?*

Signal for attention, and have a few volunteers share their thinking. Continue reading to the end of the section.

Explain that the last section of Chapter 3, "A New Union," talks about how César Chávez and Dolores Huerta got their union started. Read "A New Union" aloud. Ask and briefly discuss:

Q *What did you find out in the section you just heard?*

▶ Discuss the Reading

 Have the students use "Heads Together" to discuss the following question. Remind them to include everyone in the discussion and to refer to information in the text to support their thinking. Ask:

Q *Why were César Chávez and Dolores Huerta more successful at unionizing, or organizing, farm workers than others had been in the past?*

Signal for the students' attention and have a few volunteers share their thinking with the class. Encourage the students to use the discussion prompts.

FACILITATION TIP

Continue to build the students' intrinsic motivation during class discussions by **responding neutrally** with genuine curiosity and interest rather than praise or criticism; for example:

● *Interesting—say more about that.*

● *What you said makes me curious. I wonder…*

● *You have a point of view that's [similar to/different from] what [Jackson] just said. How is it [similar/different]?*

Students might say:

"They were successful because the workers trusted them."

"I agree with [James]. They were both Mexican American and knew about the lives of farm workers. César Chávez even worked in the fields himself."

"In addition to what [Zoe] said, we learned that Chávez and Huerta were a good team. They got a lot of people to join the union."

"I agree with [Terence]. The book said that Chávez was quiet and shy but understood the workers and Huerta was good at getting out and talking to a lot of people."

Explain that tomorrow the students will hear and discuss Chapters 4 and 5, "The Great Delano Grape Strike" and "A Long, Hard Road."

▶4 Reflect on Group Work

Ask and briefly discuss:

Q *What did your group do to make sure everyone was included? If everyone wasn't included, what do you want to do differently next time so everyone participates?*

Q *Why is it important to include everyone when you are working in groups?*

INDIVIDUALIZED DAILY READING

▶5 Use Comprehension Strategies to Read Textbooks

Have the students sit in their groups of four. Explain to them that in addition to rereading to help them understand a text, using the reading comprehension strategies they have been learning this year will also help them make sense of the text. Explain that today the students will continue to read their social studies textbooks and stop to think about which comprehension strategies they are using to help them understand what they are reading.

Direct the students' attention to the "Reading Comprehension Strategies" chart, review each strategy with the students, and remind them that these are the strategies they have learned so far

Reading Comprehension Strategies

- recognizing text features

this year. Ask the students to notice which strategies they use and where they use them during their reading today. At the end of IDR, they will share with their groups.

Have the students read their social studies textbooks independently for up to 30 minutes.

 At the end of independent reading, have each student share his reading and a strategy he used—the name of the strategy and where he used it—with his group. Have students who cannot think of a comprehension strategy they used discuss what they read.

Signal for the students' attention. As a whole class, discuss questions such as:

Q *How did making inferences about [the causes of the Civil War] help you make sense of the text?*

Q *[Jackie] said [she] was able to visualize [the hardships and oppression slaves felt prior to the Emancipation Act]. How did visualizing help you make sense of the text?*

Q *What questions do you have for [Jackie] about [her] thinking?*

EXTENSION

Explore and Discuss Expository Text Features

Show the photographs from the first three chapters of the book. Ask and discuss questions such as:

Q *What information do these photographs add to the text?*

Q *Would the information in the text be as useful to readers without the photographs? Why or why not?*

Day 3

Read-aloud

Materials

- *Farm Workers Unite* (page 15–24)
- Textbooks for students to read during IDR
- *Student Response Book,* IDR Journal section

In this lesson, the students:

- Hear expository text read aloud
- Identify what they learn from expository text
- Read independently for up to 30 minutes
- Contribute to group work
- Include one another during group work

1 ▶ Review Contributing to Group Work

Have groups sit together. Tell the students that they will be using "Heads Together" again today to talk about their thinking. Encourage them to continue to include one another and contribute responsibly to the group work.

2 ▶ Read Aloud with Brief Section Introductions

Show the cover of *Farm Workers Unite* and review that in the previous lesson the students heard Chapter 3 of the book and learned about César Chávez and Dolores Huerta and how they decided to start their own union for farm workers, the National Farm Workers Association (NFWA). Ask and briefly discuss:

Q *What have we learned so far about César Chávez and Dolores Huerta?*

Explain that today you will read from Chapters 4 and 5 (pages 15–24), which are about the Great Delano Grape Strike, a very important event in the history of the National Farm Workers Association. Read Chapters 4 and 5 aloud, following the procedure described on the next page.

Suggested Vocabulary

went on strike: stopped working because they felt their bosses weren't treating them fairly (p. 15)

retaliate: fight back; take revenge (p. 16)

vulnerable: able to be hurt easily (p. 16)

movement: large group effort (p. 16)

picket lines: workers standing in lines outside where they work to show people they are not being treated fairly (p. 17)

intimidate: frighten (p. 20)

tactics: ways of doing things (p. 20)

enthusiasm: energy and excitement (p. 21)

ELL Vocabulary

English Language Learners may benefit from discussing additional vocabulary, including:

rival: competing (p. 15)

national attention: people all over the country talking about it (p. 16)

justice: fairness (p. 16)

recognize or negotiate with: pay attention to or talk to (p. 21)

protesters: people who were trying to get fair treatment (p. 22)

hobbled: limped (p. 24)

a turning point: an important event that made things start to get better (p. 24)

Read the title of Chapter 4, "The Great Delano Grape Strike," aloud and then explain that the first section of Chapter 4, entitled "To Join or Not to Join," talks about how the Great Grape Strike started. Read the opening paragraph of the section. Stop after:

> **p. 15**   "…making their pay lower than the braceros'."

Ask:

Q   *What have you found out so far about how the strike started?*

Have one or two volunteers share what they found out.

Continue reading to the end of the section; then read the sidebars "Extract from Chávez's Speech" on page 18 and "Strikes and Picket Lines" on page 19. Show the photographs and read the captions to the students. Ask:

Q   *What did you find out in the rest of the section?*

Teacher Note ▶

Consider reading the sections "Gathering Support" and "The Strike Spreads" aloud at another time (see Extension, page 422).

Have a few volunteers share their what they found out in the rest of the section. Explain that there are two more sections in Chapter 4, entitled "Gathering Support" (page 17) and "The Strike Spreads" (pages 18–19), that you will not read aloud at this time.

Explain that Chapter 5, "A Long, Hard Road" (pages 20–24), discusses challenges the workers faced as the strike continued and how the workers and the union responded to the strike. Explain that the first section, entitled "Hard Times on the Picket Lines," talks about how the growers responded to the strike.

Teacher Note ▶

As you read each section, show the photographs to the students and read aloud the captions.

 Read the section aloud; then have the students use "Heads Together" to discuss:

Q *What was hard about picketing during the strike?*

Signal for the students' attention. Without discussing the question as a class, explain that the next two sections, entitled "The March on Sacramento" and "The United Farm Workers of America," talk about what happened as the strike continued.

 Read "The March on Sacramento" and "The United Farm Workers of America" aloud, including the sidebar text. Then, have the students use "Heads Together" to discuss:

Q *What were some changes that happened because of the strike?*

Signal for the students' attention. Have several volunteers share their thinking.

> ***Students might say:***
>
> "The biggest grower signed a contract with the union."
>
> "In addition to what [Miguel] said, after the march, some of the smaller growers signed contracts, too."
>
> "Because of the strike, the farm workers got on TV and got a lot of publicity."
>
> "I agree with what [Megan] said. Because of the strike, a lot of people all over the country learned about farm workers for the first time and supported their cause."

Discuss the Reading

Use the question that follows to facilitate a class discussion about Chapter 5. Encourage the students to include one another and contribute ideas to the discussion. Ask:

Q *Why was the march on Sacramento important to the workers and the union?*

As students respond, encourage them to refer to the text to support their thinking. Be ready to reread from the text to help them.

> **Students might say:**
>
> "The march was important because it made more people pay attention to the strike."
>
> "I agree with what [Tobias] said. It made the growers pay attention because after the march, one of the biggest growers made a contract with the union."
>
> "The march was important because it got more workers to join the union."
>
> "In addition to what [Carmen] said, after the march the two unions joined together to make a bigger, stronger union."

Explain that tomorrow the students will hear and discuss the last two chapters of *Farm Workers Unite*.

 Reflect on Group Work

Review that today the students focused on contributing their thinking during group work. Ask and briefly discuss:

Q *What did you do to make sure everyone in your group felt comfortable sharing their thinking?*

Q *Why is it important to contribute your thinking to the group discussion?*

INDIVIDUALIZED DAILY READING

 Read Textbooks/Record Facts in Their IDR Journals

Remind the students they have been reading their social studies textbook and monitoring what they are learning. Explain that today the students will continue to read their social studies textbook independently and then they will record several pieces of information they have learned.

Have the students read their social studies textbook for up to 30 minutes.

At the end of IDR, have the students write in their IDR Journals about what they read. Ask each student to write the title of the chapter she read and five or six things she learned from her reading.

After sufficient time, signal for the students' attention and briefly discuss questions such as:

Q *What did you read today?*

Q *What information did you learn from your reading?*

Q *What inferences did you make about [Reconstruction after the Civil War]?*

Q *What questions do you have for [Ronnie] about [his] thinking?*

EXTENSION

Read "Gathering Support" and "The Strike Spreads" Aloud

Introduce the section "Gathering Support," in Chapter 4 (pages 17–18) of *Farm Workers Unite,* by explaining that this section talks about how César Chávez and Dolores Huerta generated support for the strike. Read the section aloud. Ask and briefly discuss:

Q *Why did César Chávez think it was so important to get support for the Great Grape Strike?*

Introduce the section "The Strike Spreads," in Chapter 4 (pages 18–19) of *Farm Workers Unite,* by explaining that this section discusses how the strike began to grow. Read the section aloud. Ask and briefly discuss:

Q   *What are some reasons the strike grew bigger and stronger?*

Day 4

Materials

- *Farm Workers Unite* (pages 25–30)
- *Student Response Book* page 47
- *Assessment Resource Book*
- Textbooks for students to read during IDR

Read-aloud

In this lesson, the students:

- Hear expository text read aloud
- Identify what they learn from expository text
- Read independently for up to 30 minutes
- Contribute to group work
- Use discussion prompts in small group discussions

1 ▶ Review and Introduce the Reading

Have groups of four sit together. Show the cover of *Farm Workers Unite* and remind the students that they have heard part of each of the first five chapters of the book. Have them turn to the contents page from *Farm Workers Unite,* reproduced on *Student Response Book* page 47, and explain that today you will read the last two chapters of the book. Ask the students to read the chapter and section headings for Chapters 6 and 7 (pages 25–30). Ask and briefly discuss:

Q *What do you think the last two chapters of this book will be about? What makes you think so?*

2 ▶ Read Aloud with Brief Section Introductions

Read Chapters 6 and 7 aloud, stopping as described on the next page.

> ### Suggested Vocabulary
>
> **documented:** found proof (p. 28)
>
> **unemployment benefits:** small amounts of money workers can get from the government to help them when they don't have jobs (p. 30)

ELL Vocabulary

English Language Learners may benefit from discussing additional vocabulary, including:

focus its efforts on: pay more attention to (p. 25)

the media: television, radio, magazines, and newspapers (p. 27)

guarantees: promises (p. 28)

banned: made against the law (p. 28)

treated with chemicals: sprayed with dangerous substances (p. 29)

get around: not obey (p. 30)

Explain that the first section of Chapter 6, "The Great Grape Boycott" (pages 25–27), discusses what the union did after the success of the Great Grape Strike. Read the first three paragraphs of the section aloud. Stop after:

> **p. 25** "Chávez responded by asking the public to stop buying all California grapes."

Ask:

Q *What have you found out so far about the Great Grape Boycott?*

Have one or two volunteers share what they found out.

Read the last paragraph of the section aloud. Have the students use "Heads Together" to discuss the question that follows. Encourage the students to contribute their ideas to the discussion. Look for examples of groups working well together and groups having difficulty, and be ready to share your observations at the end of the lesson.

Q *Was the Great Grape Boycott successful? What did you hear that makes you think that?*

Signal for attention and have one or two volunteers share their thinking.

Explain that the next section, "Keeping the Peace," is about what happened as the boycott continued. Read the section aloud, including the sidebar on page 26. Show the photographs and read the captions.

Have the students use "Heads Together" to discuss the question that follows. Ask the students to refer to the text to support their thinking.

Q *Why was César Chávez's fast important?*

CLASS COMPREHENSION ASSESSMENT

Circulate among the groups as they work. Randomly select groups to observe and ask yourself:

Q *Are the students able to identify what they've learned from the book?*

Q *Are they contributing their thinking to the group?*

Q *Are they using prompts to extend their conversations?*

Record your observations on page 25 of the *Assessment Resource Book.*

Signal for attention and have a few volunteers share what they found out.

> **Students might say:**
>
> "César Chávez's fast reminded the workers not to fight back even though the growers were violent."
>
> "I agree with what [Tony] said. The book said his fast united the strikers and gave them the message that the union was committed to nonviolence."
>
> "In addition to what [Amelia] said, the public got the message about nonviolence, too."
>
> "After his fast, the workers never gave up and the boycott worked."

Explain that the final chapter, "New Battles, New Victories" (pages 28–30), talks about what has happened since the Great Grape Boycott. Read the first paragraph of the chapter aloud. Ask:

Q *What did you find out in the part you just heard?*

Have one or two students share what they found out. Explain that at this time you will not read aloud the next section in Chapter 7, entitled "The Campaign Against Pesticides" (pages 28–29).

Teacher Note

Consider reading the section "The Campaign Against Pesticides" at another time (see Extension, page 429).

Read the title of the last section, "The Struggle Goes On," and continue reading to the end of the chapter. Ask:

Q *What did you find out in the last part of the book?*

Have one or two students share what they found out.

 ## **Discuss the Reading**

Facilitate a class discussion about Chapters 6 and 7 using the question that follows. Encourage the students to use the discussion prompts they have learned as they participate in the discussion. Ask:

Q *Why were the Great Delano Grape Strike and the Great Grape Boycott important for farm workers?*

As students respond, encourage them to refer to the text to support their thinking. Be ready to reread from the text to help them support their thinking.

> **Students might say:**
>
> "The strike and the boycott were important because afterwards, the union had the power to keep making things better for workers."
>
> "I agree with what [Jacques] said, because the book says that the short-handled hoe was banned."
>
> "In addition to what [Veronica] said, more of the workers had homes and more of their children could go to school."

Explain that next week the students will hear and read parts of the book again and explore how the text is organized to give readers information.

Reflect on Group Work

Share some of your observations of how the students worked together in their groups. Without giving names, describe both examples of groups in which all the members were engaged and contributing and any examples of groups in which some members were not participating. You might give examples and ask questions such as those that follow.

Q *I noticed a group in which all four members were leaning into the center of the table and looking at each other. I also heard one group member ask another what she thought. How might these actions help a group work well together?*

Q *I noticed a group in which it looked like the students were working in pairs, rather than one group of four. Why might that happen? What can a group do to make sure they are working as a group during "Heads Together"?*

Explain that the students will have more opportunities to practice participating in group work next week.

INDIVIDUALIZED DAILY READING

5 **Have the Students Practice Self-monitoring/ Document IDR Conferences**

Continue to have the students read their textbooks independently and monitor their own comprehension. Remind the students that it is important to stop to think about what they are reading. When they do not understand what they are reading, they may need to reread to help them make sense of it. In addition, encourage them to continue to use the reading comprehension strategies they have learned so far this year to help them make sense of the text.

Have the students read their textbooks independently for up to 30 minutes.

Circulate among the students and ask individuals to read a passage to you and tell you what it is about. If a student is confused by any part of the textbook, have her reread that section. If several students are struggling, read the section aloud to the whole class and briefly discuss what they have learned.

Use the "IDR Conference Notes" record sheet to conduct and document individual conferences.

At the end of the reading time, have a whole-class discussion about what the students learned from the textbook.

EXTENSIONS

Read and Discuss the Appendices in *Farm Workers Unite*

Show the "Timeline of Events" (pages 33–34), "Glossary" (page 35), "Bibliography" (page 36), and "Index" (page 37) sections in *Farm Workers Unite*. Discuss the function of each section by asking questions such as:

Q *What information does the ["Glossary"] provide? How is that helpful to a reader?*

Q *How do you think the ["Timeline of Events"] might help a reader make sense of this book?*

Q *What do you notice about the ["Bibliography"]? How might a reader use it?*

Q *How do you think the ["Index"] might help a reader?*

Read "The Campaign Against Pesticides" Aloud

Introduce the section "The Campaign Against Pesticides," in Chapter 7 (pages 28–29) of *Farm Workers Unite,* by explaining that this section talks about a problem that continued for farm workers even after all the work the union did during the Great Delano Grape Strike and the Great Grape Boycott.

Read the section aloud. Ask and briefly discuss:

Q *Why do you think the growers kept using pesticides on their crops?*

Q *How was the union able to fight the use of pesticides?*

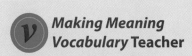

***Making Meaning Vocabulary* Teacher**

Next week you will revisit this week's reading to teach Vocabulary Week 22.

Overview

UNIT 7: ANALYZING TEXT STRUCTURE

Expository Nonfiction

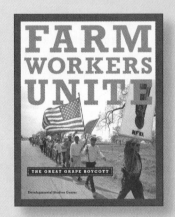

*Farm Workers Unite: The Great Grape Boycott**
(Developmental Studies Center, 2008)

The Great Delano Grape Strike and the Great Grape Boycott, masterminded by union activists César Chávez and Dolores Huerta, raised public awareness of the plight of farm workers and led to lasting improvements in migrant workers' living and working conditions.

* This book was also used in Week 3.

ALTERNATIVE BOOKS

Japanese American Internment Camps by Gail Sakurai

Arriving at Ellis Island by Dale Anderson

Comprehension Focus

- Students *use text structure* to explore expository text.

- Students explore how information is organized in textbooks.

- Students explore text structures such as chronology and compare and contrast in expository text.

- Students read independently.

Social Development Focus

- Students take responsibility for their own learning during group work.

DO AHEAD

- Prior to Day 1, prepare a sheet of chart paper with the heading "Relationships in Expository Text" (see Step 2 on page 434).

- Prior to Day 1, decide which of the students' social studies textbooks you would like them to read this week during IDR. If the textbooks are challenging for your students, plan to read aloud with the students before having them read the textbooks independently.

- Prior to Day 4, choose a section from the students' social studies textbook for the class to read during IDR.

- Make copies of the Unit 7 Parent Letter (BLM16) to send home with the students on the last day of the unit.

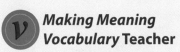

Making Meaning Vocabulary Teacher

If you are teaching Developmental Studies Center's *Making Meaning Vocabulary* program, teach Vocabulary Week 22 this week. For more information, see the *Making Meaning Vocabulary Teacher's Manual.*

Day 1

Materials

- *Farm Workers Unite* (pages 4–5 and 12–13)
- *Student Response Book* pages 47–51
- "Relationships in Expository Text" chart, prepared ahead, and a marker
- Social studies textbook for each student to read during IDR
- *Student Response Book*, IDR Journal section

Strategy Lesson

In this lesson, the students:

- *Use text structure* to explore expository text
- Explore how information can be organized in expository text
- Explore chronological relationships in expository text
- Read independently for up to 30 minutes
- Take responsibility for their own learning during group work

1 ▶ Review *Farm Workers Unite*

Have pairs sit in their groups of four. Explain that for the last several weeks the students have been working on how to be responsible group members. They have been making an effort to include everyone in their group discussions and to contribute their thinking and ideas to their small-group discussions. Ask the students to continue to take responsibility for their learning during their small-group discussions this week.

Remind the students that last week they heard *Farm Workers Unite,* a book written like many social studies textbooks. Show the cover and then have the students turn to their copy of the table of contents from *Farm Workers Unite* on *Student Response Book* page 47. Ask the students to follow along as you read the table of contents aloud. Have the students use "Heads Together" to briefly discuss what they learned in each chapter.

Signal for attention. As a class, discuss the following question:

 Q *What are some things you learned from* Farm Workers Unite *about the struggle of César Chávez and Dolores Huerta to improve the working and living conditions for migrant farm workers?*

Teacher Note ▶

If the students struggle with this question, consider rereading sections of the book and then ask the question again.

Explain that it can be helpful in understanding textbooks to think about how the information is organized. Tell the students that they will use *Farm Workers Unite* this week to explore two different ways information can be organized in nonfiction text. They will then use this information to help them make sense of their own textbooks.

2 ▶ Discuss and Notice Chronological Relationships

Have the students refer to Chapter 1, "Competition for Work," on *Student Response Book* pages 48–49 and explain that authors make deliberate choices about how to organize information in expository texts. Explain that when events are written in the order in which they occurred, they are organized chronologically. Tell the students that this chapter is organized chronologically. Ask them to follow along as you read the chapter aloud.

Read Chapter 1, "Competition for Work" (pages 5–6), aloud slowly and clearly. Ask and briefly discuss:

Q *What did you learn about the competition for work from this chapter?*

Q *What do you notice about how the authors organized information in this chapter?*

Have the students turn to *Student Response Book* pages 50–51, where the section from Chapter 3 titled "César Chávez and Dolores Huerta" (pages 12–13) is reproduced. Explain that this is another example of information organized chronologically. Ask the students to follow along as you read the text aloud. Ask them to notice how the authors use time to organize the information. Briefly discuss the following question:

Q *What do you notice about how the authors use time to organize information in this passage?*

Students might say:

"I notice that the passage starts out by mentioning that César Chávez was born in 1927."

"In addition to what [Juanita] said, it mentions important dates in César Chávez's life. Like 1942, when he was 15 and he had to drop out of school to work in the fields to help his family."

◀ Teacher Note

This lesson and the following lesson on exploring how expository texts are organized lay the foundation for work that the students will continue to do in subsequent grades. In grades 5 and 6 of the *Making Meaning* program, students explore cause and effect relationships as well as chronological and compare and contrast relationships. Mastery of these concepts is not expected at this point. Also note that for clarity the terms "chronological relationships" and "compare and contrast relationships" are used to describe the expository text structures of chronology and compare-contrast.

On a sheet of chart paper entitled "Relationships in Expository Text," write *chronological relationships*. Point out that recognizing chronological relationships can help the students make sense of their own reading of nonfiction. Explain that you will add to the chart tomorrow when the students explore another way information can be organized.

Teacher Note ▶

Save the "Relationships in Expository Text" chart for use throughout the week.

Encourage the students to look for chronological relationships in expository text when they read independently.

INDIVIDUALIZED DAILY READING

3 ▶ **Read Textbooks/Record Facts in Their IDR Journals**

Remind the students they have been reading textbooks and monitoring what they are learning. Explain that today the students will again read their social studies textbook independently, and then they will record several pieces of information they have learned.

Have the students read their social studies textbook for up to 30 minutes.

ELL Note

Consider modeling this activity for your English Language Learners.

At the end of IDR, have the students write in their IDR Journals about what they read. Ask each student to write the title of the chapter he read and five or six things he learned from his reading.

After sufficient time, signal for the students' attention and briefly discuss questions such as:

Q *What did you read today?*

Q *What information did you learn from your reading?*

Q *Did you notice if the text was organized in chronological order? If so, what did you learn in that section of the textbook?*

Q *What questions do you have for [Sly] about [his] thinking?*

Day 2

Strategy Lesson

In this lesson, the students:

- *Use text structure* to explore expository text
- Explore how information can be organized in expository text
- Explore compare and contrast relationships in expository text
- Read independently for up to 30 minutes
- Take responsibility for their own learning during group work

Materials

- *Farm Workers Unite* (pages 14–17)
- "Relationships in Expository Text" chart from Day 1 and a marker
- *Student Response Book* pages 52–55
- *Student Response Book*, IDR Journal section

 Review "Relationships in Expository Text" Chart

Have pairs sit in their groups of four. Remind the students that they will continue to take responsibility for their learning during their group work today by contributing ideas and including everyone during small group discussions.

Remind the students that they read a passage from Chapter 3 of *Farm Workers Unite* yesterday and thought about chronological relationships in the reading. Direct their attention to the "Relationships in Expository Text" chart, and review that chronological relationships are one way expository text can be organized. Explain that today the students will explore another way information can be organized.

2 Discuss and Notice Compare and Contrast Relationships

Read aloud the end of Chapter 3 starting with the subheading "A New Union," on page 14 of *Farm Workers Unite*. Point out that this is an example of another relationship that can be found in expository text: the compare and contrast relationship, in which the author describes the similarities and/or differences between two things.

Direct the students to *Student Response Book* page 52, where the passage is reproduced. Explain that they are to follow along as you reread the passage aloud. Ask the students to pay close attention to the comparisons made between César Chávez and Dolores Huerta.

 Reread the passage; then have the students use "Heads Together" to discuss:

Q *Why did Chávez and Huerta make a good team?*

Q *How did the author compare and contrast Chávez's and Huerta's personalities?*

Q *How did the author compare and contrast Chávez's and Huerta's experiences?*

Have several students share their thinking with the class.

> **Students might say:**
>
> "I think they made a good team because they each brought different things to their partnership."
>
> "I agree with [Rosa]. The book says that Chávez worked in the fields and really understood what it was like to be a farm worker and Huerta was educated and knew how to deal with the government and other unions. So together they could work with both sides."
>
> "First the authors described something about Chávez and then they described how Huerta was the opposite. Like Chávez was shy and Huerta was bold and outgoing."

▶ **3** **Identify and Discuss Compare and Contrast Relationships**

 Ask the students to turn to *Student Response Book* pages 53–55, where part of Chapter 4 of *Farm Workers Unite* is reproduced. Ask the students to follow along as you read "To Join or Not to Join" on pages 15–17 aloud. Read it aloud slowly and clearly. Have the students use "Heads Together" to discuss:

Q *What was the National Farm Workers Association's first major challenge?*

Q *What compare and contrast relationship did you notice in this passage?*

Teacher Note

The passage discusses the many reasons the National Farm Workers Association should or should not join the AWOC grape strike.

Have several students share their thinking with the class.

Point out that the authors write that there were many reasons for the National Farm Workers Association not to join the strike. Have the students find and underline this sentence on *Student Response Book* page 54 "There were also good reasons for the National Farm Workers Association to join the strike." Explain that the way this information is organized is a good example of how authors often organize information using compare and contrast relationships to help the readers make sense of the text.

 Have the students refer to *Student Response Book* pages 53–54, and use "Heads Together" to discuss the following questions:

Q *What reasons were given for the National Farm Workers Association to not join the strike?*

Q *In contrast, what reasons were given for the National Farm Workers Association to join the strike?*

Signal for the students' attention and have several volunteers share their thinking. Ask and discuss the questions that follow. Be prepared to reread parts of the book to help the students support their thinking.

Q *Why was Chávez's decision to join the AWOC grape strike so important to the migrant farm workers' struggle to get decent working and living conditions? What in the book makes you think that?*

Q *Do you agree or disagree with what [Joel] said? Explain your thinking.*

Q *What questions do you have for [Erma] about [her] thinking?*

Explain that compare and contrast is used frequently in expository texts. Write *compare and contrast* on the "Relationships in Expository Texts" chart. Explain that tomorrow the students will have an opportunity to look for chronological as well as compare and contrast relationships in their textbooks.

FACILITATION TIP

Continue to focus on **responding neutrally** with interest during class discussions by refraining from overtly praising or criticizing the students' responses. Instead, build the students' intrinsic motivation by responding with genuine curiosity and interest; for example:

- *Interesting—say more about that.*

- *What you said makes me curious. I wonder...*

- *You have a point of view that's [similar to/different from] what [Marie] just said. How is it [similar/different]?*

Reflect on Group Work

Help the students reflect on their work together by asking:

Q *What did you do to take responsibility for yourself during "Heads Together" today?*

Q *What problems did you have in your group? How did you try to solve those problems? What can you do next time to avoid those problems?*

INDIVIDUALIZED DAILY READING

 Read Textbooks/Record Facts in Their IDR Journals

Remind the students they have been reading textbooks and monitoring what they are learning. Explain that today the students will read their social studies textbook independently and then, as they did in the previous lesson, record several pieces of information they have learned.

Have the students read their social studies textbook for up to 30 minutes.

At the end of IDR, have the students write in their IDR Journals about what they read. Ask each student to write the title of the chapter she read and five or six things she learned from her reading.

 After sufficient time, signal for the students' attention. Have the students use "Heads Together" to discuss the things they learned and wrote about in their IDR Journals.

Signal for attention. Briefly discuss what the students learned from their reading today.

Day 3

Independent Strategy Practice

In this lesson, the students:

- *Use text structure* to explore expository text
- Explore how information can be organized in expository text
- Explore chronological and compare and contrast relationships in expository text
- Take responsibility for their own learning
- Read independently

Materials

- "Relationships in Expository Text" chart
- Social studies textbook for each student
- Small self-stick notes for each student
- *Assessment Resource Book*

1 ▶ Review "Relationships in Expository Text" Chart

Remind the students that over the past several days they have been exploring relationships in expository text. Direct their attention to the "Relationships in Expository Text" chart and remind the students that expository text can be organized around chronological and compare and contrast relationships. Explain that the students will learn other ways expository texts are organized as they go through middle school and high school.

Explain that today the students will practice recognizing these two relationships as they read their own social studies textbooks independently.

> *Relationships in Expository Text*
>
> - chronological
> - compare and contrast

2 ▶ Read Textbooks Independently Without Stopping

Distribute several self-stick notes to each student. Have the students flip through their textbooks and stop either at the next chapter they are to read or one that looks interesting to them. Ask them to mark where they will start reading today with a self-stick note, and then read independently for 10–15 minutes.

Think About Relationships and Prepare to Reread

Stop the students and ask them to think quietly to themselves for a moment about the following questions:

Q *What is your reading about?*

Q *Did you notice chronological, or time, relationships in your reading? If so, what is the time frame?*

Q *Did you notice compare and contrast relationships in your reading? If so, what is being compared?*

Explain that now the students will reread the same section beginning at the self-stick note. As they reread, they will mark any chronological or compare and contrast relationships they notice with self-stick notes. Encourage them to think about how recognizing these relationships helps them understand what they are reading.

 Reread Independently and Mark with Self-stick Notes

Have the students reread independently for 10 minutes, marking as they read. Circulate and look for evidence that the students are recognizing relationships as they read.

CLASS COMPREHENSION ASSESSMENT

Circulate and observe the students as they reread and ask yourself:

Q *Do the students notice how their texts are organized?*

Q *Do they recognize chronological and compare and contrast relationships in their reading?*

Record your observations on page 26 of the *Assessment Resource Book.*

Discuss Readings as a Class

Signal for attention. Have a few volunteers share with the class what they read by saying a few words about the topic and then reading a passage they marked that contains an example of a relationship. As the students share passages, facilitate a discussion by asking:

Q *What kind of relationship do you think [Mindy] marked there? Why do you think so?*

Q *What questions can we ask [Mindy] about the passage [she] read?*

Q *[Mindy], how does recognizing that [compare and contrast] relationship help you better understand the topic you're reading about?*

Remind the students that the purpose of studying relationships in expository text is to help them make sense of their own independent reading. Tell the students that they will have another opportunity tomorrow to explore relationships in the textbook.

Day 4

Materials

- Social studies textbook for each student
- "Relationships in Expository Text" chart
- *Assessment Resource Book*
- Unit 7 Parent Letter (BLM16)

Independent Strategy Practice

In this lesson, the students:

- *Use text structure* to explore expository text read independently
- Explore how information can be organized in expository text
- Explore chronological and compare and contrast relationships in expository text
- Take responsibility for their own learning

1 Review Taking Responsibility

Have the students sit in their groups of four. Remind the students that over the past several days they have been working in small groups and noticing how they are taking responsibility for their learning. Explain that at the end of the lesson they will discuss what they did to take responsibility today.

2 Read Textbooks Independently

Teacher Note ▶

Prior to this activity, select a passage for the students to read.

Explain that today all of the students will read the same section of their social studies textbook and then discuss the reading in their groups.

Have the students read independently for 10 minutes and think about any chronological and compare and contrast relationships they notice. After 10 minutes, stop them and ask them to reread the same passage and notice any information they might have missed or misunderstood during the first reading.

3 Think About Relationships and Discuss the Reading

After another 10 minutes, stop the students and ask them to think quietly to themselves for a moment about the questions that follow.

Q *What information did you learn from your reading?*

Q *Did you notice chronological, or time, relationships in your reading? If so, what is the time frame?*

Q *Did you notice compare and contrast relationships in your reading? If so, what is being compared?*

After a moment, have the students use "Heads Together" to discuss these questions. Encourage the students to use the discussion prompts during their conversation.

4 ▶ Discuss the Reading as a Class

Signal for attention. Have a few volunteers share with the class information they learned from the reading. Facilitate a whole-class discussion using the following questions:

Q *What [compare and contrast] relationship did you notice in the text?*

Q *What did you learn from the [compare and contrast] relationship?*

Q *Do you agree or disagree with [Lewis]? Explain your thinking.*

Remind the students that the purpose for studying relationships in expository text is to help them make sense of their own independent reading. Encourage them to continue to look for these relationships as they read expository text during IDR and throughout the school day.

5 ▶ Reflect on Taking Responsibility

Ask and briefly discuss:

Q *What did you do to take responsibility for your learning this week?*

Q *What do you want to continue to work on the next time you work with a partner on in a group?*

Teacher Note

This is the last week in Unit 7. If you feel your students need more experience with analyzing expository text before moving on, you may want to repeat Weeks 3 and 4 of this unit with an alternative textbook.

You will reassign partners for Unit 8.

INDIVIDUAL COMPREHENSION ASSESSMENT

Before continuing with Unit 8, take this opportunity to assess individual students' progress in reading and making sense of expository nonfiction. Please refer to pages 44–45 in the *Assessment Resource Book* for instructions.

SOCIAL SKILLS ASSESSMENT

Take this opportunity to assess your students' social skill development using the Social Skills Assessment record sheet on pages 2–3 of the *Assessment Resource Book*.

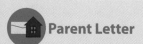

Parent Letter

Send home with each student the Parent Letter for this unit (see "Do Ahead," page 431). Periodically, have a few students share with the class what they are reading at home.

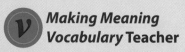

Making Meaning Vocabulary Teacher

Next week you will revisit this week's reading to teach Vocabulary Week 23.

Determining Important Ideas and Summarizing

NARRATIVE NONFICTION

During this unit, the students continue to make inferences to understand text. They also think about important and supporting ideas in text and use important ideas to build summaries. During IDR, the students explore the important ideas in their independent reading. Socially, they give reasons for their opinions, discuss their opinions respectfully, and reach agreement.

Week 1 *Flight* by Robert Burleigh

Week 2 *A Picture Book of Amelia Earhart* by David A. Adler

Week 3 *In My Own Backyard* by Judi Kurjian

Week 4 *A Picture Book of Rosa Parks* by David A. Adler

Week 5 Student-selected text

UNIT 8: DETERMINING IMPORTANT IDEAS AND SUMMARIZING
Narrative Nonfiction

Flight
by Robert Burleigh, illustrated by Mike Wimmer
(PaperStar, 1997)

Charles Lindbergh becomes the first person to fly solo across the Atlantic Ocean.

ALTERNATIVE BOOKS

Come Back, Salmon by Molly Cone

Seeker of Knowledge by James Rumford

Comprehension Focus

- Students *make inferences* to understand text.

- Students *think about important and supporting ideas* in a text.

- Students read independently.

Social Development Focus

- Students take responsibility for their learning and behavior.

- Students develop the group skills of giving reasons for their opinions and reaching agreement.

DO AHEAD

- Prior to Day 1, decide how you will randomly assign partners to work together during the unit.

- Collect a variety of fiction and narrative nonfiction texts, including biographies and autobiographies, for the students to read during IDR.

- Make a transparency of "Excerpt 1 from *Flight*" (BLM29).

- Make transparencies of "Excerpt 2 from *Flight*" (BLM30–BLM32).

- Prepare to model distinguishing between important and supporting ideas (see Day 4, Step 1 on page 462).

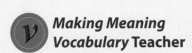

Making Meaning Vocabulary Teacher

If you are teaching Developmental Studies Center's *Making Meaning Vocabulary* program, teach Vocabulary Week 23 this week. For more information, see the *Making Meaning Vocabulary Teacher's Manual*.

Read-aloud

In this lesson, the students:

- *Make inferences* as they hear a nonfiction text
- Read independently for up to 30 minutes
- Give reasons for their opinions

1 Pair Students and Learn a Prompt for Justifying Opinions

Randomly assign partners and have them sit together. Review that the students have practiced several social skills, including asking clarifying questions, confirming that they understood another person's thinking by repeating back what they heard, and using prompts to add to a discussion. Explain that in the next few weeks they will focus on explaining their thinking more clearly by giving reasons for their opinions.

Write the following prompt on the board: "The reason I think this is _____." Tell the students that you would like them to use this prompt when they answer a question or give an opinion during a book discussion.

Point out that the students have already been giving reasons for their opinions when they have answered the questions *Why do you think so?* and *What in the text makes you think that?* Now the focus is on consciously using the prompt without waiting to be asked to explain their thinking.

Materials

- *Flight*
- Map of the world
- "Reading Comprehension Strategies" chart
- Small self-stick notes for each student

***Being a* Writer™ Teacher**

You can either have the students work with their *Being a Writer* partner or assign them a different partner for the *Making Meaning* lessons.

Teacher Note ▶

You might model using the prompt by saying, "Most Americans are related to immigrants or are immigrants themselves. The reason I think this is that almost everyone came to this country from somewhere else" or "Harriet Tubman was a moral person. The reason I think this is that she believed slavery and discrimination were wrong and acted on this her whole life."

2 ▶ Introduce *Flight*

Review that the students have been making inferences to help them make sense of poems, stories, and books. Ask them to continue to think about making inferences as they hear the book *Flight* today. Show the cover of the book and read the names of the author and illustrator aloud.

Explain that the book tells the true story of Charles Lindbergh's historic flight from New York to Paris in 1927. Lindbergh was the first person to fly solo across the Atlantic Ocean. Point out that in 1927, the airplane was a fairly new invention. (The Wright brothers' famous first flight of a motorized airplane occurred at Kitty Hawk, North Carolina, in 1903.) People rarely saw airplanes overhead. Lindbergh's flight made him world-famous and changed the way people thought about air travel.

3 ▶ Read *Flight* Aloud

Read the book aloud, showing the illustrations, and stopping as described on the next page.

Suggested Vocabulary

cockpit: area in the front of the plane where the pilot sits (p. 7)

aloft: up in the air (p. 8)

periscope: tube containing mirrors that enables someone to see around things (p. 10)

drones: makes a continuous humming sound (p. 10)

sentries: guards (p. 11)

throttle: lever that controls the speed of an airplane (p. 16)

sod: grass (p. 27)

aviators: people who fly airplanes; pilots (p. 29)

ELL Vocabulary

English Language Learners may benefit from discussing additional vocabulary, including:

goggles: special glasses that protect one's eyes (p. 8)

diary: book used to record personal thoughts or activities (p. 11)

He follows two compasses and the stars to navigate: He uses two instruments that tell his direction and the stars to help him fly in the right direction (p. 13)

 ELL Note

Consider previewing this book with your English Language Learners prior to today's lesson. Explain Charles Lindbergh's flight across the Atlantic to them.

◀ **Teacher Note**

Display a map of the world to show Lindbergh's route and how far he flew.

Read the first page of the story twice. Then continue reading. Stop after:

p. 8   "Over thirty hours away."

 Have the students use "Turn to Your Partner" to discuss:

Q *What did you learn in the part of the story you just heard?*

Without sharing as a class, reread the last sentence on page 8 and continue reading to next stopping point:

p. 13   "He has completed one-third of the flight."

 Have the students use "Turn to Your Partner" to discuss:

Q *What happened in the part of the story you just heard?*

 Without sharing as a class, reread the last sentence on page 13 and continue reading. Follow the same procedure at the remaining stops:

p. 20   "It is 10:52 in the morning, New York time."

p. 24   "It is 4:52 in the afternoon, New York time. Lindbergh's thirty-fourth hour in the air."

p. 32   "It is 1927, and his name is Charles Lindbergh."

FACILITATION TIP

During this unit, we invite you to continue practicing **responding neutrally** with interest during class discussions. This week continue to respond neutrally by refraining from overtly praising or criticizing the students' responses. Try responding neutrally by nodding, asking them to say more about their thinking, or asking other students to respond.

4 Discuss the Story as a Class

Facilitate a discussion of the story, using the following questions. Be ready to reread passages to help the students recall what they heard. Remind them to use "The reason I think this is _____" and the other discussion prompts they have learned to add to one another's thinking. Ask:

Q *What is this book about?*

Reread the following passage on page 8: "He has been up all night getting ready…I have been waiting my entire life for this flight." Ask:

Q *How do you think Charles Lindbergh feels at this point in the book? What in the book makes you think that?*

Students might say:

"He's scared and nervous, but he's going to do it anyway."

"I agree with [Sarah]. The reason I think this is he thinks about not doing it, but then decides to go ahead."

"I think he knows he's going to be famous, so that's why he decides to fly."

Reread the following passage on page 13: "Now he can no longer follow the land's edge for direction…The slightest movement could send him miles off course and risk the fuel supply." Ask:

Q *What does this passage mean? Why does it make sense that he is concerned about this?*

As the students make inferences about the story, point them out. (For example, you might say, "The story does not directly say that Charles Lindbergh was afraid to begin his flight, but you inferred that from clues in the story.")

▶5 Reflect on Giving Reasons for Opinions

Facilitate a brief discussion about how the students did using the prompt to give reasons for their opinions. Share your own observations, and explain that you would like them to continue to focus on giving reasons for their opinions throughout the week.

INDIVIDUALIZED DAILY READING

▶6 Mark and Discuss Comprehension Strategies

Direct the students' attention to the "Reading Comprehension Strategies" chart and remind them that these are the strategies they have learned so far this year. Ask them to notice which strategies they use and where they use them during their reading today.

Explain that the students will use self-stick notes to mark places in a book where they use a strategy and that they should write the name of the strategy on the self-stick note. At the end of independent reading, they will share in pairs one of the passages they marked

Reading Comprehension Strategies

- recognizing text features

and the strategy they used. Ask the students to be prepared to talk about how each strategy helped them understand what they read.

Have the students read independently for up to 30 minutes.

As the students read, circulate among them. Ask individual students questions such as:

Q *What is your book about?*

Q *What strategies are you using as you read?*

Q *How does this passage help you [visualize]? How does [visualizing] this passage help you understand the story?*

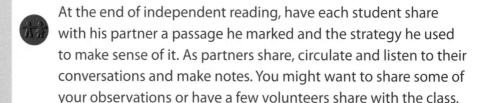 At the end of independent reading, have each student share with his partner a passage he marked and the strategy he used to make sense of it. As partners share, circulate and listen to their conversations and make notes. You might want to share some of your observations or have a few volunteers share with the class.

EXTENSION

Learn More About Charles Lindbergh

Have interested students research the life of Charles Lindbergh. The website charleslindbergh.com is a comprehensive source of information on the Internet. Additional resources include a PBS documentary titled *Lindbergh* (visit pbs.org/wgbh/amex/lindbergh) and a film titled *Lindbergh's Great Race: "Are There Any Mechanics Here?"*

Day 2

Guided Strategy Practice

In this lesson, the students:

- *Make inferences* as they hear a nonfiction text
- *Think about what is important* in the text
- Use "Think, Pair, Write"
- Read independently for up to 30 minutes
- Give reasons for their opinions

About Determining Important and Supporting Ideas

The focus of the next two weeks is *determining important and supporting ideas,* a strategy that helps readers understand and retain what they read. In the *Making Meaning* program, the focus is on helping the students distinguish between important and supporting ideas, rather than on identifying the one "main idea." The students explore these ideas through teacher modeling, discussion, and referring back to the text to support their opinions. The goal, as with all the reading comprehension strategies, is for the students to use the strategy to make sense of their independent reading. (For more about *determining important ideas,* please see volume 1, page xvi.)

▶ 1 Use "Think, Pair, Write" to Think About What Is Important

Review that the students heard *Flight* and made inferences to figure out what happens in the story and why. Explain that today they will use inference in a new way—to help them think about what is most important for them to understand and remember in the story.

Explain that you will reread the first part of *Flight* aloud and the students will use "Think, Pair, Write" to take notes about what they think is important in the story.

Have the students turn to "Think, Pair, Write About *Flight*" on *Student Response Book* page 56. Explain that during the reading you will stop several times. At the first two stops, you will model thinking about what is important so the students can follow along before trying it on their own. At the last two stops, they will use "Think,

Materials

- *Flight* (pages 4–16)
- *Student Response Book* page 56
- Chart paper and a marker
- "Reading Comprehension Strategies" chart
- Small self-stick notes for each student

◀ **Teacher Note**

You may need to remind the students that in "Think, Pair, Write" they think quietly for a moment, talk in pairs about their thinking, and then individually write their ideas.

Pair, Write" to think about what is important in the part of the story they just heard, turn to their partner to share their thinking, and individually write their own ideas in their own *Student Response Book*.

2 ▶ **Reread Pages 4–10 of** *Flight* **and Model Thinking About What Is Important**

Read the first three pages of the story aloud twice. Stop after:

> **p. 6** "Alone."

Model thinking quietly for a moment; then think aloud about what seems important in the passage (for example, "What seems most important to understand and remember in this passage is that Lindbergh is about to attempt what no one has done before, to fly from New York to Paris").

Model writing a note about this on chart paper (for example, "Lindbergh will attempt what no one has done before, to fly from New York to Paris"). Ask the students to write the same note on their *Student Response Book* page.

Continue reading, stopping after:

> **p. 10** "At this rate, he will have enough fuel to reach his destination, but only if he stays on course."

Once again, model thinking quietly for a moment; then think aloud about what seems important in the passage (for example, "What seems most important to understand and remember is that Lindbergh is nervous and afraid, but he takes off anyway").

Model writing a note about this where everyone can see it (for example, "He's afraid, but he takes off anyway"). Ask the students to write the same note on their *Student Response Book* page. Emphasize that thinking about what's important sometimes means saying in a few words what the author says over several pages.

3 ▸ Reread Pages 11–16 with "Think, Pair, Write"

Remind the students that at the next two stops they will practice thinking about what is important on their own and then share their thinking with their partner.

Reread the last sentence you read on page 10 ("At this rate…but only if he stays on course") and continue reading. Stop after:

> **p. 13** "He has completed one-third of the flight."

Ask:

Q *What is most important to understand and remember in the part I just read?*

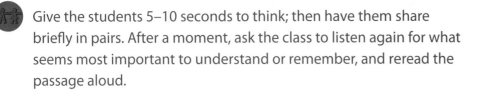

Give the students 5–10 seconds to think; then have them share briefly in pairs. After a moment, ask the class to listen again for what seems most important to understand or remember, and reread the passage aloud.

Have the students record what they think is most important to understand or remember on *Student Response Book* page 56. Then have a few volunteers share what they wrote with the class.

Facilitate a brief class discussion by asking:

Q *Why does that idea seem most important?*

Q *What other ideas seemed most important as you listened to the passage? Why?*

Reread the last sentence on page 13, and continue reading to the next stopping point:

> **p. 16** "To sleep is to die!"

Ask:

Q *What seems most important to understand and remember in the part I just read?*

Teacher Note

Circulate as partners talk and notice whether they are able to identify important ideas in the passage. One important idea is that Lindbergh is now flying over the ocean, so he doesn't have landmarks to guide him. If the students have difficulty, reread parts of the passage to individual students and ask questions such as:

Q *What is this part mainly about?*

Q *If you had to tell what this part is about in one sentence, what would you say?*

Teacher Note

Students may have different ideas about what is important in a passage. Give them time to consider different points of view before giving your own opinion. Encourage them to explain their thinking and to refer to the text to support their opinions.

Teacher Note

Again circulate as partners
talk and notice whether they
are able to identify important
ideas in the passage. Important
ideas include that Lindbergh
made it through a storm cloud
and that he is struggling to
stay awake. Reread parts of the
passage to individual students
who have difficulty and ask:

Q *If you had to tell what this
part is about in one sentence,
what would you say?*

 Again, have the students think, and then briefly share in pairs.
Reread the passage aloud; then have the students record what they
think is most important to understand or remember on *Student
Response Book* page 56.

Have a few volunteers share with the class what they wrote and
facilitate a brief class discussion by asking:

Q *Why does that idea seem most important?*

Q *What other ideas seemed most important as you listened to the
passage? Why?*

Tell the students that *thinking about what is important* is a strategy
good readers use to help them identify and remember the essential
ideas in a text. Explain that in the next lesson you will read the rest
of the story and the students will continue to think about what's
important in it.

 4 ▶ Reflect on "Think, Pair, Write"

Facilitate a brief discussion of how the students did giving reasons
for their opinions when they talked in pairs during "Think, Pair, Write."

INDIVIDUALIZED DAILY READING

ELL Note

You might want to model
this activity for your English
Language Learners. In addition,
you may want to preview the
questions with them prior to
having these students read.

 5 ▶ Discuss Reading Comprehension Strategies

Continue to have the students use self-stick notes to mark places
they use reading comprehension strategies. Refer to the "Reading
Comprehension Strategies" chart and review the strategies.

Have the students read independently for up to 30 minutes.

As the students read, circulate among them. Ask individual students
questions such as:

Q *What strategies are you using as you read?*

Q *How does [making inferences] in this passage help you understand the story?*

At the end of independent reading, have a few students share with the class a passage they marked and the strategy they used to make sense of it. Remind the students to give reasons for their thinking and to ask each other clarifying questions.

Allow time for any student who has finished a book to add it to the "Reading Log" section of her *Student Response Book*.

Day 3

Materials

- *Flight* (pages 17–32)
- *Student Response Book* page 56
- "Reading Comprehension Strategies" chart
- Small self-stick notes for each student

Guided Strategy Practice

In this lesson, the students:

- *Make inferences* as they hear a story
- *Think about what is important* in the text
- Use "Think, Pair, Write"
- Read independently for up to 30 minutes
- Give reasons for their opinions

1 ▶ Review Giving Reasons for Opinions

Explain that today the students will again use "Think, Pair, Write" to help them think about what is important in a text. Remind them to practice giving reasons for their opinions, using "The reason I think this is _____."

2 ▶ Review Thinking About What Is Important

Remind the students that in the previous lesson they heard the first part of *Flight* again and used "Think, Pair, Write" to think about what is important in the story. Have them open to *Student Response Book* page 56 and review the important ideas they recorded. Ask:

Q *What are some important ideas we identified in the first part of* Flight?

Explain that today you will reread the rest of the story aloud, stopping three times. As you did yesterday, you will model thinking about what is important at the first stop. At the next two stops, the students will use "Think, Pair, Write" to think about what is important in the passage they just heard, share their thinking in pairs, and write their own ideas on *Student Response Book* page 56.

Reread Pages 17–32 with Modeling and "Think, Pair, Write"

Remind the students that in the last part of the story they heard, Lindbergh had made it halfway to Paris and was fighting to stay awake. Reread the last sentence on page 16, and continue reading. Stop after:

p. 22 "He wants to complete his dream."

Model thinking quietly for a moment; then think aloud about what seems important in the passage. (For example, you might say, "What seems most important to understand and remember in this part of the story is that Lindbergh makes it across the ocean and is now over land again on the other side.")

Model writing a note about this where everyone can see it (for example, "Lindbergh made it across the ocean"). Ask the students to write the same note in their own *Student Response Books*.

Ask the students to think about what is most important in the next passage you read. Reread the last sentence on page 22, and continue reading. Stop after:

p. 27 "It is 10:22, Paris time. The flight has taken thirty-three and a half hours."

Ask:

Q *What is most important to understand and remember in the part I just read?*

 Give the students 5–10 seconds to think; then have them share briefly in pairs. After a moment, ask the class to listen again for what seems most important to understand or remember, and reread the passage aloud.

Have the students record what they think is most important to understand or remember in the passage on *Student Response Book* page 56. Then have a few volunteers share what they wrote with the class, and facilitate a brief class discussion by asking:

Q *Why does that idea seem most important?*

◀ **Teacher Note**

Important ideas include that Lindbergh successfully flew from the United States to Paris, France, across the Atlantic Ocean.

Q *What other ideas seemed most important as you listened to the
passage? Why?*

Reread the last sentence on page 27 and continue reading.
Stop after:

> **p. 32** "It is 1927, and his name is Charles Lindbergh."

Again, have the students think, and then briefly share in pairs.
Reread the passage aloud; then have the students record what they
think is most important to understand or remember on *Student
Response Book* page 56.

Have a few volunteers share what they wrote with the class.
Facilitate a brief class discussion by asking:

Q *Why does that idea seem most important?*

Q *What other ideas seemed most important as you listened to the
passage? Why?*

Remind the students that thinking about what is important in
a story helps them identify what is essential to understand and
remember. Explain that in the next lesson they will think more
about what is important in *Flight*.

4▶ Reflect on "Think, Pair, Write"

Facilitate a brief discussion about how the students did working in
pairs during "Think, Pair, Write." Ask:

Q *How did you and your partner do giving reasons for your thinking
about what was important today?*

Q *Did anyone change your mind about what was important in a
passage after hearing your partner's thinking? Tell us about that.*

Teacher Note ▶

The important ideas in this
passage include that Charles
Lindbergh has become a
hero all over the world for
being the first man to fly
across the Atlantic Ocean.

INDIVIDUALIZED DAILY READING

 **Discuss Reading Comprehension Strategies/
Document IDR Conferences**

Continue to have the students place self-stick notes in their
independent reading books where they use reading comprehension
strategies. Ask and briefly discuss:

Q *Which of these strategies have you used in your independent
reading this week? How did [questioning] help you understand
what you were reading?*

Remind the students that using these strategies will help them
understand and enjoy what they are reading. However, if they are
having difficulty using these strategies and comprehending the text
they are reading, they should think about selecting a different text.

Have the students read independently for up to 30 minutes.

Use the "IDR Conference Notes" record sheet to conduct and
document individual conferences.

At the end of independent reading, conduct a brief discussion with
the whole class. Ask and briefly discuss:

Q *Which strategy do you use most frequently when you
read independently?*

Q *How does that strategy help you understand what you
are reading?*

Q *What should you do if you don't understand what you are reading?*

Day 4

Materials

- *Flight*
- Transparency of "Excerpt 1 from *Flight*" (BLM29)
- Transparency pens in two colors
- *Student Response Book* pages 57–58
- *Assessment Resource Book*
- Transparencies of "Excerpt 2 from *Flight*" (BLM30–BLM32)
- "Reading Comprehension Strategies" chart
- Small self-stick notes for each student
- *Student Response Book,* IDR Journal section

Guided Strategy Practice

In this lesson, the students:

- *Distinguish between important and supporting ideas* in a text
- Use "Think, Pair, Write"
- Read independently for up to 30 minutes
- Reach agreement

1 ▶ Model Distinguishing Between Important and Supporting Ideas

Review that in previous lessons the students heard you reread *Flight* and used "Think, Pair, Write" to think about the important ideas in the story.

Place the transparency of "Excerpt 1 from *Flight*" on the overhead projector. Point out that this passage comes from the very beginning of the story, and then read it aloud. Remind the students that in a previous lesson they discussed the important idea in the passage—that Lindbergh was going to attempt what no one had done before. Explain that the sentence "And yet—he is about to attempt what no one has done before: To fly—without a stop—from New York to Paris, France" expresses the important idea in the passage. Underline the passage on the transparency.

Using a different colored pen, underline the sentence fragment "Over 3,600 miles away" and explain that it contains a detail about how long the flight from New York to Paris will be. Explain that details, examples, and descriptions that tell more about the important ideas are called *supporting ideas*.

Ask:

Q *What else in this passage supports the important idea that Lindbergh was going to attempt what no one had done before, to fly from New York to Paris?*

Have a few volunteers share their thinking with the class, and underline the supporting ideas on the transparency.

Students might say:

"I think 'The airplane has a name painted on its side: *Spirit of St. Louis*' is a supporting idea. The reason I think this is because it's a detail about the main point, which is that Lindbergh will cross the ocean."

"I agree with [Tracy]. In addition, I think that Lindbergh's height is a supporting idea. It's a detail."

Point out that readers usually don't remember every word or detail as they read, so they need to be thinking about what ideas are the *most* important to understand and remember. Good readers need to be able to tell the difference between important and supporting ideas as they read. Explain that today the students will practice identifying important and supporting ideas in another passage from *Flight*.

2 ▶ **Agree on One Important and One Supporting Idea**

Have the students turn to *Student Response Book* pages 57–58. Point out that this is the part of the story in which Charles Lindbergh lands in Paris and is mobbed by thousands of people. Read the excerpt (found on BLM30–BLM32) aloud as the students follow along.

Explain that the students will reread the excerpt independently and think quietly about one important and one supporting idea in the passage. They will then discuss their thinking in pairs. Partners will come to agreement on one important and one supporting idea, and each partner will underline these in his own *Student Response Book*. The students may use two different colored pens, or a pencil and a pen, to distinguish between the important and supporting ideas they underline.

Teacher Note

If the students have difficulty identifying supporting ideas, review that supporting ideas are details, examples, or descriptions that tell more about an important idea. Ask:

Q *Where in the passage are other details about Lindbergh's goal for his flight?*

 Note

To support your students, show and discuss the illustrations on pages 26–31 again; then read the excerpt aloud as they follow along, stopping intermittently to talk about what is happening. The students might benefit from an explanation of the following words and passages:

- "'the sod coming up to meet me'"
- "dazed"
- "'drowning in a great sea'"
- "deafened"

Teacher Note

Initially, students often have difficulty distinguishing between important and supporting ideas. Having the students identify only one important and one supporting idea helps to focus their thinking.

CLASS COMPREHENSION ASSESSMENT

Circulate as the pairs work and notice which sentences the students underline. Ask yourself:

Q *Are the students able to identify an important idea in the passage?*

Q *Are they able to identify a supporting idea?*

Q *Is there evidence that they see the difference between important and supporting ideas in the passage?*

Record your observations on page 27 of the *Assessment Resource Book*.

3 ▶ **Discuss Important and Supporting Ideas as a Class**

When the students finish their partner work, place the transparencies of "Excerpt 2 from *Flight*" on the overhead projector.

Facilitate a discussion by asking the questions that follow. Remind the students to give reasons for their opinions. Ask:

Q *What is an important idea in this part of the story? Why do you think that information is important?*

Q *Do others agree that this information is important? Why or why not?*

Students might say:

"I think 'the plane touches the ground' is important. The reason I think this is because Lindbergh finally got to the end of his flight. He made it."

"I think 'newspaper headlines all over the world are beginning to blazon the news' is important because it shows how great the flight was."

"I agree with [Philip]. I underlined that, too, and also 'American hero safe in Paris!' because it says he was a hero and safe."

Q *What is a supporting idea? Why do you think that information is supporting?*

Students might say:

"I thought 'closer, closer, closer' is supporting. The reason I think this is because it doesn't really tell you anything. His landing is important, but this just describes the plane's movement."

"I thought 'policemen guard the plane' was less important. This seems like a detail."

"I disagree with [Leon]. I think that 'policemen guard the plane' is important because it means the plane is important."

As the students share, underline the important and supporting information on the transparency using two different colored pens. Ask and discuss as a class:

Q *Over the past couple of days we've been talking about important ideas in* Flight. *Now that you've thought about some of the important ideas, what would you say this story is about?*

4 **Add to the "Reading Comprehension Strategies" Chart**

Direct the students' attention to the "Reading Comprehension Strategies" chart and add *determining important and supporting ideas* to it. Remind the students that distinguishing between important and supporting information can help them better understand and remember what they've read, and that the goal is for them to use the strategy as they read independently.

Tell the students that they will continue to think about important and supporting information in the coming week.

> Reading Comprehension Strategies
>
> - recognizing text features

5 **Reflect on Reaching Agreement**

Facilitate a brief discussion about how the students worked together. Ask:

Q *How did you and your partner do agreeing on one important and one supporting idea?*

Q *What did you do if you didn't agree at first?*

INDIVIDUALIZED DAILY READING

 ### Write About Reading Comprehension Strategies in Their IDR Journals

Ask the students to continue to mark passages with self-stick notes where they use reading comprehension strategies to make sense of what they are reading.

Have them read independently for up to 30 minutes.

At the end of independent reading, facilitate a brief whole-class discussion by asking:

Q *What strategy did you use today?*

Q *How did that strategy help you understand what you were reading?*

Q *What should you do if you don't understand what you are reading?*

Then have each student write in her IDR Journal about a strategy she used and how it helped her understand her reading. If time permits, have a few students share their writing with the class.

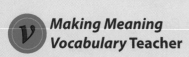 ### *Making Meaning Vocabulary* Teacher

Next week you will revisit this week's reading to teach Vocabulary Week 24.

Week 2

Overview

UNIT 8: DETERMINING IMPORTANT IDEAS AND SUMMARIZING
Narrative Nonfiction

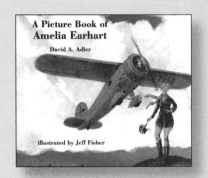

A Picture Book of Amelia Earhart
by David A. Adler, illustrated by Jeff Fisher
(Holiday House, 1998)

This biography of Amelia Earhart focuses on her courage as a pioneering pilot and her impact on women's roles in the United States.

ALTERNATIVE BOOKS

A Picture Book of Jackie Robinson by David A. Adler

A Boy Called Slow by Joseph Bruchac

Comprehension Focus

• Students *make inferences* to understand text.

• Students *think about important and supporting ideas* in a text.

• Students read independently.

Social Development Focus

• Students take responsibility for their learning and behavior.

• Students develop the group skills of giving reasons for their opinions and reaching agreement.

DO AHEAD

• Make transparencies of the "Excerpt from *A Picture Book of Amelia Earhart*" (BLM33–BLM34).

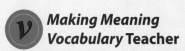

Making Meaning Vocabulary Teacher

If you are teaching Developmental Studies Center's *Making Meaning Vocabulary* program, teach Vocabulary Week 24 this week. For more information, see the *Making Meaning Vocabulary Teacher's Manual.*

Day 1

Materials

- *A Picture Book of Amelia Earhart*
- Map of the world
- Small self-stick notes for each student

Teacher Note

Because *making inferences* and *identifying important ideas* are key comprehension strategies, the students focus on these strategies again this week. This additional practice will help to prepare them for *summarizing,* which is the focus of the later weeks of this unit. As always, the goal is that the students use the strategies to make sense of what they read independently.

Teacher Note ▶

Display a map of the world to point out the places described in the book and Earhart's various routes.

 Note

Consider previewing the book with your students prior to today's read-aloud.

Read-aloud

In this lesson, the students:

- *Make inferences* as they hear a biography
- Read independently for up to 30 minutes
- Give reasons for their opinions

1 Review Giving Reasons for Opinions

Have partners sit together. Review that last week the students used the prompt "The reason I think this is _____" to give reasons for their opinions. Ask them to continue using the prompt as they talk in pairs and with the whole class this week.

2 Introduce *A Picture Book of Amelia Earhart*

Show the cover of *A Picture Book of Amelia Earhart* and read the title and the names of the author and illustrator aloud. Point out that the book is a biography and remind the students that earlier in the year they heard *A Picture Book of Harriet Tubman,* which is another biography by the same author.

Tell them that Amelia Earhart was the first woman to fly across the Atlantic Ocean alone, not long after Charles Lindbergh completed his flight. She completed many other pioneering flights, and she affected the way people thought about women and what women are capable of.

3 Read *A Picture Book of Amelia Earhart* Aloud

Read the book aloud, showing the illustrations and stopping as described on the next page.

Suggested Vocabulary

absorbed: soaked up; learned (p. 10)

domestic: having to do with the home (p. 14)

pontoons: objects on a plane that help it float (p. 16)

stationery: writing paper and envelopes (p. 20)

endorsements: support for products (p. 20)

aviation: the science of building and flying airplanes (p. 24)

pop off: (idiom) die (p. 26)

ELL Vocabulary

English Language Learners may benefit from discussing additional vocabulary, including:

shocking: surprising (p. 5)

I have a reputation for brains: I am known for being smart (p. 7)

paralyzed: unable to move or feel a part of the body (p. 9)

confetti: small pieces of paper (p. 19)

heroine: brave girl or woman (p. 19)

lectures: talks given to teach something (p. 20)

courageous: brave (p. 28)

Stop after:

p. 7   "And she wrote, 'Did I tell you I have a reputation
for brains?'"

Have the students use "Turn to Your Partner" to discuss:

Q   *What did you learn about Amelia in the part of the story you
just heard?*

Without sharing as a class, reread the last sentence and continue reading to the next stop. At each of the following stops, have the students use "Turn to Your Partner" to share what they have learned very briefly. Then reread the last sentence before the stop and continue reading to the next stopping point.

p. 16   "Amelia described the flight as 'a grand experience,'
but since she didn't pilot the plane, she said she felt
like 'baggage.'"

p. 28   "She certainly was."

p. 30   "There is little evidence that there is any truth to
these theories."

◀   **Teacher Note**

Circulate as partners talk. Notice whether the students are using the prompt. If they are not, encourage them to do so. Be ready to share your observations at the end of the lesson.

4 ▶ **Discuss the Reading as a Class**

Facilitate a discussion of the story using the following questions. Be ready to reread passages aloud and show illustrations again to help the students recall what they heard. Remind them to use the discussion prompts they have learned to add to one another's thinking.

Q *What are some of the ways that Amelia Earhart challenged the way people thought women should behave and live? Why do you think she did this?*

Q *Amelia was the first woman to fly across the Atlantic Ocean when she joined Bill Stultz and Slim Gordon in the* Friendship *on June 18, 1928. On page 16, it says, "Amelia described the flight as 'a grand experience,' but since she didn't pilot the plane, she said she felt like 'baggage.'" What do you think she meant by this?*

Students might say:

"She showed women could do things that people thought only men could do, like fly planes alone."

"Amelia enjoyed the flight, but she wished she could have flown the plane. Maybe she was a little disappointed."

"I agree with [Boris]. She watched the maps. She didn't actually fly the plane."

Q *Amelia wrote to her husband, "Women must try to do things as men have tried. When they fail, their failures must be but a challenge to others." What do you think she meant by "their failures must be but a challenge to others?"*

Students might say:

"I think she was saying that just because one woman fails at something doesn't mean another woman shouldn't try again."

"I agree with [Shauna]. She failed to fly all the way around the world, but she was saying that the next person who tries might make it."

As the students make inferences, point them out. (For example, you might say, "The story doesn't directly say that Amelia was a little disappointed about not actually flying the *Friendship,* but you figured it out from clues in the story.")

Reflect on Giving Reasons for Opinions

Facilitate a brief discussion about how the students did using the prompt to give reasons for their opinions. Share your own observations, and explain that you would like the students to continue to focus on giving reasons for their opinions throughout the week.

INDIVIDUALIZED DAILY READING

 Think About Important Ideas

Remind the students that they have been thinking about important ideas in texts. Explain that you want them to use self-stick notes to mark at least one important idea in their reading today.

Have the students read independently for up to 30 minutes.

As the students read, circulate among them. Ask individual students questions such as:

Q *What is your book about?*

Q *Why do you think the idea you marked is important?*

Q *What other ideas might be important in this section?*

At the end of independent reading, have a few volunteers each share one important idea they found in their reading.

Day 2

Materials

- *A Picture Book of Amelia Earhart* (pages 3–16)
- *Student Response Book* page 59
- Small self-stick notes for each student

Guided Strategy Practice

In this lesson, the students:

- *Make inferences* as they hear a biography
- *Think about what is important* in the text
- Use "Think, Pair, Write"
- Read independently for up to 30 minutes
- Reach agreement

▶ 1 Review *A Picture Book of Amelia Earhart*

Show the cover of the book and ask:

Q *What do you remember about* A Picture Book of Amelia Earhart?

Review that last week the students learned about distinguishing between important and supporting ideas to help them make sense of text. Remind them that because it's difficult to remember everything, good readers think about what is most important to understand or remember as they read.

Tell the students that today they will practice thinking about what's important as they hear the first part of *A Picture Book of Amelia Earhart* again.

▶ 2 Reread Pages 3–5 and Model Thinking About What Is Important

Have the students turn to "Think, Pair, Write About *A Picture Book of Amelia Earhart*" on *Student Response Book* page 59. Explain that you will reread the first part of the story aloud, stopping several times during the reading. The students will use "Think, Pair, Write" to think about what is important in the part they just heard, agree in pairs on one important idea, and record the important idea in their own *Student Response Book*. Tell the students that you will model this for the class at the first stop.

Read pages 3–5 of the story aloud twice. Stop after:

> **p. 5**   "But, Amelia wrote later, 'Some elders have to be shocked for everybody's good now and then.'"

Model thinking quietly for a moment; then think aloud about what seems important in the passage. (For example, you might say, "What seems most important to understand and remember in this passage is that as a young girl Amelia did things that some people thought were shocking. The reason I think this is important is because this might give you an idea of how she will be later in her life.")

Model writing a note about this, and ask the students to write the same note in their *Student Response Books*. (For example, you might say, "As a young girl, Amelia did things that shocked some people.")

3 Reread Pages 6–16 with "Think, Pair, Write"

Ask the students to listen for what's important in the next passage. Reread the last sentence on page 5 and continue reading. Stop after:

> **p. 10**   "Some years later she explained that 'though I had seen one or two at county fairs before, I now saw many of them…I hung around in my spare time and absorbed all I could.'"

Ask:

Q *What seems most important to understand and remember in the part I just read?*

 Give the students 5–10 seconds to think; then have them share briefly in pairs. After a moment, ask the class to listen again for what seems most important to understand or remember, and reread the passage aloud.

Ask partners to agree on one idea that seems the most important in the passage, and then individually record that idea on *Student Response Book* page 59. Have a few volunteers share what they wrote with the class, and facilitate a brief class discussion by asking:

Q *Why does that idea seem most important?*

Q *Do others agree that this idea seems most important? Why or why not?*

Teacher Note

If necessary, model again by thinking aloud, recording your thinking, and asking the students to copy your note into their *Student Response Books*. (You might write "What seems most important in this part of the story is that at first Amelia was not that interested in airplanes, but that later in her life she became really fascinated by them.")

Q *What other ideas seem most important? Why?*

Reread the last sentence on page 10 and continue reading. Follow the same procedure at the following stops:

p. 12 "Another time, her airplane turned over in heavy rain, and Amelia, held in by her safety belt, hung upside down."

p. 16 "Amelia described the flight as 'a grand experience,' but since she didn't pilot the plane, she said she felt like 'baggage.'"

Explain that in the next lesson, the students will think more about what is important in *A Picture Book of Amelia Earhart*.

 Teacher Note

Important ideas in these passages include that Amelia took her first plane ride and became determined to learn how to fly and that she became the first woman to fly in a plane across the Atlantic, though she would have been happier as the pilot than as a passenger.

4 ▶ Reflect on Reaching Agreement

Have partners report briefly how they did today reaching agreement about important ideas. Point out that reaching agreement means partners need to keep talking until they agree. Sometimes partners have to convince each other of their thinking. This helps them learn to work together, and it also forces them to think more clearly about the book.

INDIVIDUALIZED DAILY READING

5 ▶ Think About Important Ideas

Have the students read independently for up to 30 minutes. Continue to have the students use self-stick notes to mark important ideas in their books. As the students read, circulate among them. Ask individual students questions such as:

Q *What is your book about?*

Q *Why do you think the idea you marked is important?*

Q *What other ideas might be important in this section?*

At the end of independent reading, have a few volunteers share one important idea they found in their reading.

Day 3

Guided Strategy Practice

In this lesson, the students:

- *Distinguish between important ideas and supporting ideas* in a text
- Read independently for up to 30 minutes
- Reach agreement

▶ 1 Review Important Ideas

Have the students turn to *Student Response Book* page 59. Remind them that in the previous lesson they heard the first part of *A Picture Book of Amelia Earhart* and used "Think, Pair, Write" to think about and record what is important in the story. Ask:

Q *What information in the first part of the story did we think was important to understand or remember?*

Remind the students that distinguishing between important ideas and supporting ideas (like details, examples, and descriptions) helps readers understand texts more deeply. Explain that today the students will think about what is important and supporting in a selection from *A Picture Book of Amelia Earhart*.

▶ 2 Identify Important and Supporting Ideas

Place the transparency of the excerpt on the overhead projector, and have the students turn to *Student Response Book* page 60. Point out that the excerpt is from the part of the story in which Amelia attempts to fly around the world. Read the excerpt aloud, slowly and clearly, as the students follow along in their *Student Response Books*.

Direct the students' attention to the first two paragraphs by darkening the rest of the excerpt with a sheet of paper on the overhead projector. Explain that today they will focus their discussion on just these two paragraphs, and they will work with the rest of the excerpt tomorrow.

Materials

- *A Picture Book of Amelia Earhart*
- *Student Response Book* pages 59–60
- Transparencies of the "Excerpt from *A Picture Book of Amelia Earhart*" (BLM33–BLM34)
- Transparency pens in two colors
- Small self-stick notes for each student

ELL Note

English Language Learners may benefit from extra support to make sense of the excerpt. Show and discuss the illustrations on pages 26–28 of *A Picture Book of America Earhart* again; then read the excerpt aloud as they follow along, stopping periodically to talk about what is happening. The students might benefit from an explanation of the following words and passages:

- "'If I should pop off, it will be doing the thing I've always wanted to do.'"
- "'…their failures must be but a challenge to others.'"

Reread the paragraphs aloud; then think aloud about what seems important in the paragraphs. (For example, you might say, "One idea that seems important to understand and remember in this paragraph is that Amelia planned to fly around the world. The reason I think this is because it is a main event in the story.") Underline "In 1937 she planned to fly around the world" on the transparency.

 Remind the students that supporting ideas are details, examples, and descriptions that tell more about the important ideas. First in pairs, and then as a class, have the students discuss:

Q *Which sentences in the paragraph are supporting ideas that tell more about Amelia's planned trip around the world?*

As the students identify supporting ideas, underline them on the transparency using a different colored pen.

> ***Students might say:***
>
> "I think the sentence 'On June 1, 1937, Amelia Earhart and her navigator, Fred Noonan, began the trip' is a supporting detail. The reason I think this is because the date that they started the trip is a detail that doesn't seem as important to remember."
>
> "I think 'it will be doing the thing I've always wanted to do' is supporting. The reason I think this is because it is a detail to tell how Amelia felt about her flight."
>
> "I disagree with [Cammy]. I think that sentence shows something important about Amelia's character."

 3 ▶ **Think About a Specific Idea**

Direct the students' attention to the following sentence in the second paragraph: "They flew to South America, and then to Africa, India, Burma, Thailand, Singapore, Indonesia, Australia, and New Guinea." Have the students use "Turn to Your Partner" to discuss:

Q *Is this sentence an important idea or a supporting idea? Why do you think so?*

Have one or two students share their thinking with the class. Remind the students to use the discussion prompts they have learned to connect their comments to those of others.

Students might say:

"I think the sentence is a supporting idea. The reason I think this is that knowing exactly where they went doesn't seem that important to remember."

"In addition to what [Patrick] said, it's more important to know that she was trying to go around the world."

Remind the students that good readers don't necessarily remember everything they read in a text, but they do remember what's important. Distinguishing between important and supporting ideas helps them identify what they want to remember.

Explain that in the next lesson they will think about what is important and supporting in the rest of the excerpt.

Keep the transparencies with the underlined sentences for Day 4.

INDIVIDUALIZED DAILY READING

4 ▶ **Have the Students Think About Important Ideas/ Document IDR Conferences**

Have the students continue to use self-stick notes to mark important ideas in their book.

Have the students read independently for up to 30 minutes. Use the "IDR Conference Notes" record sheet to conduct and document individual conferences.

At the end of independent reading, have volunteers share one important idea they found in their reading with the class. Remind the students to ask clarifying questions and to use the prompt "The reason I think this is _____" to support their thinking.

Ask and briefly discuss questions such as:

Q *What idea did you think was important?*

Q *Why do you think that is important?*

Q *How did thinking about what is important help you make sense of
the text you are reading?*

EXTENSION

Distinguish Between Facts and Opinions

Explain that when the students read an expository or other
nonfiction text it is important that they recognize when the author
is stating facts and when the author is stating opinions. Recognizing
the difference between facts and opinions helps readers judge the
accuracy or truthfulness of what they are reading.

Explain that a fact is a statement that can be proved true
by observation or by checking a reliable source, such as an
encyclopedia. (For example, the statement "In 1932, Amelia Earhart
became the first woman to fly alone across the Atlantic Ocean" is
a fact. It can be proved true by checking newspapers and other
historical records.) An opinion is a statement of what someone
thinks, feels, or believes about something. (For example, the
statement "Amelia was the bravest woman who ever lived" is an
opinion. It is a statement of what someone thinks or believes to be
true, but it is not a provable fact.)

Write the sentences below on a sheet of chart paper. Then have
the students use "Think, Pair, Share" to first think about, and then
discuss, whether each statement is a fact or an opinion.

Fact or Opinion?

- Amelia was born in Kansas in 1897.

- Amelia took flying lessons in California.

- Amelia was a better pilot than Charles Lindbergh.

- In 1937, Amelia disappeared trying to fly around the world.

- Amelia should not have tried to fly around the world.

Day 4

Guided Strategy Practice

In this lesson, the students:

- *Distinguish between important ideas and supporting ideas* in a story
- Use "Think, Pair, Write"
- Read independently for up to 30 minutes
- Reach agreement

1 Review Important and Supporting Ideas

Have the students turn to *Student Response Book* page 60. Place the transparency on the overhead projector. Remind the students that they discussed important and supporting ideas in the first two paragraphs of the excerpt together yesterday. Explain that today the students will use "Think, Pair, Write" to think about what ideas are important or supporting in the rest of the excerpt.

2 Identify Important and Supporting Ideas in the Rest of the Excerpt

As you read the rest of the excerpt aloud, have the students follow along and think about what is important and supporting.

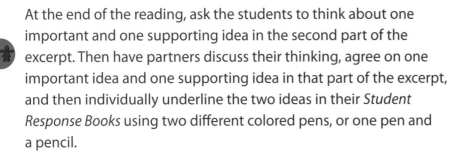

At the end of the reading, ask the students to think about one important and one supporting idea in the second part of the excerpt. Then have partners discuss their thinking, agree on one important idea and one supporting idea in that part of the excerpt, and then individually underline the two ideas in their *Student Response Books* using two different colored pens, or one pen and a pencil.

Materials

- *A Picture Book of Amelia Earhart*
- *Student Response Book* page 60
- Transparencies of the "Excerpt from *A Picture Book of Amelia Earhart*" from Day 3
- Transparency pens in two colors
- *Assessment Resource Book*
- *Student Response Book*, IDR Journal section
- Small self-stick notes for each student

··········

CLASS COMPREHENSION ASSESSMENT

Circulate among the pairs and notice which sentences the students underline. Ask yourself:

Q *Are the students making reasonable distinctions between important and supporting information?*

Q *Are they supporting their thinking by referring to the story?*

Record your observations on page 28 of the *Assessment Resource Book*.

3 ▶ Discuss Important and Supporting Ideas as a Class

After a few minutes, facilitate a class discussion using the following questions:

Q *What sentence did you and your partner agree was an important idea? Explain your thinking.*

Q *What sentence did you and your partner agree was a supporting detail? Explain your thinking.*

Q *Do you agree with [Hiroko and Jim]? Why or why not?*

> **Students might say:**
>
> "My partner and I underlined 'They never made it.' We think that is important because it is an important event in the story."
>
> "We underlined 'She risked her life to prove that in the air, and elsewhere, women were up to the challenge.' It's an important idea because that's what this book is about—how Amelia changed how the world looked at women."
>
> "We think the last paragraph on the first page is supporting. It supports how Amelia was a pioneer."

As the students share, underline the important and supporting ideas on the transparency using two different colored pens.

Remind the students that the purpose of learning to identify important and supporting ideas in a text is to help them think about what's important to understand or remember in their own reading. Explain that in the coming weeks they will continue to think about important and supporting ideas in text they hear and read independently.

◀ **Teacher Note**
In Week 3, the students focus on building summaries from important ideas. If you feel your students need more experience identifying important ideas and distinguishing between important and supporting ideas before continuing, you may wish to repeat this week's lessons with an alternative book before going on to Week 3. Alternative books are listed on this week's Overview page.

4 ▶ Reflect on Reaching Agreement

Facilitate a brief discussion about how the students did reaching agreement during "Think, Pair, Write." Ask questions such as:

Q *How did you come to agreement today during "Think, Pair, Write"? If you didn't agree, how did you solve the problem?*

Q *How did giving reasons for your opinions help you reach agreement?*

INDIVIDUALIZED DAILY READING

5 ▶ Document IDR Conferences/Have the Students Write About an Important Idea in Their IDR Journals

Have the students continue to use self-stick notes to mark important ideas as they read.

Have the students read independently for up to 30 minutes. Use the "IDR Conference Notes" record sheet to conduct and document individual conferences.

At the end of independent reading, have the students write in their IDR Journals about one important idea they marked in their reading and why they thought it was important. Have a few students share their writing with the class.

 ***Making Meaning Vocabulary* Teacher**
Next week you will revisit this week's reading to teach Vocabulary Week 25.

Week 3

Overview

UNIT 8: DETERMINING IMPORTANT IDEAS AND SUMMARIZING

Narrative Nonfiction

In My Own Backyard
by Judi Kurjian, illustrated by David R. Wagner
(Charlesbridge, 1993)

A child looks out a bedroom window and imagines how the landscape has changed over the ages.

ALTERNATIVE BOOKS

Eleanor by Barbara Cooney

Dandelions by Eve Bunting

Comprehension Focus

• Students *think about important and supporting ideas* in a text.

• Students use important ideas to *build summaries.*

• Students read independently.

Social Development Focus

• Students relate the value of respect to their behavior.

• Students develop the group skills of giving reasons for their opinions and discussing their opinions respectfully.

DO AHEAD

• Make a transparency of the "Summary of *A Picture Book of Amelia Earhart*" (BLM35).

• Collect sample book and movie summaries, enough for one per pair of students (see Day 1, Step 4 and the Teacher Note on page 488).

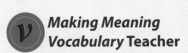

Making Meaning Vocabulary Teacher

If you are teaching Developmental Studies Center's *Making Meaning Vocabulary* program, teach Vocabulary Week 25 this week. For more information, see the *Making Meaning Vocabulary Teacher's Manual.*

Day 1

Materials

- *A Picture Book of Amelia Earhart* (from Unit 8, Week 2)
- Transparency of the "Summary of *A Picture Book of Amelia Earhart*" (BLM35)
- Book and movie summaries, collected ahead (one summary per pair)
- *Student Response Book* page 61
- (Optional) *Student Response Book* page 62

Strategy Lesson

In this lesson, the students:

- Hear, read, and discuss summaries
- Explore what a summary is
- Read independently for up to 30 minutes
- Give reasons for their opinions

About Summarizing

During the next three weeks, the focus of instruction is *summarizing,* a key strategy for helping readers understand and communicate what they read. The students continue to identify important ideas, a critical step in summarizing. Through teacher modeling, class and partner discussions, and guided practice, the students learn to put a text's important ideas together in a concise summary. The goal is for the students to be able to use summarization both orally and in writing to communicate with others about the texts they read.

1 ▶ Review Giving Reasons for Opinions

Ask partners to sit together. Remind them that they learned the prompt "The reason I think this is _____" to give reasons for their opinions in discussion. Explain that you would like them to continue using the prompt in both partner and whole-class discussions this week.

Teacher Note ▶

If necessary, write the prompt where everyone can see it.

2 ▶ Review *A Picture Book of Amelia Earhart*

Show the students the cover of *A Picture Book of Amelia Earhart.* Review that in the previous week the students heard you read the book and made inferences as they thought about the important and supporting ideas in it. Remind the students that the book is a biography that tells the story of Amelia Earhart's life. Ask:

Q *What do you remember from the book about Amelia Earhart's life?*

Stimulate the students' recollection by reading each of the following sentences aloud and asking the students to remember what was happening in that part of the story. For each sentence, have a volunteer share what was happening:

p. 5 "The Earhart girls' behavior was shocking to some people."

p. 12 "'As soon as I left the ground,' she wrote later, 'I knew I myself had to fly.'"

p. 16 "…she said she felt like 'baggage.'"

p. 22 "'Have you come far?' the first person to see her asked. 'From America,' Amelia Earhart told him."

p. 27 "They never made it."

▶3 Read and Discuss a Summary of the Book

Place the transparency of "Summary of *A Picture Book of Amelia Earhart*" on the overhead projector. Explain that this is a summary of the book and that a summary is a brief description of what a text is about. Ask the students to follow along as you read it aloud.

After reading the summary, have the students turn to "Summary of *A Picture Book of Amelia Earhart*" on *Student Response Book* page 61. Point out that this is the summary you just read. Ask the students to read it again quietly to themselves.

After the reading, facilitate a whole-class discussion using the following questions. Remind the students to use "The reason I think this is _____" as they talk.

Q *What does this summary of the book do?*

Q *What kind of information is in the summary?*

Students might say:

"The summary tells you what the book is about."

"It gives you the story, but in a shorter version."

"It has the main stuff about her life. The reason I think this is because it doesn't tell everything—like when she got married."

"I agree with [Cory]. The summary has the important ideas from the book—like when she flew around the world and how she disappeared."

◀ **Teacher Note**

Have students who are unable to read the summary on their own read it with a partner, or you might reread it aloud yourself as the students read along.

Q *Why might you want to read a summary of a book?*

Students might say:

"You might want to know what the book is about before
 you read it."

"From the summary, you can figure out if the book
 sounds interesting."

4 ▸ Explore Other Summaries

Teacher Note ▸

You can find book summaries on
the back covers of books as well
as on Internet bookseller sites.
You might also collect reviews
that summarize movies the
students might be familiar with.

If you do not have enough
summaries for all the
pairs, have them read the
summary of *Flight* on *Student
Response Book* page 62.

Explain that you collected summaries from various sources for
the students to read today. Distribute the summaries, one to each
pair. Have each pair read their summary quietly, and then discuss
the following questions. Write the questions where everyone can
see them:

- *What book or movie is your summary about?*

- *What did you learn about the book or movie from the summary?*

When most pairs have had a chance to talk, have a few pairs share
with the class what their summary is about and what they learned
from the summary. Follow up by asking:

Q *How might this summary be helpful to you or others who read it?*

Explain that *summarizing* is *using important information in a text
to say briefly what the text is about*. Readers summarize to help
them make sense of what they are reading and to remember the
important information. They also summarize to communicate to
others what a text is about.

Explain that during the next few weeks the students will learn
how to summarize so they can write summaries of their own
independent reading books to share with the class.

5 ▸ Reflect on Giving Reasons for Opinions

Facilitate a brief discussion about how the students did using the
prompt to give reasons for their opinions.

INDIVIDUALIZED DAILY READING

 ## Self-monitor to Think About What Is Important

Remind the students that they have been thinking about important ideas in texts. Explain that today you will stop them periodically during IDR to have them think about how well they are recognizing what is important in their reading to that point.

Have the students read books at appropriate levels independently for up to 30 minutes. Stop them at 10-minute intervals and have them think about the following questions:

Q *What seems important to understand in the reading so far?*

Q *What might the author want you to be thinking at this point?*

At the end of independent reading, have a few volunteers share an important idea in their reading. Remind the students to use evidence from the text to support their thinking.

Day 2

Materials

* *In My Own Backyard*

Read-aloud

In this lesson, the students:

* Think about life in the past
* Hear and discuss a story
* *Make inferences*
* Read independently for up to 30 minutes
* Give reasons for their opinions

▶1 Review Summaries and Summarizing

Remind the students that in the previous lesson they heard a summary of *A Picture Book of Amelia Earhart*. Review that a summary is a brief description of what a text is about. It includes important information or ideas from the text.

Explain that you will read a book aloud today, and in the next two days the class will build a summary of it together using the important ideas.

▶2 Introduce *In My Own Backyard*

Tell the students that to prepare to hear today's book, you would like them to think quietly for a moment about the following questions:

Q *Think about the piece of land our school is sitting on. What do you think it might have looked like 100 years ago, or before the school was built?*

Q *What do you think it might have looked like a thousand years ago? A million years ago?*

Have several students share their ideas and explain their thinking. If they have difficulty responding, think aloud about how the school site might have looked in the past. (For example, you might say, "A hundred years ago, there might have been a farm on this land.

A thousand years ago, perhaps a community of Native Americans lived here. A million years ago, there might have been only animals roaming here, animals that are now extinct.")

Show the cover of *In My Own Backyard* and read the author's and illustrator's names aloud. Explain that in the book a child is looking out a bedroom window when suddenly the backyard begins to go back in time. Ask them to think about what they just discussed as they listen to the story.

3 Read *In My Own Backyard* Aloud

Read the book aloud, showing the illustrations and stopping as described below.

Suggested Vocabulary

scythe: tool used for cutting grasses and crops (p. 6; refer to the illustration on p. 7)

waterwheel: large wheel turned by water, used in the past to power machines in mills and factories (p. 6; refer to the illustration on p. 7)

coral: groups of the hard skeletons of tiny sea creatures (p. 24)

algae: water plants that have no roots or stems (p. 26)

sponges and sea fans: sea creatures that live on rocks and surfaces under water (p. 26)

ELL Vocabulary

English Language Learners may benefit from discussing additional vocabulary, including:

brook: small stream (p. 6)

settlers: people who make a home in a new place (p. 10)

celebration: happy gathering (p. 12)

blizzard: heavy snowstorm (p. 14)

tropical plants: plants that grow in hot, moist climates (p. 20)

ancestors: family members from a long time before (p. 22)

fossils: remains of plants and animals that lived long ago (p. 30)

Stop after:

p. 6   "What I was seeing out my window was my backyard one
hundred years ago!"

Have the students use "Turn to Your Partner" to discuss:

Q *What does the child see outside the window?*

Without sharing as a class, reread the last sentence on page 6 and continue reading to the next stop. Stop after:

p. 12 "Newly-picked corn, squash, acorns, and berries made me think that this must be a harvest celebration before the first settlers came from Europe."

 Have the students use "Turn to Your Partner" to discuss:

Q *What does the child see in the part of the story I just read?*

 Without sharing as a class, reread the last sentence before the stop and continue reading to the next stop. Repeat this procedure at the next four stops:

p. 16 "I could see paintings on a flat rock wall of the shelter where they slept."

p. 20 "A baby stegosaurus grazed right in front of my window!"

p. 24 "Around the coral and seaweed, unusual fish wore hard shells."

p. 30 "Ever since that day, I've looked for bones and fossils that might have been left in that most amazing place: my own backyard."

4 ▶ **Discuss the Reading as a Class**

Facilitate a discussion of the story using the following questions. Remind the students to use "The reason I think this is _____" and other discussion prompts they have learned to add to one another's thinking.

Teacher Note ▶

Be ready to reread the text and show illustrations again to help the students recall what they heard.

Q *What does the child learn about the past by looking out the window?*

Students might say:

"The child sees what the place was like at different times in history."

"Farmers lived on the land a hundred years ago."

"I agree with [Stacy]. Before the farmers there were pioneers and Native Americans."

"A really long time ago it was all covered by water."

Q *The setting is the time and place a story happens. What is the setting of this story?*

Q *Why do you think the child calls the backyard "that most amazing place"?*

Students might say:

"One reason I think it's an amazing place is because the book says dinosaurs used to live on the land. That's pretty amazing!"

"I agree with [Leon]. It's pretty amazing to think that cave dwellers used to live where you're living now."

As the students make inferences about the story, point them out (for example, "The book does not say directly that the child imagines that the backyard is changing to show how it was in the past, but you figured that out from clues in the story").

Explain that in the next lesson they will think about what information is important to know and remember in this story, and prepare to write a summary of it.

INDIVIDUALIZED DAILY READING

 Self-monitor to Think About What Is Important

Have the students independently read books at appropriate levels for up to 30 minutes. Continue to have the students think about what they are reading. Stop them at 10-minute intervals and have them think about the following questions:

Q *What seems important to understand in the reading so far?*

Q *What might the author want you to be thinking at this point?*

As they read, circulate among the students and ask individuals to read a selection aloud to you and explain what they think is important so far.

At the end of independent reading, have a few volunteers share how they are doing at identifying important ideas as they read. Remind the students to use evidence from the text to support their thinking.

Day 3

Guided Strategy Practice

In this lesson, the students:

* *Distinguish between important ideas and supporting ideas* in a text
* Read independently for up to 30 minutes
* Give reasons for their opinions
* Discuss their opinions respectfully

▶ 1 Review Important and Supporting Ideas

Remind the students that in the past few weeks, they have been thinking about important and supporting ideas in books such as *Flight* and *A Picture Book of Amelia Earhart*. Review that *distinguishing between important ideas and supporting ideas* is a comprehension strategy that helps readers identify what is essential to know and remember in a text.

Explain that distinguishing between important and supporting ideas is also necessary to summarize a text, because a summary is made up of the important information. Tell them that today they will think about what is important in *In My Own Backyard* and get ready to write a summary of the book together.

▶ 2 Reread the Story

Explain that as you reread *In My Own Backyard,* you will stop several times to have the students think about what is important in the part of the story they just heard and share their thinking in pairs.

Reread the story, slowly and clearly, stopping after:

> **p. 6** "What I was seeing out my window was my backyard one hundred years ago!"

Materials

* *In My Own Backyard*
* Chart paper and a marker
* *Assessment Resource Book*
* Small self-stick notes for each student

Ask:

Q *What is most important to understand or remember about what you've heard so far?*

 Have the students use "Think, Pair, Share" to discuss their ideas. Then have a couple of volunteers share their ideas with the class. Record the ideas on a chart entitled "Important Ideas in *In My Own Backyard*."

> **Students might say:**
>
> "The child looks out the window into the backyard."
>
> "The yard starts changing into a farm 100 years ago."

Follow this procedure at the next five stops, recording a couple of ideas on the chart at each stop.

p. 12 "Newly-picked corn, squash, acorns, and berries made me think that this must be a harvest celebration before the first settlers came from Europe."

p. 16 "I could see paintings on a flat rock wall of the shelter where they slept."

p. 22 "The trees had green trunks, but I could not see very far between them because the air was thick with mist."

p. 28 "It was hard to believe that this place was my backyard four billion years ago, at the beginning of life on our planet."

p. 30 "Ever since that day, I've looked for bones and fossils that might have been left in that most amazing place: my own backyard."

Teacher Note ▶

If the students have difficulty identifying important ideas in the passages, you may want to teach this lesson over two days. Follow the procedure you used in Days 2 and 3 of Week 2, in which the students hear the passage, discuss important ideas in pairs, hear the passage again, and record their ideas.

CLASS COMPREHENSION ASSESSMENT

Circulate as partners talk. Ask yourself:

Q *Are the students able to identify important information in the text?*

Q *Are they referring to the text to support their thinking?*

Record your observations on page 29 of the *Assessment Resource Book*.

Discuss Important Ideas as a Class

Review the ideas on the "Important Ideas in *In My Own Backyard*" chart. Facilitate a discussion using the following questions. Remind the students to give reasons for their opinions.

Q *Are there any important ideas that we need to add to the chart? Explain your thinking.*

Q *Are there any ideas on the chart that you think are supporting ideas? Why do you think that?*

Q *Do you agree or disagree with [Rosa]? Why?*

> **Students might say:**
>
> "I think the idea that the Native Americans are having a celebration is a supporting idea. I don't think we need to remember that."
>
> "I agree with [Huan]. The important idea is that Native Americans lived on the land before settlers came. The information about the celebration is a detail."
>
> "I think it's supporting that the ice was a mile thick. That's another detail."

Make adjustments to the chart as needed during this discussion, adding important ideas and crossing out supporting information. If the students have difficulty thinking about what is important and what is supporting, you might think aloud to model your own thinking and revise the chart as needed.

Explain that in the next lesson the students will use the ideas on the chart to write a summary of the story as a class.

 Reflect on Discussing Opinions Respectfully

Point out that it is normal for people to have different opinions when discussing what is important and supporting in a text. Remind the students of any disagreements that arose during today's whole-class discussion.

Teacher Note

On Day 4, the class will write a summary of *In My Own Backyard,* using the important ideas. Examples of some of the important ideas are:

- The child looks out the window.
- The child wonders who has stood there before.
- The yard becomes a farm 100 years ago.
- Pioneers came in covered wagons.
- Native Americans lived on the land.
- Ice covered everything.
- People wore animal skins.
- Dinosaurs and strange animals lived there.
- Everything was under water.
- The only thing alive was algae.
- Everything returns to normal.
- The child looks for bones and fossils.

Ask:

Q *When someone disagrees with you, how do you like them to tell you that?*

Q *If they don't tell you in that way, how might you feel? Why?*

Q *How can we make sure that we can disagree respectfully during our discussions?*

Tell the students that they will continue to discuss their opinions in the coming weeks and that you would like them to focus on doing this respectfully.

Save the "Important Ideas in *In My Own Backyard*" chart for Day 4.

INDIVIDUALIZED DAILY READING

▶ **5** **Discuss Important and Supporting Ideas/Document IDR Conferences**

Remind the students that they have been thinking about both important and supporting ideas in texts. Explain that you want them to use self-stick notes to mark one important idea and one supporting idea in their reading today.

Have the students read independently for up to 30 minutes. Use the "IDR Conference Notes" record sheet to conduct and document individual conferences.

At the end of independent reading, have volunteers share the important and supporting ideas they marked. Remind them to ask clarifying questions and to use the prompt "The reason I think this is _____" to support their thinking.

Conduct a whole-class discussion by asking and briefly discussing questions such as:

Q *What passage did you mark as important?*

Q *How did you know that idea was important?*

Q *What passage did you mark as supporting? How does this passage you marked support the important ideas in your reading?*

Day 4

Materials

- *In My Own Backyard*
- "Important Ideas in *In My Own Backyard*" chart (from Day 3)
- Transparency of the "Summary of *A Picture Book of Amelia Earhart*" (BLM35)
- *Student Response Book* page 62
- Chart paper or a blank transparency and a marker
- "Reading Comprehension Strategies" chart
- Small self-stick notes for each student
- *Student Response Book,* IDR Journal section

Important Ideas in In My Own Backyard

- The child looks out the window.
- The child wonders who has stood there before.

Guided Strategy Practice

In this lesson, the students:

- *Build a summary* as a class
- Read independently for up to 30 minutes
- Give reasons for their opinions

1 Review Important Ideas and Summarizing

Direct the students' attention to the "Important Ideas in *In My Own Backyard*" chart and remind them that in the previous lesson they made a list of important ideas in the story. Review that identifying what is important is necessary for summarizing a text and that summarizing is a powerful strategy for remembering important information and communicating it to others.

Explain that today the class will use the ideas on the chart to write a summary of *In My Own Backyard*. Remind them that they will be writing their own summaries in the next couple of weeks.

2 Review the Summary of *A Picture Book of Amelia Earhart*

Put the transparency of the "Summary of *A Picture Book of Amelia Earhart*" on the overhead projector and have the students turn to *Student Response Book* page 62, where they will find the summary. Explain that this summary, which they read earlier in the week, can serve as a model for the summary they will write today.

Ask the students to reread the summary quietly to themselves (or read it aloud again as they follow along); then have the students use "Think, Pair, Share" to discuss:

Q *What do you notice in the summary of* A Picture Book of Amelia Earhart *that might serve as a model when we summarize* In My Own Backyard?

Students might say:

"The first sentence just tells you what the story is about."

"It tells about the story from the beginning to the end. The reason I think this is that the summary starts at the beginning of her life and goes to the end."

"It doesn't say everything that's in the book."

"It's not too long."

If the students have difficulty answering the question, suggest some ideas like those in the "Students might say" note. Be sure to point out that the summary begins with a general statement of what the book is about followed by important events or ideas from the book.

 ## **Model Starting the Summary of *In My Own Backyard***

On a blank transparency or sheet of chart paper, write the title "Summary of *In My Own Backyard.*" Explain that you will begin the summary and that the class will write the rest of it together.

Tell the students that you want to begin the summary with a general statement of what the book is about. Ask:

Q *In a sentence, what is* In My Own Backyard *about?*

Students might say:

"It's about a child who looks out the window and sees the backyard go back in time."

"It's about what happened in a place in the past."

Using the students' suggestions, model writing an opening sentence about the book (for example, "In this story, a child imagines what life in her backyard was like in the past"). If the students cannot come up with a general opening sentence, provide one yourself.

Explain that the rest of the summary will be made up of ideas on the "Important Ideas in *In My Own Backyard*" chart. To model adding to the summary, think aloud about selecting information on the chart for the second sentence. (For example, you might say, "Since this story moves backward in time, it probably makes sense to tell what the child saw in the order it happened. The first thing the child saw was the farmers who lived on the land one hundred years ago.")

Model writing the second sentence of the summary. (For example, you might write "First, the child sees farmers who lived on the land one hundred years ago.")

Follow this procedure to provide the third sentence of the summary. If possible, model combining two or three pieces of information on the chart into a single sentence. Point out that combining information in this way helps to keep the summary brief. (For example, "Pioneers came in covered wagons" and "Native Americans lived on the land" can be combined into the sentence "Then the child sees other people from further back in time, like pioneers and Native Americans.")

4 ▶ Complete the Summary as a Class

Referring to the "Important Ideas in *In My Own Backyard*" chart, elicit suggestions for what to add to the summary by asking:

Q *What information do you think should come next in the summary? Why do you think that?*

Teacher Note ▶

If the students are unable to suggest sentences, continue to model by thinking aloud and adding your own sentences to the chart.

Use the students' suggestions to add sentences to the chart, shaping and combining their ideas as necessary to keep the summary clear and concise. (For example, you may need to model the use of words such as *then, next,* and *after that* to connect sentences and show the sequence of events.)

The completed summary might look like this:

Summary of In My Own Backyard

In this story, a child imagines what life in her backyard was like in the past. First she sees farmers working on the land one hundred years ago. Then she sees other people from further back in time, such as pioneers and Native Americans. Then ice covers the land, and people in animal skins appear. Next, in the time before humans, dinosaurs and other strange animals live on the land. Finally, the land is covered by water, and the child sees the very beginning of life, when the only living thing is algae.

The child comes back to the present and decides to start looking for bones and fossils in that "most amazing place," the backyard.

When the summary is finished, reread it aloud and ask:

Q *Do you think someone who hasn't read* In My Own Backyard *could get a good idea of what the book is about from reading this summary? If not, what can we add?*

5 ▶ Add to the "Reading Comprehension Strategies" Chart

Direct the students' attention to the "Reading Comprehension Strategies" chart and add *summarizing* to it. Review that *summarizing* is *using important information in a text to say briefly what the text is about.* Readers summarize to help them make sense of important information in a text and also to communicate to others what a text is about.

Tell the students that during the next couple of weeks they will practice summarizing with the goal of writing a summary of their own book to share with their classmates.

◀ **Teacher Note**

Save the "Summary of *In My Own Backyard*" chart for use in Weeks 4 and 5 of this unit.

Reading Comprehension Strategies

- recognizing text features

---

6 Reflect on Today's Partner and Class Conversations

Facilitate a brief discussion about today's conversations and how the students did giving reasons for their opinions and discussing their opinions respectfully. Report any examples you noticed of students disagreeing respectfully and giving reasons for their opinions.

INDIVIDUALIZED DAILY READING

7 Document IDR Conferences/Write About Important and Supporting Ideas in Their IDR Journals

Have the students continue to use self-stick notes to mark one important idea and one supporting idea in their reading.

Have the students read independently for up to 30 minutes. Use the "IDR Conference Notes" record sheet to conduct and document individual conferences.

At the end of independent reading, have the students write in their IDR Journals about the important and supporting ideas they marked in their reading and why they thought the ideas were important or supporting.

EXTENSION

Research Your Community's Past

Have the students research and report on how their community has changed over time. Some students might focus on recent history, investigating what the community was like during the 1980s, 1970s, 1960s, and so on. Other students might investigate periods further back in time, such as life in the area 100 years ago, 200 years ago, and so on. Your community library and historical society are likely sources of information.

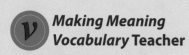

***Making Meaning
Vocabulary* Teacher**

Next week you will revisit this week's reading to teach Vocabulary Week 26.

UNIT 8: DETERMINING IMPORTANT IDEAS AND SUMMARIZING
Narrative Nonfiction

A Picture Book of Rosa Parks
by David A. Adler, illustrated by Robert Casilla
(Holiday House, 1993)

Rosa Park's refusal to give up her seat on a public bus sparks a protest that changes history.

ALTERNATIVE BOOKS

George Washington Carver by Andy Carter and Carol Saller

Freedom School, Yes! by Amy Littlesugar

Comprehension Focus

- Students *think about important and supporting ideas* in a text.

- Students use important ideas to *summarize*.

- Students read independently.

Social Development Focus

- Students relate the value of respect to their behavior.

- Students develop the group skills of giving reasons for their opinions and discussing their opinions respectfully.

DO AHEAD

- Make transparencies of the excerpts from *A Picture Book of Rosa Parks* (BLM36–BLM41).

- Prepare charts with directions for taking notes (see Day 2, Step 4 on page 514 and Day 3, Step 4 on page 518).

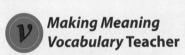

***Making Meaning Vocabulary* Teacher**

If you are teaching Developmental Studies Center's *Making Meaning Vocabulary* program, teach Vocabulary Week 26 this week. For more information, see the *Making Meaning Vocabulary Teacher's Manual*.

Day 1

Materials

- *A Picture Book of Rosa Parks*
- Small self-stick notes for each student

 Note

Preview the book with your English Language Learners prior to today's read-aloud. Help your students understand the background knowledge needed to make sense of the story.

Read-aloud

In this lesson, the students:

- *Identify important ideas* in a text
- Read independently for up to 30 minutes
- Give reasons for their opinions
- Discuss their opinions respectfully

1 ▶ Review the Social Focus and Summarizing

Ask partners to sit together. Remind the students that they have been focusing on giving reasons for their opinions and on discussing their opinions respectfully. Explain that you would like them to continue practicing these skills in the coming week.

Explain that this week the students will continue to learn about using important ideas to summarize a text. Remind them that *summarizing* is an important strategy because it helps readers understand a text and communicate what it is about.

2 ▶ Introduce *A Picture Book of Rosa Parks*

Tell the students that today you will read *A Picture Book of Rosa Parks* aloud. Show the cover and read the author's and illustrator's names aloud.

Remind the students that earlier in the year they heard *The Bat Boy & His Violin* and *Teammates,* two stories that were set in the United States during the first half of the 20th century. They learned about segregation and laws in the South that discriminated against blacks. Some of these laws required black people to ride at the back of a public bus and to give up their seat for a white rider. Explain that Rosa Parks took an important action that began to change those unfair laws.

Facilitate a brief discussion about what the students think they know about Rosa Parks, and ask them to keep these things in mind as they listen to the story.

3 Read *A Picture Book of Rosa Parks* Aloud

As you read, have the students listen for important ideas. Tell them that you will stop several times to have partners talk about what seems important about the part they just heard.

Read the book aloud, showing the illustrations and stopping as described on the next page.

Suggested Vocabulary

discrimination: unfair treatment (p. 8)

tailor's assistant: helper for someone who makes or fits clothes (p. 18)

appealed to a higher court: asked for another opinion from a different court (p. 20)

bus boycott: show of protest by refusing to ride buses (p. 21)

humiliated: made to feel ashamed (p. 21)

kicked about by the brutal feet of oppression: treated poorly (p. 21)

demonstrations: groups of people saying in public how they feel about political issues (p. 25)

nationality: country from which a person comes or to which a person belongs (p. 28)

ELL Vocabulary

English Language Learners may benefit from discussing additional vocabulary, including:

tortured: hurt badly (p. 10)

barber: person who cuts hair (p. 14)

struggle: fight (p. 14)

fare: money; cost to ride the bus (p. 16)

arrested: taken away by police officers (p. 18)

court: place where a judge or jury decides whether someone has broken the law (p. 20)

found guilty: determined to have broken the law (p. 20)

minister: religious leader (p. 21)

retired: stopped working (p. 27)

Have the students use "Think, Pair, Share" to discuss the following question at each stop:

Q *What's most important to understand or remember about the part you just heard?*

> **p. 10**   "Rosa's grandfather, Sylvester Edwards, carried a shotgun to protect his family from the Klan."

> **p. 20**   "Many walked, some as far as twelve miles."

> **p. 30**   "…with the respect all people deserve."

Teacher Note ▶

If necessary, explain that in the bus boycott African Americans refused to ride and the city's buses lost a great deal of money.

4   Discuss the Story as a Class

Facilitate a discussion of the story using the following questions. Remind the students to use "The reason I think this is _____" and other discussion prompts they have learned to add to one another's thinking.

Q *What were some of the important ideas you heard in this reading? Why do those ideas seem important?*

Students might say:

"Rosa Parks did not give up her seat on the bus to a white man. They arrested her and she went to jail. The reason I think it's important is because that's what started everything."

"The black leaders organized a bus boycott. The reason I think it is important is that I think this helped get the laws changed."

"To add to what [Natasha] said, Rosa was brave. The reason I think this is that she wasn't afraid to get arrested."

Explain that in the next lesson the students will think about important ideas in an excerpt from this book.

INDIVIDUALIZED DAILY READING

 5 ▶ Discuss Important and Supporting Ideas

Remind the students that they have been thinking about both important and supporting ideas in texts. Explain that you want each student to use self-stick notes to mark one important idea and one supporting idea in the reading today.

Have the students read independently for up to 30 minutes. As they read, circulate among them. Ask individual students questions such as:

Q *What is your book about?*

Q *Why do you think this passage is important?*

Q *How does this passage you marked support the important ideas in your reading?*

Q *Why do you think this passage is supporting?*

At the end of independent reading, have volunteers share the important and supporting ideas they marked and the reasons for their thinking.

EXTENSION

Read an Interview with Rosa Parks

Have the students read and discuss an interview with Rosa Parks. They can find one by searching the Internet with the keywords "Rosa Parks" and "interview." Before they read the interview, you might have the students brainstorm questions they would want to ask Rosa Parks.

Day 2

Materials

- Transparencies of sections 1–3 of the "Excerpt from *A Picture Book of Rosa Parks*" (BLM36–BLM38)
- *Student Response Book* pages 63–64
- Chart with directions for taking notes, prepared ahead (see Step 4)

Guided Strategy Practice

In this lesson, the students:

- *Identify important ideas* in a text
- Read independently for up to 30 minutes
- Give reasons for their opinions
- Discuss their opinions respectfully

1 ▶ Review Important Ideas and Summarizing

Review that *determining important and supporting ideas* helps readers better understand what they read by helping them identify what is essential to know or remember in a text. Remind them that summaries are made up of important information in a text and that summarizing helps readers understand a text and communicate what it is about.

Explain that this week the students will use important ideas in the excerpt from *A Picture Book of Rosa Parks* to practice writing a summary of the story together. This week's activities will prepare them to write summaries of their own books for their classmates.

2 ▶ Model Taking Notes and Underlining Important Ideas in Section 1

Place the transparency of section 1 of the excerpt from *A Picture Book of Rosa Parks* on the overhead projector, and explain that this is the part of the story when Rosa Parks takes a stand against discrimination.

As the students follow along, read the section aloud. Then think aloud about what the section is about. On the transparency, model writing a brief note in the margin and underlining the sentences that seem most important.

(For example, you might say, "The main event in this paragraph is that Rosa got on the bus and sat in the middle section. I will underline the sentence 'She got on the Cleveland Avenue bus and took a seat in the middle section.'" Then write the note: "She got on the bus and sat in the middle section.")

3 ▶ Practice Taking Notes and Underlining Important Ideas in Section 2

Explain that the full excerpt, divided into sections, is reproduced on *Student Response Book* pages 63–64. Direct the students to the first section and have them write the note you modeled in their own margin and underline the sentence you underlined.

 Ask them to read the second section in pairs and together discuss what is most important in that section.

After several minutes, bring the students' attention back to the whole class. Ask:

Q   *What is this section about? What is most important in this section?*

Q   *Which sentences give you the most important information?*

> **Students might say:**
>
> "In this section, I think it is most important that Rosa Parks did not move from her seat because she thought the law was unfair."
>
> "I think the sentence, 'James Blake called the police, and Rosa Parks was arrested' is an important sentence. The reason I think this is because it is an important event."

As the students respond, jot notes in the margin of the transparency and underline sentences. If the students have difficulty identifying the most important ideas in the section, model again by thinking aloud, writing a note in the margin, and underlining important sentences, such as those listed in the "Students might say" note.

Have the students copy your notes and underlining in their own *Student Response Books*.

◀ **Teacher Note**

The copied notes give the students a record of your modeled thinking as they take notes and underline important ideas in the rest of the excerpt.

Have Partners Take Notes and Underline Important Ideas in Section 3

Direct the students' attention to the chart you prepared ahead, and explain the following directions. Make sure the chart is posted where all the students can see it:

1. Read section 3 with your partner.

2. Discuss what it is about.

3. Write notes in the margin that tell what this section is about.

4. Underline sentences that seem most important.

Circulate as pairs work and notice whether they are able to identify and take notes about important ideas in a section. If they are having difficulty, support them by asking questions such as:

Q *What happens in this section? Tell me in your own words.*

If you notice many students struggling with identifying or taking notes about the major ideas, bring the class together and go through this section of the excerpt in the more directed way you did for the first two sections.

> **Teacher Note** ▶
>
> Identifying and taking notes about important ideas can be challenging. It can be difficult for students (and even adults) to sort out major ideas from supporting details, especially in very concise texts. The students will benefit from repeated experiences hearing and thinking about important and supporting ideas.

Discuss Important Ideas in Section 3 as a Class

Facilitate a discussion about section 3 of the excerpt, using the following questions. As the students report their thinking, jot notes and underline sentences on the transparency of the excerpt. Remind the students to give reasons for their opinions.

Q *What did you and your partner think is important to know and remember in this section? What sentences did you underline that talked about that directly? What notes did you write?*

Q *Why did you think that idea is important?*

Q *Do you agree or disagree with [Rita and Art]? Why?*

Reflect on Discussing Opinions Respectfully

Facilitate a brief discussion of how the students interacted. Ask:

Q *Did people disagree with you today? If so, did they disagree in a way that felt comfortable for you? Why or why not?*

Q *What might we want to do differently tomorrow so we know we are discussing our opinions respectfully?*

Explain that in the next lesson the students will take notes and underline important sentences in the rest of the excerpt.

Save your marked transparencies of the excerpt from *A Picture Book of Rosa Parks* for Days 3 and 4.

INDIVIDUALIZED DAILY READING

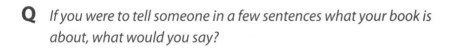

Practice Orally Summarizing Reading

Have the students read independently for up to 30 minutes.

At the end of independent reading, explain that you would like the students to think about a brief summary of the book they are reading by reflecting on some of the important ideas they have found. Have the students share their thinking, first in pairs, and then as a whole class. Ask questions such as:

Q *If you were to tell someone in a few sentences what your book is about, what would you say?*

Day 3

Materials

- Transparencies of the "Excerpt from *A Picture Book of Rosa Parks*" (BLM36–BLM41)
- *Student Response Book* pages 63–64
- Chart with directions for taking notes, prepared ahead (see Step 4)

Guided Strategy Practice

In this lesson, the students:

- *Identify important ideas* in a text
- Read independently for up to 30 minutes
- Give reasons for their opinions
- Discuss their opinions in a respectful way

1 ▶ **Review Important Ideas in the First Part of *A Picture Book of Rosa Parks***

Show the transparencies of the first three sections of *A Picture Book of Rosa Parks* and review the notes you wrote and the sentences you underlined yesterday. Remind the students that they thought about the most important ideas in the first three sections of the story.

Explain that today the students will identify important ideas in the rest of the story using the same process they used yesterday. This will prepare them to summarize the story tomorrow.

2 ▶ **Model Taking Notes and Underlining Important Ideas in Section 4**

Place the transparency of section 4 of the excerpt from *A Picture Book of Rosa Parks* on the overhead projector. As the students follow along, read the paragraph. Then think aloud about what this section is about. On the transparency, model writing a brief note about this in the margin and underlining sentences that seem most important in the section. (For example, you might say, "What seems important in this section is that people protested Rosa's arrest by not riding buses. I'll underline the first sentence that talks about that and write a note that says, 'People refused to ride buses in protest of Rosa's arrest.'")

Ask:

Q *What sentences in this section support the important idea I underlined?*

Students might say:

"'They found other ways to get to work' is a supporting idea. It tells you what they did instead of riding the bus."

Direct the students to section 4 on *Student Response Book* page 63, and have them write the notes you modeled in the margin of their own page and underline the sentences you underlined.

3 Practice Taking Notes and Underlining Important Ideas in Section 5

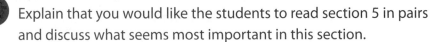

Explain that you would like the students to read section 5 in pairs and discuss what seems most important in this section.

After allowing several minutes for partners to talk, bring their attention back to the whole class. Ask:

Q *What's this section about? What seems most important in this section?*

Q *Which sentences give you the most important information?*

Students might say:

"In this section, I think it is most important that the boycott was led by Dr. Martin Luther King Jr."

"I agree with [Tariq]. I think 'The bus boycott was led by Dr. Martin Luther King Jr., the new minister at the Dexter Avenue Baptist Church,' is an important sentence."

"In addition to what [Eryn] said, I think the last sentence of the paragraph is important because it explains the reason for the boycott."

As the students respond, jot notes in the margin of the transparency and underline sentences. If the students have difficulty identifying the most important ideas in the section, model again by thinking aloud, writing notes in the margin, and underlining important sentences, such as those listed in the "Students might say" note.

Have the students copy your notes and underlines in their own *Student Response Books.*

4 ▶ **Have Partners Continue to Take Notes and Underline Important Ideas in Section 6**

Explain the following directions, which you have written on a chart and posted where everyone can see them:

1. *Read section 6 (the last three paragraphs) with your partner.*

2. *Discuss what it is about.*

3. *Write notes in the margin that tell what this section is about.*

4. *Underline sentences that seem most important.*

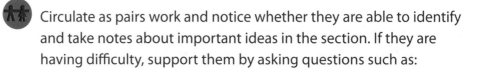

Circulate as pairs work and notice whether they are able to identify and take notes about important ideas in the section. If they are having difficulty, support them by asking questions such as:

Q *What happens in this section? Tell me in your own words.*

If you notice many students struggling with identifying the major ideas or taking notes, bring the class together and go through this section of the excerpt together in the more directed way you did for the prior two sections.

Teacher Note ▶

Keep in mind that identifying important ideas and taking notes about them can be challenging. It can be difficult for students to sort out major ideas from supporting details, especially in very concise texts. Students will benefit from repeated experiences hearing and thinking about important and supporting ideas.

5 ▶ **Discuss Important Ideas in Section 6 as a Class**

Facilitate a discussion about section 6 of the excerpt, using the following questions. As the students report their thinking, jot notes and underline sentences on the transparencies. Remind the students to give reasons for their opinions.

Q *What did you and your partner think this section is about? What sentences did you underline that talked about that directly? What notes did you take?*

Q *Why did you think that idea was important?*

Q *Do you agree or disagree with [Trevor and Bonnie]? Why?*

Explain that in the next lesson the students will use their notes and underlined passages to write a summary of the story together.

Save your marked transparencies of the excerpt from *A Picture Book of Rosa Parks* for Day 4.

INDIVIDUALIZED DAILY READING

6 ▶ Document IDR Conferences/Have the Students Practice Orally Summarizing Reading

Have the students read independently for up to 30 minutes.

Use the "IDR Conference Notes" record sheet to conduct and document individual conferences.

At the end of independent reading, ask each student to summarize his reading for his partner by telling his partner in a few sentences what he read. Have a few volunteers share with the class.

Day 4

Materials

- *Student Response Book* pages 63–64
- Chart paper and a marker
- "Summary of *In My Own Backyard*" chart (from Week 3)
- Transparencies of the "Excerpt from *A Picture Book of Rosa Parks*" with notes (from Days 2 and 3)
- Paper and pencil for each student
- *Assessment Resource Book*
- *Student Response Book,* IDR Journal section

Teacher Note

This lesson may take longer than one class period.

Guided Strategy Practice

In this lesson, the students:

- *Build a summary* as a class
- Read independently for up to 30 minutes
- Give reasons for their opinions
- Discuss their opinions respectfully

▶ 1 Review Important Ideas and Summarizing

Have partners sit together. Explain that today they will use their notes and the important ideas they underlined to write a summary of the excerpt from *A Picture Book of Rosa Parks.*

Have them open to *Student Response Book* pages 63–64 and review their notes and underlining.

▶ 2 Model Writing the First Few Sentences of the Summary

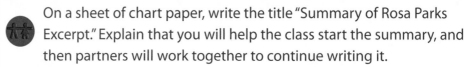

On a sheet of chart paper, write the title "Summary of Rosa Parks Excerpt." Explain that you will help the class start the summary, and then partners will work together to continue writing it.

Review that a summary should give readers a good idea of what the piece of text is about. Refer to the summary of *In My Own Backyard,* and remind the students that a summary begins with a general statement about the text's topic and continues with important ideas in the text. Ask:

Q *In one or two sentences, how might you say what* A Picture Book of Rosa Parks *is about?*

Have a few volunteers share their thinking with the class. Then ask the students to listen and watch as you think aloud and write an opening sentence on the chart (for example, "This story describes how Rosa Parks took an important action that challenged segregation laws in the South").

Place the transparency of the first two sections of the excerpt on the overhead projector. Read the note(s) you wrote and the sentences you underlined. Think aloud about how you might summarize these sections; then add a few sentences to the summary on the chart (for example, "Rosa refused to give up her seat on a bus to a white passenger").

Ask the students to copy the charted sentences onto their own paper.

3 ▶ Practice Adding to the Summary Together

Direct the students to the next section of the excerpt, on *Student Response Book* page 63. Have them reread their notes and the sentences they underlined; then have them use "Turn to Your Partner" to discuss how they might summarize this section.

After a minute or two, bring partners' attention back to the whole class. Ask one or two volunteers for sentences to summarize this section.

As the students respond, add to the summary on the chart. If the students have difficulty generating sentences that summarize this section, model again by thinking aloud and adding your own sentences.

Again, have the students copy your sentences onto their own paper, and tell them that they will write the rest of the summary in pairs.

4 ▶ Have Partners Write the Rest of the Summary

Explain that you would like partners to work together to write the rest of the summary, looking at one section at a time and reviewing their notes and underlined sentences.

As you circulate, support the students by asking them questions to
help them summarize. If you notice many students having difficulty,
bring the class together and summarize the remaining sections of
the excerpt together in a more directed manner, as you did earlier
in the lesson.

A completed summary might look like this:

> ### Summary of the Rosa Parks Excerpt
>
> This excerpt describes how Rosa Parks took an
> important action that challenged segregation laws in the
> South. Rosa refused to give up her seat on the bus to a
> white passenger. She was arrested and went to jail. Black
> leaders, including Dr. Martin Luther King Jr., organized a
> bus boycott to try to get the laws changed. The boycott
> lasted over a year. Finally the Supreme Court ruled that
> segregation on buses was illegal.

 Discuss Summaries as a Class

Facilitate a discussion using the following questions. Remind the
students to give reasons for their opinions.

Q *What did you and your partner include in your summary? How
does that capture what's important in the excerpt?*

Have a few volunteers read their summaries aloud, and then ask the class:

Q *Do you agree that [Shel and Rachael] captured the important ideas of the excerpt in their summary? Why or why not?*

Q *What did you include in your summary that is [similar to/different from] what [Shel and Rachael] included in their summary?*

Explain that in the coming weeks the students will use what they have learned about summarizing to write a summary of their own independent reading books.

◢ 6 Reflect on Discussing Opinions Respectfully

Facilitate a brief discussion of how the students did giving reasons for their opinions and discussing their opinions respectfully.

Collect the students' summaries and save them for Week 5, Day 1.

INDIVIDUALIZED DAILY READING

◢ 7 Document IDR Conferences/Have the Students Summarize Reading in Their IDR Journals

Have the students read independently for up to 30 minutes.

Use the "IDR Conference Notes" record sheet to conduct and document individual conferences.

At the end of independent reading, ask each student to verbally summarize her reading for her partner. Then have each student write a brief summary of her reading in her IDR Journal.

Have several volunteers read their summaries to the whole class. Facilitate a discussion using questions such as:

Q *Based on the summary [Matthias] just gave, what was [his] reading about?*

Q *Can you get an idea of what [Amanda's] book is about from the summary [she] gave? Why or why not?*

Q *What questions do you want to ask [Jonah] about the book [he] summarized?*

EXTENSION

Analyze Summaries

Collect the students' excerpt summaries and make a copy of each with the students' names obscured. Place the students in groups of four and randomly distribute the summaries, four to each group. Have each group read the summaries and discuss the following questions:

Q *Which summaries give a good idea of what this whole excerpt is about? Why do you think so?*

Have a whole-class discussion to share what groups discussed. Groups may want to read aloud summaries they agreed gave them a good idea of the excerpt. (Be sure to facilitate this activity in such a way as to keep the authors of the summaries anonymous.)

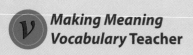

*Making Meaning
Vocabulary Teacher*

Next week you will revisit this week's reading to teach Vocabulary Week 27.

Week 5

Overview

UNIT 8: DETERMINING IMPORTANT IDEAS AND SUMMARIZING

Narrative Nonfiction

Comprehension Focus

- Students *think about important and supporting ideas* in a text.

- Students use important ideas to *summarize*.

- Students read independently.

Social Development Focus

- Students take responsibility for their learning and behavior.

- Students develop the group skills of supporting one another's independent work and giving feedback in a caring way.

- Students have a class meeting to discuss working independently.

DO AHEAD

- Collect short stories, articles, picture books, and other short pieces of writing at various reading levels (see Day 1, Step 2 on page 526).

- Prepare a chart for independent reading (see Day 1, Step 3 on page 527).

- Make copies of the Unit 8 Parent Letter (BLM17) to send home with the students on the last day of the unit.

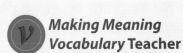

Making Meaning Vocabulary Teacher

If you are teaching Developmental Studies Center's *Making Meaning Vocabulary* program, teach Vocabulary Week 27 this week. For more information, see the *Making Meaning Vocabulary Teacher's Manual*.

Day 1

Materials

- "Summary of *In My Own Backyard*" chart (from Week 3)

- Short texts at appropriate levels (see Step 2)

- Chart for independent reading, prepared ahead (see Step 3)

- Small self-stick notes for each student

- Paper and a pencil for each student

Teacher Note ▶

Post the charted summary of *In My Own Backyard* where everyone can see it. Also, hand out the students' summaries of *A Picture Book of Rosa Parks* and encourage the students to refer to these summaries as they write their own summaries this week.

Independent Strategy Practice

In this lesson, the students:

- *Think about important ideas* in a text read independently
- Support one another's independent work

1 Review Important Ideas and Summarizing

Review that over the past weeks the students watched you model identifying important ideas in and writing a summary of *In My Own Backyard*. They also identified important ideas in and wrote a summary of *A Picture Book of Rosa Parks* together. Tell them that this week they will identify important ideas and write summaries of their own independent reading books to share with their classmates next week.

Explain that today each student will select his text and read it, marking important ideas he wants to include in his summary. Tomorrow, the students will write their summaries.

2 Select Texts to Read Independently and Summarize

Explain that the students should select a whole, short piece of text to read and summarize. Direct their attention to the short texts you collected (short stories, picture books, and articles from magazines and newspapers). Invite them to choose a text from this collection or choose a short piece of their own. Students reading chapter books may choose to read and summarize a whole chapter in this lesson. Encourage the students to choose a text that they would be interested in summarizing for their classmates.

Give the students time to select their book or article.

Prepare to Read Independently and Identify Important Ideas

Explain the following directions, which you have posted where all the students can see them:

1. *Read your text through once independently.*

2. *Read your text again, using self-stick notes to mark important ideas for your summary.*

3. *Talk with your partner about the important ideas that you might want to include in your summary tomorrow.*

Remind the students to give reasons for their opinions when talking in pairs and to discuss their opinions in a respectful way.

 Read Independently and Identify Important Ideas

 Have the students read, reread, mark important ideas, and discuss their texts. As the students work, circulate and support them by asking individual students questions such as:

Q *What are some important ideas you marked that you want to include in your summary?*

Q *Why do those ideas seem important?*

 Discuss as a Whole Class

When most students have finished, facilitate a whole-class discussion using the following questions. Remind the students who share to briefly tell what their text is about. Ask:

Q *What is one important idea that you want to make sure to include in your summary tomorrow? Why does that idea seem important?*

Q *Was it hard or easy to identify important ideas in your text? Explain your thinking.*

6▶ **Reflect on Supporting One Another's Independent Work**

Point out that the students had to work independently today and that they will work independently again tomorrow. Ask:

Q *How did you do working independently today?*

Q *How did your classmates help or hinder your independent work?*

Q *What might we want to work on tomorrow to help one another work better independently?*

Ask the students to put their text, with self-stick notes in place, in a safe location until tomorrow's lesson.

Day 2

Independent Strategy Practice

In this lesson, the students:

- *Think about important ideas* in a text read independently
- *Build a summary* of their own text
- Support one another's independent work

▶1 Review Supporting One Another's Independent Work

Explain that today the students will write a summary of the short text they selected and read yesterday. Remind them that they will be working independently and that you would like them to focus on taking responsibility for their own independent work and helping others to work independently. Ask:

Q *What will you do today to help your partner and others around you to work independently?*

Tell the students that you will check in to see how they did at the end of the lesson.

▶2 Write Opening Sentences for Summaries

Have the students spend a moment reviewing the important ideas they marked in their text yesterday. Then remind them that summaries usually begin with a general sentence about what the text is about and continue with the important ideas. Direct their attention to the opening sentence on the charted summary of *In My Own Backyard* and their summaries of *A Picture Book of Rosa Parks*. Have them think quietly about this question:

Q *How might you say in one sentence what your text is about?*

Materials

- Students' marked short texts from Day 1
- "Summary of *In My Own Backyard*" chart (from Week 3)
- Students' summaries of *A Picture Book of Rosa Parks* (from Week 4)
- Paper and a pencil for each student

Teacher Note

This lesson may take longer than one class period.

After a moment, have the students share in pairs. Bring their attention back to you and ask them each to write a summary opening sentence on a sheet of paper.

Ask a few volunteers to read their opening sentence aloud to the class. Point out that the students might want to come back and revise their opening sentence once they have started writing their summary. Encourage them to do so if they need to.

3 ▶ Write Summaries

Ask the students to identify the first important idea they want to write about in their summary and begin writing. Remind them that they will share their summary with the class, so the summaries must give a good idea of what their text is about.

As the students write their summaries, circulate and support them by having individual students read some important ideas they marked aloud to you, and then asking:

Q *How might you communicate those ideas briefly in your own words?*

During the writing, you might stop the class periodically and have a few students read what they have written so far to provide examples for those who are having trouble getting started.

4 ▶ Reflect on Writing Summaries and Working Together

 When most students have finished writing, bring them together for a brief discussion. Explain that tomorrow they will have a chance to revise (or finish, if necessary) their summary. Use "Turn to Your Partner" as needed during this discussion to increase accountability and to encourage participation.

Ask:

Q *Do you think your summary in its current form would give another reader a good idea of what your text is about? Why or why not?*

Q *What might you want to add, or how else might you want to revise your summary tomorrow?*

Q *What did you do today to help your partner and others around you work independently?*

Collect the students' summaries and save them for Day 3.

Day 3

Materials

- Students' marked short texts from Day 1
- Students' summaries from Day 2
- Chart paper and a marker
- *Assessment Resource Book*

Independent Strategy Practice

In this lesson, the students:

- Give each other feedback about their summaries
- Revise their summaries
- Give feedback in a caring way

▶1 Get Ready to Give Feedback in a Caring Way

Explain that today the students will read in pairs the summaries they wrote. Partners will give each other feedback about the summaries to help each other revise or add to their summaries, if necessary. Ask:

Q *If your partner has a suggestion for how to make your summary stronger, how do you want your partner to give you that feedback?*

Q *What are some words we can use to give each other feedback in a caring way?*

As the students suggest ideas, record these on a sheet of chart paper entitled "Words to Use When Giving Feedback." If the students do not generate any ideas, offer some like those suggested in the "Students might say" note

> **Students might say:**
>
> "I'm confused about this part. What are you trying to say?"
>
> "This part is really clear, but I'm not sure I understand this part."
>
> "I wonder if this part would be clearer if you said…"
>
> "You might consider adding…"
>
> "Have you thought about…?"

Encourage the students to use some of the ideas on the chart today to give feedback when working in pairs.

2 Discuss Summaries in Pairs and Revise as Needed

Distribute the students' summaries and have partners read their summaries to each other and discuss the following questions. Write the questions where everyone can see them:

- *Does this summary begin with a general sentence describing what this text is about?*

- *Does this summary give some important ideas in the text?*

- *What do you understand about the text from this summary?*

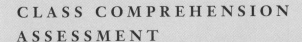

◀ **Teacher Note**

Any student who did not finish writing his summary yesterday can get feedback on the part he wrote and finish writing the summary today.

> ### CLASS COMPREHENSION ASSESSMENT
>
> Circulate as partners share and discuss their summaries, and ask yourself:
>
> **Q** *Do the students' summaries successfully communicate what their texts are about?*
>
> **Q** *Is there evidence in the partners' feedback that they understand something about the texts being summarized?*
>
> **Q** *Are the students revising or adding to their summaries based on the feedback?*
>
> Record your observations on page 31 of the *Assessment Resource Book*.

When most partners have had a chance to talk, briefly interrupt the students and ask them to revise or add to their summaries based on the feedback they received.

3 Discuss Giving Feedback on Summaries as a Class

When partners have discussed their summaries and made any necessary revisions, bring their attention back to the whole class and ask:

Q *What did your partner say about your summary that was helpful?*

Q *Did you revise your summary based on what your partner said? How?*

Q *How did you and your partner give each other feedback in a caring way? How did that help your work?*

Explain that the students will have an opportunity in the coming week to share their summaries with the whole class. Collect the students' summaries and save them for Unit 9, Week 1.

Teacher Note

Next week, the students will add a paragraph of opinion to the summary they wrote today. A student whose summary does not communicate what a text is about may have difficulty adding an opinion paragraph to it. If necessary, give feedback about the summaries and have the students write new drafts based on your feedback before beginning Unit 9.

Day 4

Class Meeting

In this lesson, the students:

- Have a class meeting to discuss how they are working independently and supporting one another's independent work
- Read independently for up to 30 minutes
- Take responsibility for themselves

1 Gather for a Class Meeting

Tell the students that today they will have a class meeting. Before the class meeting, make sure the "Class Meeting Ground Rules" chart is posted where everyone can see it. Review the procedure for coming to a class meeting and remind the students that they have been working towards becoming a caring and safe community of readers.

Have partners sit together and ask them to make sure they can see each member of the class.

2 Introduce and Discuss the Topic

Review the "Class Meeting Ground Rules." Explain that during today's class meeting the students will talk about how they have been working independently and supporting one another's independent work. Ask:

Q *How have you been doing working independently?*

Q *What helps or hinders your ability to work independently?*

Q *Why is it important that we support one another's ability to work independently in our class?*

Materials

- Space for the class to sit in a circle
- "Class Meeting Ground Rules" chart
- Chart paper and a marker
- *Student Response Book,* IDR Journal section
- *Assessment Resource Book*
- Unit 8 Parent Letter (BLM17)

> ### Class Meeting Ground Rules
>
> - one person talks at a time
> - listen to one another

◀ **Teacher Note**

Use "Turn to Your Partner" as needed during this discussion to increase participation, especially if you are hearing from only a few students. You can also use "Turn to Your Partner" if many students want to speak at the same time.

Students might say:

"I can concentrate better when it's quiet and I don't hear other
people talking."

"If everyone else is working independently, it helps me to work
independently, too."

"It's important to support each other because we want to help
each other learn, not bother each other."

3 **Discuss Ways to Support One Another**

Have the students use "Think, Pair, Share" to think about and discuss:

Q *What are some ways that we can try to support one another when
we work independently?*

Students might say:

"We can agree to work quietly during independent work time."

"I think we can support one another by not banging our desks or
sharpening our pencils while people are trying to read or write."

"In addition to what [Xavier] said, I think we can support our
partner by getting everything we need before the work starts so
we don't have to get up and distract people."

Have a few pairs share their ideas with the whole class; write their
responses on a sheet of chart paper. If necessary, suggest some
solutions like those in the "Students might say" note to stimulate
their thinking.

Review the suggestions on the chart and ask:

Q *Is there anything on this list that you can't agree to try in the
coming days?*

Make adjustments to the list only if the students give reasonable
explanations for why certain solutions are unfeasible. Explain that
you would like the students to use the suggestions on the chart in
the coming days.

4 ▶ Adjourn the Meeting

Briefly discuss how the students felt they did following the ground rules during the class meeting. Review the procedure for returning to their desks, and then adjourn the meeting.

Display the chart where everyone can see it. Hold the students accountable by checking in periodically in the coming days to see how they are doing supporting one another's independent work.

Teacher Note

This is the last week in Unit 8. You will reassign partners for Unit 9.

INDIVIDUALIZED DAILY READING

5 ▶ Document IDR Conferences/Have the Students Summarize Reading in Their IDR Journals

Have the students read independently for up to 30 minutes.

Use the "IDR Conference Notes" record sheet to conduct and document individual conferences.

At the end of independent reading, ask partners to verbally summarize their reading for one another. Then have each student write a brief summary of his reading in his IDR Journal.

Have several volunteers read their summaries to the whole class. Facilitate a discussion using questions such as:

Q *Based on the summary [Moriah] just gave, what was [her] reading about?*

Q *Can you get an idea of what [Anil's] book is about from the summary [he] gave? Why or why not?*

Q *What questions do you want to ask [Jolene] about the book [she] summarized?*

INDIVIDUAL COMPREHENSION ASSESSMENT

Before continuing with Unit 9, take this opportunity to assess individual students' progress in determining important ideas and summarizing to make sense of what they read. Please refer to pages 46–47 in the *Assessment Resource Book* for instructions.

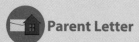

Parent Letter

Send home with each student the Parent Letter for this unit (see "Do Ahead," page 525). Periodically, have a few students share with the class what they are reading at home.

Unit 9

Revisiting the Reading Life

During this unit, the students use important ideas to build summaries. They also synthesize by making judgments and forming opinions about text, using evidence from the text to support their conclusions. They continue to develop the group skills of giving reasons for their opinions and discussing their opinions respectfully. During IDR, the students continue to practice self-monitoring and reflect on the reading strategies they use that help them understand what they are reading. They have a class meeting to discuss their growth as readers and as members of a classroom community.

Week 1 **Student-selected book**

Week 1

Overview

UNIT 9: REVISITING THE READING LIFE

Comprehension Focus

• Students *use important ideas* to *build summaries.*

• Students *synthesize* by making judgments and forming opinions about text, using evidence from the text to support their conclusions.

• Students reflect on their growth as readers over the year.

• Students read independently.

Social Development Focus

• Students analyze the effect of their behavior on others and on the group work.

• Students develop the group skills of giving reasons for their opinions and discussing their opinions respectfully.

• Students have a class meeting to discuss how they have grown as readers and as members of a classroom community.

DO AHEAD

• Prior to Day 1, decide how you will randomly assign partners to work together during the unit.

• Prepare to model a book recommendation (see Day 1, Step 2 on page 542) and have each student select a favorite book to recommend for summer reading (see Day 1, Steps 3–5 on pages 543–544).

• Make copies of the Unit 9 Parent Letter (BLM18) to send home with the students on the last day of the unit.

Day 1

Materials

- Book to model (see Step 2)
- Students' books to recommend for summer reading (see "Do Ahead" and the "Teacher Note" on page 543)
- Students' summaries from Unit 8, Week 5, Day 2
- "Self-monitoring Questions" chart

Being a Writer™ **Teacher**

You can either have the students work with their *Being a Writer* partner or assign them a different partner for the *Making Meaning* lessons.

Teacher Note

The book you choose for modeling making a book recommendation (see Step 2) could be a *Making Meaning* book that the students liked when you read it earlier this year, another popular book you have read aloud from the *Making Meaning* alternative book lists, or a book the students have not heard before. You might also want to collect other books to read aloud for the Extensions on Days 1 and 2.

Guided Strategy Practice

In this lesson, the students:

- Begin working with new partners
- Prepare to recommend a book for summer reading
- Read independently for up to 30 minutes

1 ▶ Pair Students and Get Ready to Work Together

Randomly assign partners and have them sit together. Tell them that during this last week of the *Making Meaning* program, they will review the comprehension strategies they have learned, think about how they have grown as readers and as members of a community, share their favorite books, and plan their summer reading.

Tell them that at the end of this week they will also be asked to list some things they really enjoyed about working with partners this year. Encourage them to focus during the coming week on enjoying their partner work and using the skills they have learned to help them in their work together.

Explain that today they will discuss how to make summer reading book recommendations to their classmates. They will use the books and the summaries they wrote last week and find an interesting short passage to read to the class. Tell the students you will use one of your favorite books to model ways to share a book with others.

2 ▶ Model a Book Recommendation

Model recommending a book to the class by showing the book, reading the title and author's name, briefly summarizing the book, saying what you liked about it, and reading a short passage aloud. (For example, you might say, "The book I want to recommend for your summer reading is *Charlotte's Web*, by E. B. White, illustrated by Garth Williams. It's a story about a pig named Wilbur, who is destined to become 'smoked bacon and ham' until his friend Charlotte, a beautiful gray spider, finds a way to save him. I like the warm friendship between the pig and the spider, and the barnyard animals all have their own funny personalities.")

3 ▶ Discuss What to Share in a Book Recommendation

Explain that the students will have some time today to plan what they want to say to their classmates about their book. They will also choose a short passage from the book to read aloud. Ask:

Q *What information might be important to share when you recommend your book? Why?*

Q *What might be important to include when you tell what your book is about?*

Q *What might you want to look for in a passage to read aloud to the class?*

Students might say:

"It is important to share what the book is about."

"It is important to include the important ideas, but you don't want to tell the whole story."

"I want to read an exciting or interesting part. This way people might want to read the book."

4 ▶ Prepare to Share a Book Recommendation

Distribute the books and the students' summaries from Unit 8, Week 5, Day 2. Have the students use their books and summaries to plan what they will say about their book and to identify the passage they will read aloud. If you think it will be helpful, have the students quietly practice reading their passage aloud before sharing as a class.

Teacher Note

As the students prepare their book recommendations, circulate among them. Encourage them in their preparation by asking questions such as:

Q *What passage are you planning to read? Why did you choose that passage?*

Q *How are you going to summarize the book?*

Q *What did you especially like about this book?*

5 ▶ Discuss Book Recommendations in Pairs

Have partners share their book recommendations and passages with each other and discuss the following questions. Write the questions where everyone can see them:

- *Does the recommendation summarize the book?*

- *Does the recommendation give just enough information?*

- *Does the recommendation make you want to read the book?*

- *Does the passage pique your interest?*

6 ▶ Discuss Working Together

When partners have discussed their book recommendations, bring the attention back to the whole class and ask:

Q *What did your partner do that was helpful?*

Q *How did you and your partner give each other feedback in a caring way? How did that help you?*

Explain that the students will have an opportunity in the coming days to share their book recommendations with the whole class.

INDIVIDUALIZED DAILY READING

7 ▶ Review and Discuss Self-monitoring

Direct the students' attention to the "Self-monitoring Questions" chart and remind them that a comprehension technique they learned this year is to stop and think about what they are reading and ask themselves questions to help them track their understanding. Tell them that they will practice this self-monitoring technique today during independent reading.

Have the students read independently for up to 30 minutes. Stop them at 10-minute intervals and have them monitor their comprehension by thinking about the questions on the chart.

Self-monitoring Questions

- *What is happening in my story right now?*

- *Does the reading make sense?*

At the end of independent reading, facilitate a whole-class discussion about how self-monitoring helps the students track their understanding.

Discuss questions such as:

Q *How does stopping and checking your understanding help you?*

Q *What are some things you do when you do not understand?*

E X T E N S I O N

Introduce a Second Summer Reading Book Recommendation and Read Aloud

Tell the students that you will make another summer reading book recommendation by first summarizing the book and then reading the book aloud. Refer to the "Reading Comprehension Strategies" chart and remind the students to think about the comprehension strategies they are using as they listen.

Introduce the book by reading the information on the cover and providing any necessary background information and a brief summary. Read the book aloud, showing the illustrations. You might stop periodically to have partners discuss what they have heard so far.

Discuss the reading as a class. Use "Turn to Your Partner" as appropriate to encourage thinking and participation. Be ready to reread passages to help the students recall what they heard. Ask questions such as:

Q *What is the story about?*

Q *What do you want to add to the summary [Danny] just gave?*

Q *Is this a book you would recommend to someone? Why or why not?*

Q *What comprehension strategies did you use as you listened to this story? How did that help you?*

Day 2

Materials

- Students' books to recommend for summer reading
- *Student Response Book* page 65
- "Reading Comprehension Strategies" chart

Guided Strategy Practice

In this lesson, the students:

- Begin their summer reading list
- Recommend books for summer reading
- Make choices about books they want to read
- Read independently for up to 30 minutes
- Discuss opinions respectfully

 ## Introduce the Summer Reading List

Confirm that each student has selected a book to recommend for summer reading. Explain that today the students will begin to share their book recommendations with the class. Tell them that they will have the opportunity to share their books over the next two days.

Have the students turn to *Student Response Book* page 65, "Summer Reading List." Explain that as they hear book recommendations in the coming days they will list the books they might be interested in reading this summer. Point out that the "Summer Reading List" has space for the book title, author, and a few words to remind them about the book.

Remind the students that yesterday you recommended a book for their summer reading. Invite the students to add that book to their summer reading list, if they wish. Write the title and author on the board so interested students can copy this information.

Review What to Share in a Book Recommendation

Briefly review sharing book recommendations by discussing questions such as:

Q *What might be important to include when you tell what your book is about?*

Q *What is important to remember when reading your passage aloud?*

 ## Share Book Recommendations

Call on a volunteer to share her book recommendation with the class. Remind the student to show the cover and read the title and the names of the author and illustrator aloud before telling about the book and reading the selected passage.

When the student has finished, facilitate a brief class discussion using questions such as:

Q *What questions do you want to ask [Desiree] about the book [she] shared?*

Q *What did you hear about this book or in the passage that intrigued you?*

Q *[Desiree], what were you thinking when you chose that passage?*

Q *Do you have enough information to decide whether you want to add this book to your summer reading list? If not, what else do you want to know?*

Ask the student who shared the book to write the book's title and author clearly on the board. Have the students copy this information onto their summer reading list if they are interested in reading the book over the summer.

Have several more students share their books and passages with the class. After each student shares, allow time for questions and discussion and for interested students to add to their reading list.

Discuss Working Together

Have the students who shared their recommendations today talk briefly about how they felt the class treated them while they were sharing. Ask:

Q *What made you feel like your classmates were interested in what you were sharing?*

Q *If you weren't sure that your classmates were interested, what made you unsure?*

Open the discussion to the whole class, and ask:

Q *What should we do the same way, or differently, as we continue to share our book recommendations?*

Remind the students of your expectation that they will do their part to help create a safe, caring community in the class. Tell them that more students will share their book recommendations tomorrow.

INDIVIDUALIZED DAILY READING

 Read Independently and Discuss Reading Comprehension Strategies

Refer to the "Reading Comprehension Strategies" chart and review that the students learned and practiced each of these strategies this year. Review that the goal of learning comprehension strategies is to help them actively think about what they are reading in order to make sense of it. Remind the students to think about the comprehension strategies they are using as they read independently.

Have the students read independently for up to 30 minutes.

Reading Comprehension Strategies

- *recognizing text features*

As the students read, circulate among them. Ask individual students questions such as:

Q *What is this passage about?*

Q *What comprehension strategies are you using to help you understand what you are reading? Tell me what you thought about when you used that strategy.*

You might need to encourage the students' thinking with questions such as:

Q *What are some questions that come to your mind about what you are reading?*

Q *Have any pictures come to your mind about the reading? If so, what have you visualized? What helped bring this picture to your mind?*

Q *What do you think is an important idea in this story?*

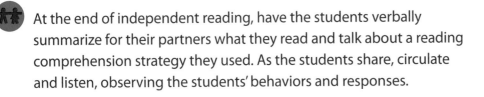 At the end of independent reading, have the students verbally summarize for their partners what they read and talk about a reading comprehension strategy they used. As the students share, circulate and listen, observing the students' behaviors and responses.

EXTENSION

Introduce a Third Summer Reading Book Recommendation and Read Aloud

Tell the students that you will make another summer reading book recommendation by first summarizing the book and then reading the book aloud. Refer to the "Reading Comprehension Strategies" chart and remind the students to think about the comprehension strategies they are using as they listen.

Introduce the book by reading the information on the cover and providing any necessary background information and a brief summary. Read the book aloud, showing the illustrations. You might stop periodically to have partners discuss what they have heard so far.

Discuss the reading as a class. Use "Turn to Your Partner" as appropriate to encourage thinking and participation. Be ready to reread passages to help the students recall what they heard. Ask questions such as:

Q *What is the story about?*

Q *What do you want to add to the summary [Rian] just gave?*

Q *Is this a book you would recommend to someone? Why or why not?*

Q *What comprehension strategies did you use as you listened to this story? How did that help you?*

Day 3

Guided Strategy Practice and Reflection

In this lesson, the students:

- Recommend books for summer reading
- Make choices about books they want to read
- Think and write about how they have grown as readers
- Read independently for up to 30 minutes
- Discuss opinions respectfully

1 ▶ Discuss Sharing Ideas Respectfully

Remind the students that yesterday they began to share book recommendations for summer reading. They will hear several more book recommendations today and consider these books for their summer reading list. Explain that they will also spend some time reflecting on their own reading lives.

Discuss how the students will interact kindly and respectfully during today's sharing. Ask:

Q *How do you want your classmates to respond to your book recommendation, whether they would choose to read your book or not? Why?*

Q *How can you let your classmates know that you are interested in the book they are sharing and that you appreciate the work they've done to share it with you?*

Encourage the students to keep these things in mind as they participate today.

Materials

- Students' books to recommend for summer reading
- *Student Response Book* pages 2 and 65–66

Continue to Share Book Recommendations

Have several more students share their books and passages with the class. Remind each student to begin by showing the cover of the book and reading the title and the author's name aloud.

Facilitate a brief class discussion after each student shares, and have the student write the book's title and author on the board for interested students to copy. Use questions such as:

Q   *What questions do you want to ask [Tito] about the book [he] shared?*

Q   *What did you hear about the book or in the passage that intrigued you?*

Q   *[Tito], what were you thinking when you chose that passage?*

Q   *Do you have enough information to decide whether you want to add this book to your summer reading list? If not, what else do you want to know?*

After the students have shared their book recommendations, end the sharing time for today. (If some students have not shared, assure them that they will have time later to share their book recommendations.) Ask:

Q   *If you hear about a book you are interested in reading, how might you find that book this summer to read?*

Students might say:

"I might find the book at the public library."

"If a friend has the book, I could borrow it from her."

"I might look for it at the bookstore or on the Internet."

If the students have difficulty answering this question, suggest some ideas like those in the "Students might say" note.

Teacher Note ▶

If all the students are not able to share their book recommendations, make time later in the day or on another day for them to share before proceeding with the Day 4 lesson.

Teacher Note

You might consider taking your students on a short field trip to a local library.

Reflect on Our Reading Lives

Explain that the students will now have a chance to think about how they have grown and changed as readers over the year. Remind them that they started the year thinking about their reading lives, and tell them that they will think about this again now that they are nearing the end of the year.

Ask the students to close their eyes and think quietly as you pose the following questions. Give them time to think between the questions.

Q *What are some of your favorite books now? Why?*

Q *Where is your favorite place to read?*

Q *What does the word* reading *mean to you?*

Q *When you don't understand something you are reading, what do you do?*

Q *What kinds of books did you read for the first time this year? What topics did you read about for the first time?*

Ask the students to turn to *Student Response Book* page 66, "Thoughts About My Reading Life." Have them write today's date and record their answers to these questions.

 Reflect on Growth as Readers

Give the students a few minutes to review what they wrote on *Student Response Book* page 66, "Thoughts About My Reading Life;" then have them turn to "Thoughts About My Reading Life" from the beginning of the year, on *Student Response Book* page 2. Ask them to reread what they wrote at the beginning of the year, then spend a few quiet moments thinking about how they have changed and grown as readers this year.

 After a few moments, have the students use "Turn to Your Partner" to share how they have changed as readers.

Tell them that they will share some of their thoughts during a class meeting tomorrow.

INDIVIDUALIZED DAILY READING

5▶ **Read Independently and Discuss Reading Comprehension Strategies**

Have the students read independently for up to 30 minutes.

As the students read, circulate among them. Ask individual students questions such as:

Q *What is this passage about?*

Q *What comprehension strategies are you using to help you understand what you are reading? Tell me what you thought about when you used that strategy.*

You might need to encourage the students' thinking with questions such as:

Q *What are some questions that come to your mind about what you are reading?*

Q *Have any pictures come to your mind about the reading? If so, what have you visualized? What helped bring this picture to your mind?*

Q *What do you think is an important idea in this story?*

At the end of independent reading, have partners verbally summarize what they read and talk about a reading comprehension strategy they used. As the students share, circulate and listen, observing the students' behaviors and responses.

EXTENSION

Review the Summer Reading Lists

Have the students review the books on their summer reading lists. Ask:

Q *What kinds of books did you choose for summer reading? Does that surprise you? Why or why not?*

You might ask the students to put a star next to the books they want to read first. Encourage them to read as many of the books on their list as they can this summer. Also encourage them to talk with family members and friends about the books they are reading and to add any interesting books to their reading list.

Day 4

Materials

- *Student Response Book* page 67
- Space for the class to sit in a circle
- "Class Meeting Ground Rules" chart
- *Assessment Resource Book*
- Small self-stick notes for each student
- *Student Response Book,* IDR Journal section
- Unit 9 Parent Letter (BLM18)

Reflection and Class Meeting

In this lesson, the students:

- Think and write about how they have grown as members of the class community
- Have a class meeting to discuss how they have grown as readers and as members of the class community
- Read independently for up to 30 minutes

1 ▶ Reflect on Our Classroom Community

Have partners sit together. Remind the students that yesterday they reflected on and wrote about their growth as readers. Explain that the students will now have a chance to think about how they did creating a safe and caring community this year and how they personally have changed as members of the community. Tell the students that later they will have a chance to share their thoughts about how they have grown as readers and as members of a classroom community during a class meeting.

 Use "Think, Pair, Share" to have the students think about and discuss the following questions. After asking each question, have the students close their eyes. Give them a few seconds to think quietly before signaling them to talk to their partner; then ask:

Q *Think about how you worked with your first partner this year. Think about how you are working with your partner now. How have you grown in your ability to work with a partner?*

Q *How have we done at becoming a caring and safe community this year? What makes you think so?*

Q *How has being part of this community helped you this year?*

Q *What three things did you like most about working with partners?*

After the students have discussed the questions, ask them to turn to *Student Response Book* page 67, "Thoughts About Our Classroom Community." Have them record their answers for these questions.

 ## Gather for a Class Meeting

Review the procedure for coming to a class meeting, and have the students move to the circle with their *Student Response Books* and with partners sitting together. Explain that during the first part of the class meeting they will discuss how they have grown as readers and during the second part of the class meeting they will talk about their classroom community and what they enjoyed about working with a partner.

Make sure the students can see each member of the class, and briefly review the "Class Meeting Ground Rules" chart.

 ## Discuss Growth as Readers

Remind the students that one of the ways they built their reading community this year was to share their reading lives with one another. Explain that one of the purposes of this class meeting is to talk about ways they have changed and grown as readers. Facilitate a discussion using questions such as:

Q *How do you think you have changed or grown as a reader? What makes you think that?*

Q *Do others think they have changed or grown in a similar way? Why do you think so?*

Q *In what ways are you the same kind of reader as you were at the beginning of the year?*

Q *What questions do you want to ask [Lionel] about what [he] said?*

 Use "Turn to Your Partner" as needed during this discussion to increase accountability and participation.

◀ Teacher Note

You may want to hold the class meeting later in the day or on the following day.

Class Meeting Ground Rules

- *one person talks at a time*
- *listen to one another*

Students might say:

"My favorite books used to be the books about Ramona. I still like those books, but my new favorite books are mysteries."

"At the beginning of the year, I wrote 'I don't know' for the question 'When you don't understand something you are reading, what do you do?' At the end of the year, I wrote, 'I ask myself questions, and then I read it again.'"

"In September, I wrote that I wanted to read about space this year, and I did. I read a bunch of books about the solar system."

"I used to think reading meant reading words. Now I think reading means thinking about a story."

You might want to share some of your general observations about ways your students have changed or grown as readers over the year. (For example, you might say, "I noticed that all of you have improved in your ability to choose books that are at the right reading level for you and that you are choosing books now that are at a higher reading level than you were at the beginning of the year.")

 ## Discuss Our Community and Partner Work

Explain that the second purpose of this class meeting is to talk about the classroom community and to share some of their favorite things about working with a partner this year. Facilitate a discussion using questions such as:

Q *How did we do creating the kind of classroom we wanted this year? What makes you think so?*

Q *How has being part of this community helped you this year?*

Q *What are three things that you liked most about working with partners this year?*

Students might say:

"At first it was hard, but we got better and better at it."

"I think the more we got to know each other, the more we were a community."

"I agree with [Franklin]. Being in this community has helped me because I used to be too shy to say anything to the class. I don't feel that way anymore."

"In addition to what [Teresa] said, I liked working with a partner. I liked having someone to talk to, not having to be quiet all the time, and getting to work with different partners."

You might want to share some of your general observations about ways your students have changed or grown as members of the community over the year. (For example, you might say, "I remember how some students didn't want to work with an assigned partner at the beginning of the year. Now you are much better at working with any partner. I also noticed that you relied much more heavily on me at the beginning of the year to help you solve your problems. Now you are able to solve many problems by yourselves.") Ask:

Q *What is one thing you learned about working well with a partner that you want to take with you next year?*

▶5 Reflect and Adjourn the Class Meeting

Facilitate a brief discussion about how the students did following the ground rules during the class meeting, and adjourn the meeting.

INDIVIDUALIZED DAILY READING

▶6 Write About Reading Comprehension Strategies in Their IDR Journals

Have the students read independently for up to 30 minutes.

Have the students use self-stick notes to mark places where they notice they are using a reading comprehension strategy.

As the students read, circulate among them. Ask individual students questions such as:

Q *What is your reading about?*

Q *I notice that you placed a self-stick note in this part of your book. What comprehension strategy helped you understand this part?*

FACILITATION TIP

Reflect on your experience over the past year using the facilitation tips included in the *Making Meaning* program. Did using the facilitation techniques feel natural to you? Have you integrated them into your class discussions throughout the school day? What effect did using the facilitation techniques have on your students? We encourage you to continue to use the facilitation techniques and reflect on students' responses as you facilitate class discussions in the future.

At the end of independent reading, have each student summarize his reading and write about a comprehension strategy he used—the name of the strategy and where he used it—in his IDR Journal.

SOCIAL SKILLS ASSESSMENT

Take this opportunity to reflect on your students' social development over the year. Review the Social Skills Assessment record sheet on pages 2–3 of the *Assessment Resource Book* and note student growth. Use this information to help you plan for next year. Ask yourself questions such as:

Q *What was challenging for my students this year in terms of their social development?*

Q *How might I help next year's students grow socially?*

Q *What skills should I emphasize with the students next year to help them build a safe and caring reading community?*

EXTENSION

End-of-year "Summer Reading Fair"

Have the students invite other third- or fourth-grade classes to a "Summer Reading Fair." Have the students present their book recommendations to small groups of students. The invited students will have an opportunity to listen to book recommendations, preview the books, and get a glimpse of the reading life of the students. Students might also make posters to advertise their favorite books. If there is a school library or librarian available, you might want to involve the library in the activity.

Parent Letter

Send home with each student the Parent Letter for this unit (see "Do Ahead," page 541).

Appendices

Grade 4

Lesson	Title	Author	Form	Genre/Type
Unit 1 Week 1	*A Bad Case of Stripes*	David Shannon	picture book	fiction
	The Old Woman Who Named Things	Cynthia Rylant	picture book	realistic fiction
Week 2	*Song and Dance Man*	Karen Ackerman	picture book	realistic fiction
Unit 2 Week 1	*Digging Up Tyrannosaurus Rex*	John R. Horner and Don Lessem	picture book	expository nonfiction
Week 2	"Tying the Score"		article	expository nonfiction
	"Food for Thought"		article	expository nonfiction
Week 3	*Italian Americans*	Carolyn P. Yoder	chapter book	expository nonfiction
Unit 3 Week 1	*Slinky Scaly Slithery Snakes*	Dorothy Hinshaw Patent	picture book	expository nonfiction
Week 2	*Animal Senses*	Pamela Hickman	chapter book	expository nonfiction
Week 3	*Animal Senses*	Pamela Hickman	chapter book	expository nonfiction
Unit 4 Week 1	*Thunder Cake*	Patricia Polacco	picture book	realistic fiction
	The Princess and the Pizza	Mary Jane and Herm Auch	picture book	fiction
Week 2	*Chicken Sunday*	Patricia Polacco	picture book	realistic fiction
Week 3	*The Bat Boy & His Violin*	Gavin Curtis	picture book	historical fiction
	Teammates	Peter Golenbock	picture book	narrative nonfiction
Week 4	*Basket Moon*	Mary Lyn Ray	picture book	realistic fiction
Unit 5 Week 1	*Hurricane*	David Wiesner	picture book	realistic fiction
Week 2	*My Man Blue*: "My Man Blue," "When We First Met," "Second Son"	Nikki Grimes	poetry collection	poetry
Week 3	*My Man Blue*: "Grounded," "The Watcher"	Nikki Grimes	poetry collection	poetry
Unit 6 Week 1	*Amelia's Road*	Linda Jacobs Altman	poetry collection	realistic fiction
Week 2	*Peppe the Lamplighter*	Elisa Bartone	picture book	historical fiction
Week 3	*Coming to America*	Betsy Maestro	picture book	expository nonfiction
Week 4	*A Picture Book of Harriet Tubman*	David A. Adler	picture book	narrative nonfiction
Unit 7 Week 1	"Virtual Worlds: Community in a Computer"		article	expository nonfiction
	"School Uniforms: The Way to Go"		article	expository nonfiction
Week 2	"How to Make Ooblek"		functional text	expository nonfiction
	"Simon's Sandwich Shop"		functional text	expository nonfiction
	"City of Lawrence Street Map"		functional text	expository nonfiction
Week 3	*Farm Workers Unite: The Great Grape Boycott*		textbook	expository nonfiction
Week 4	*Farm Workers Unite: The Great Grape Boycott*		textbook	expository nonfiction
Unit 8 Week 1	*Flight*	Robert Burleigh	picture book	narrative nonfiction
Week 2	*A Picture Book of Amelia Earhart*	David A. Adler	picture book	narrative nonfiction
Week 3	*In My Own Backyard*	Judi Kurjian	picture book	narrative nonfiction
Week 4	*A Picture Book of Rosa Parks*	David A. Adler	picture book	narrative nonfiction
Week 5	Student-selected text			
Unit 9 Week 1	Student-selected book			

Grade K

Brave Bear	Kathy Mallat
Building Beavers	Kathleen Martin-James
Cat's Colors	Jane Cabrera
"Charlie Needs a Cloak"	Tomie dePaola
Cookie's Week	Cindy Ward
A Day with a Doctor	Jan Kottke
A Day with a Mail Carrier	Jan Kottke
Flower Garden	Eve Bunting
Friends at School	Rochelle Bunnett
Getting Around By Plane	Cassie Mayer
Henry's Wrong Turn	Harriet M. Ziefert
I Want to Be a Vet	Dan Liebman
I Was So Mad	Mercer Mayer
If You Give a Mouse a Cookie	Laura Joffe Numeroff
Knowing about Noses	Allan Fowler
A Letter to Amy	Ezra Jack Keats
Maisy's Pool	Lucy Cousins
Moon	Melanie Mitchell
My Friends	Taro Gomi
Noisy Nora	Rosemary Wells
On the Go	Ann Morris
A Porcupine Named Fluffy	Helen Lester
Pumpkin Pumpkin	Jeanne Titherington
A Tiger Cub Grows Up	Joan Hewett
Tools	Ann Morris
When Sophie Gets Angry— Really, Really Angry...	Molly Bang
Whistle for Willie	Ezra Jack Keats

Grade 1

Caps for Sale	Esphyr Slobodkina
Chrysanthemum	Kevin Henkes
Curious George Goes to an Ice Cream Shop	Margret Rey and Alan J. Shalleck (editors)
A Day in the Life of a Garbage Collector	Nate LeBoutillier
Did You See What I Saw? Poems about School	Kay Winters
Dinosaur Babies	Lucille Recht Penner
Down the Road	Alice Schertle
An Elephant Grows Up	Anastasia Suen
An Extraordinary Egg	Leo Lionni
George Washington and the General's Dog	Frank Murphy
A Good Night's Sleep	Allan Fowler
A Harbor Seal Pup Grows Up	Joan Hewett
Hearing	Sharon Gordon
In the Tall, Tall Grass	Denise Fleming
It's Mine!	Leo Lionni
Julius	Angela Johnson
A Kangaroo Joey Grows Up	Joan Hewett
A Look at Teeth	Allan Fowler
Matthew and Tilly	Rebecca C. Jones
McDuff and the Baby	Rosemary Wells
Peter's Chair	Ezra Jack Keats
Quick as a Cricket	Audrey Wood
Raptors!	Lisa McCourt
Sheep Out to Eat	Nancy Shaw
The Snowy Day	Ezra Jack Keats
Throw Your Tooth on the Roof	Selby B. Beeler
When I Was Little	Jamie Lee Curtis
Where Do I Live?	Neil Chesanow

Grade 2

Alexander and the Terrible, Horrible, No Good, Very Bad Day	Judith Viorst
The Art Lesson	Tomie dePaola
Beatrix Potter	Alexandra Wallner
Bend and Stretch	Pamela Hill Nettleton
Big Al	Andrew Clements
Chester's Way	Kevin Henkes
Eat My Dust! Henry Ford's First Race	Monica Kulling
Erandi's Braids	Antonio Hernández Madrigal
Fathers, Mothers, Sisters, Brothers: A Collection of Family Poems	Mary Ann Hoberman
Fishes (A True Book)	Melissa Stewart
Galimoto	Karen Lynn Williams
The Ghost-Eye Tree	Bill Martin Jr. and John Archambault
The Incredible Painting of Felix Clousseau	Jon Agee
It Could Still Be a Worm	Allan Fowler
Jamaica Tag-Along	Juanita Havill
little blue and little yellow	Leo Lionni
McDuff Moves In	Rosemary Wells
Me First	Helen Lester
The Paper Crane	Molly Bang
The Paperboy	Dav Pilkey
Plants that Eat Animals	Allan Fowler
POP! A Book About Bubbles	Kimberly Brubaker Bradley
Poppleton	Cynthia Rylant
Poppleton and Friends	Cynthia Rylant
Sheila Rae, the Brave	Kevin Henkes
Snails	Monica Hughes
The Tale of Peter Rabbit	Beatrix Potter
A Tree Is Nice	Janice May Udry
What Mary Jo Shared	Janice May Udry

Grade 3

Alexander, Who's Not (Do you hear me? I mean it!) Going to Move	Judith Viorst
Aunt Flossie's Hats (and Crab Cakes Later)	Elizabeth Fitzgerald Howard
Boundless Grace	Mary Hoffman
Brave Harriet	Marissa Moss
Brave Irene	William Steig
Cherries and Cherry Pits	Vera B. Williams
City Green	DyAnne DiSalvo-Ryan
A Day's Work	Eve Bunting
Fables	Arnold Lobel
Flashy Fantastic Rain Forest Frogs	Dorothy Hinshaw Patent
The Girl Who Loved Wild Horses	Paul Goble
Have You Seen Bugs?	Joanne Oppenheim
Julius, the Baby of the World	Kevin Henkes
Keepers	Jeri Hanel Watts
Knots on a Counting Rope	Bill Martin Jr. and John Archambault
Lifetimes	David L. Rice
Mailing May	Michael O. Tunnell
The Man Who Walked Between the Towers	Mordicai Gerstein
Miss Nelson Is Missing!	Harry Allard and James Marshall
Morning Meals Around the World	Maryellen Gregoire
Officer Buckle and Gloria	Peggy Rathmann
The Paper Bag Princess	Robert Munsch
Reptiles	Melissa Stewart
The Spooky Tail of Prewitt Peacock	Bill Peet
What Is a Bat?	Bobbie Kalman and Heather Levigne
Wilma Unlimited	Kathleen Krull

Grade 5

Big Cats	Seymour Simon
Chinese Americans	Tristan Boyer Binns
Earthquakes	Seymour Simon
Everybody Cooks Rice	Norah Dooley
Harry Houdini: Master of Magic	Robert Kraske
Heroes	Paul Dowswell
Hey World, Here I Am!	Jean Little
Letting Swift River Go	Jane Yolen
Life in the Rain Forests	Lucy Baker
The Lotus Seed	Sherry Garland
Richard Wright and the Library Card	William Miller
A River Ran Wild	Lynne Cherry
Something to Remember Me By	Susan V. Bosak
Star of Fear, Star of Hope	Jo Hoestlandt
The Summer My Father Was Ten	Pat Brisson
Survival and Loss: Native American Boarding Schools	
Uncle Jed's Barbershop	Margaree King Mitchell
The Van Gogh Cafe	Cynthia Rylant
Wildfires	Seymour Simon

Grade 6

America Street: A Multicultural Anthology of Stories	Anne Mazer, ed.
And Still the Turtle Watched	Sheila MacGill-Callahan
Asian Indian Americans	Carolyn P. Yoder
Baseball Saved Us	Ken Mochizuki
Chato's Kitchen	Gary Soto
Dear Benjamin Banneker	Andrea Davis Pinkney
Encounter	Jane Yolen
Every Living Thing	Cynthia Rylant
Life in the Oceans	Lucy Baker
New Kids in Town: Oral Histories of Immigrant Teens	Janet Bode
Out of This World: Science Fiction Stories	Edward Blishen, ed.
Rosie the Riveter: Women in a Time of War	
The Strangest of Strange Unsolved Mysteries, Volume 2	Phyllis Raybin Emert
Train to Somewhere	Eve Bunting
Voices from the Fields	S. Beth Atkin
Volcano: The Eruption and Healing of Mount St. Helens	Patricia Lauber
Whales	Seymour Simon
Why Mosquitoes Buzz in People's Ears	Verna Aardema

Grade 7

Ancient Ones: The World of the Old-Growth Douglas Fir	Barbara Bash
Children of the Wild West	Russell Freedman
Death of the Iron Horse	Paul Goble
The Dream Keeper and Other Poems	Langston Hughes
Finding Our Way	René Saldaña, Jr.
the flag of childhood: poems from the middle east	Naomi Shahib Nye, ed.
The Friendship	Mildred D. Taylor
It's Our World, Too!	Phillip Hoose
The Land I Lost	Huynh Quang Nhuong
Life in the Woodlands	Roseanne Hooper
New and Selected Poems	Gary Soto
Only Passing Through: The Story of Sojourner Truth	Anne Rockwell
Roberto Clemente: Pride of the Pittsburgh Pirates	Jonah Winter
Shattered: Stories of Children and War	Jennifer Armstrong, ed.
Sports Stories	Alan Durant, ed.
The Village That Vanished	Ann Grifalconi
What If...? Amazing Stories	Monica Hughes, ed.
Wolves	Seymour Simon
The Wretched Stone	Chris Van Allsburg

Grade 8

the composition	Antonio Skármeta
The Giver	Lois Lowry
Immigrant Kids	Russell Freedman
In the Land of the Lawn Weenies	David Lubar
Life in the Polar Lands	Monica Byles
Nellie Bly: A Name to Be Reckoned With	Stephen Krensky
The People Could Fly	Virginia Hamilton
Satchel Paige	Lesa Cline-Ransome
Sharks	Seymour Simon
She Dared: True Stories of Heroines, Scoundrels, and Renegades	Ed Butts
When I Was Your Age: Original Stories About Growing Up, Volume One	Amy Ehrlich, ed.

Bibliography

Anderson, Richard C., Elfrieda H. Hiebert, Judith A. Scott, and Ian A. G. Wilkinson. *Becoming a Nation of Readers: The Report of the Commission on Reading*. Washington, DC: The National Institute of Education, 1985.

Anderson, Richard C., and P. David Pearson. "A Schema-Theoretic View of Basic Process in Reading Comprehension." In *Handbook of Reading Research*, P. David Pearson (ed.). New York: Longman, 1984.

Armbruster, Bonnie B., Fred Lehr, and Jean Osborn. *Put Reading First: The Research Building Blocks for Teaching Children to Read*. Jessup, MD: National Institute for Literacy, 2001.

Asher, James. "The Strategy of Total Physical Response: An Application to Learning Russian." *International Review of Applied Linguistics* 3 (1965): 291–300.

———. "Children's First Language as a Model for Second Language Learning." *Modern Language Journal* 56 (1972): 133–139.

Beck, Isabel L., and Margaret G. McKeown. "Text Talk: Capturing the Benefits of Read-Aloud Experiences for Young Children." *The Reading Teacher* 55:1 (2001): 10–19.

Beck, Isabel L., Margaret G. McKeown, and Linda Kucan. *Bringing Words to Life: Robust Vocabulary Instruction*. New York: Guilford Press (2002).

Block, C. C., and M. Pressley. *Comprehension Instruction: Research-Based Best Practices*. New York: Guilford Press, 2001.

Calkins, Lucy M. *The Art of Teaching Reading*. New York: Addison-Wesley Longman, 2001.

Contestable, Julie W., Shaila Regan, Susie Alldredge, Carol Westrich, and Laurel Robertson. *Number Power: A Cooperative Approach to Mathematics and Social Development Grades K–6*. Oakland, CA: Developmental Studies Center, 1999.

Cummins, James. "The Role of Primary Language Development in Promoting Educational Success for Language Minority Students." In *Schooling and Language Minority Students: A Theoretical Framework*. Los Angeles, CA: California State University, Evaluation, Dissemination, and Assessment Center, 1981.

Cunningham, Anne E., and Keith E. Stanovich. "What Reading Does for the Mind." *American Educator* Spring/Summer (1998): 8–15.

Developmental Studies Center. *Blueprints for a Collaborative Classroom*. Oakland, CA: Developmental Studies Center, 1997.

———. *Ways We Want Our Class to Be*. Oakland, CA: Developmental Studies Center, 1996.

DeVries, Rheta, and Betty Zan. *Moral Classrooms, Moral Children*. New York: Teachers' College Press, 1994.

Dewey, J. *Democracy and Education*. New York: Macmillan, 1916.

Bibliography

Farstrup, Alan E., and S. Jay Samuels. *What Research Has to Say About Reading Instruction*. 3rd Ed. Newark, DE: International Reading Association, 2002.

Fielding, Linda G., and P. David Pearson. "Reading Comprehension: What Works." *Educational Leadership* 51:5 (1994): 1–11.

Fountas, Irene C. and Gay Su Pinnell. *Leveled Books, K–8: Matching Texts to Readers for Effective Teaching*. Portsmouth, NH: Heinemann, 2006.

———. *Leveled Books for Readers Grade 3–6*. Portsmouth, NH: Heinemann, 2002.

———. *Matching Books to Readers: Using Leveled Books in Guided Reading, K–3*. Portsmouth, NH: Heinemann, 1999.

Gambrell, Linda B., Lesley Mandel Morrow, Susan B. Neuman, and Michael Pressley, eds. *Best Practices in Literacy Instruction*. New York: Guilford Press, 1999.

Hakuta, Kenji, Yoko Goto Butler, and Daria Witt. *How Long Does It Take English Learners to Attain Proficiency?* Santa Barbara, CA: University of California, Linguistic Minority Research Institute, 2000.

Harvey, Stephanie. *Nonfiction Matters: Reading, Writing, and Research in Grades 3–8*. York, ME: Stenhouse Publishers, 1998.

Harvey, Stephanie, and Anne Goudvis. *Strategies That Work: Teaching Comprehension to Enhance Understanding*. York, ME: Stenhouse Publishers, 2000.

Harvey, Stephanie, Sheila McAuliffe, Laura Benson, Wendy Cameron, Sue Kempton, Pat Lusche, Debbie Miller, Joan Schroeder, and Julie Weaver. "Teacher-Researchers Study the Process of Synthesizing in Six Primary Classrooms." *Language Arts* 73 (1996): 564–574.

Herrell, Adrienne L. and Michael L. Jordan. *Fifty Strategies for Teaching English Language Learners*. Upper Saddle River, NJ: Merrill, 2000.

International Reading Association. "What Is Evidence-Based Reading Instruction? A Position Statement of the International Reading Association." Newark, DE: International Reading Association, 2002.

Johnson, David W., Roger T. Johnson, and Edythe Johnson Holubec. *The New Circles of Learning: Cooperation in the Classroom*. Alexandria, VA: Association for Supervision and Curriculum Development, 1994.

Kagan, Spencer. *Cooperative Learning*. San Juan Capistrano, CA: Resources of Teachers, 1992.

Kamil, Michael L., Peter B. Mosenthal, P. David Pearson, and Rebecca Barr, eds. *Handbook of Reading Research, Volume III*. Mahwah, NJ: Lawrence Erlbaum Associates, 2000.

Keene, Ellin O., and Susan Zimmermann. *Mosaic of Thought: Teaching Comprehension in a Reader's Workshop*. Portsmouth, NH: Heinemann, 1997.

Kohlberg, Lawrence. *The Psychology of Moral Development*. New York: Harper and Row, 1984.

Kohn, Alfie. *Beyond Discipline: From Compliance to Community*. Association for Supervision and Curriculum Development, 1996.

———. *Punished by Rewards: The Trouble with Gold Stars, Incentive Plans, A's, Praise, and Other Bribes*. New York: Houghton Mifflin Company, 1999.

Krashen, Stephen D. *Principles and Practice in Second Language Acquisition*. New York: Prentice-Hall, 1982.

Moss, Barbara. "Making a Case and a Place for Effective Content Area Literacy Instruction in the Elementary Grades." *The Reading Teacher* 59:1 (2005): 46–55.

NEA Task Force on Reading. *Report of the NEA Task Force on Reading 2000*.

Neufeld, Paul. "Comprehension Instruction in Content Area Classes." *The Reading Teacher* 59:4 (2005): 302–312.

Nucci, Larry P., ed. *Moral Development and Character Education: A Dialogue*. Berkeley, CA: McCutchan Publishing Corporation, 1989.

Optiz, Michael F., ed. *Literacy Instruction for Culturally and Linguistically Diverse Students*. Newark, DE: International Reading Association, 1998.

Pearson, P. David, J. A. Dole, G. G. Duffy, and L. R. Roehler. "Developing Expertise in Reading Comprehension: What Should Be Taught and How Should It Be Taught?" In *What Research Has to Say to the Teacher of Reading*, J. Farstup and S. J. Samuels (eds.). Newark, DE: International Reading Association, 1992.

Piaget, Jean. *The Child's Conception of the World*. Trans. Joan and Andrew Tomlinson. Lanham, MD: Littlefield Adams, 1969.

———. *The Moral Judgment of the Child*. Trans. Marjorie Gabain. New York: The Free Press, 1965.

Pressley, Michael. *Effective Beginning Reading Instruction: The Rest of the Story from Research*. National Education Association, 2002.

———. *Reading Instruction That Works*. New York: Guilford Press, 1998.

Pressley, Michael, Janice Almasi, Ted Schuder, Janet Bergman, Sheri Hite, Pamela B. El-Dinary, and Rachel Brown. "Transactional Instruction of Comprehension Strategies: The Montgomery County, Maryland, SAIL Program." *Reading and Writing Quarterly: Overcoming Learning Difficulties* 10 (1994): 5–19.

Routman, Regie. *Reading Essentials: The Specifics You Need to Teach Reading Well*. Portsmouth, NH: Heinemann, 2003.

Serafini, Frank. *The Reading Workshop: Creating Space for Readers*. Portsmouth, NH: Heinemann, 2001.

Soalt, Jennifer. "Bringing Together Fictional and Informational Texts to Improve Comprehension." *The Reading Teacher* 58:7 (2005): 680–683.

Taylor, Barbara M., Michael Pressley, and P. David Pearson. *Research-Supported Characteristics of Teachers and Schools That Promote Reading Achievement*. National Education Association, 2002.

Trelease, Jim. *The Read-Aloud Handbook*. New York: Penguin Books, 1995.

Weaver, Brenda M. *Leveling Books K–6: Matching Readers to Text*. Newark, DE: International Reading Association, 2000.

Williams, Joan A. "Classroom Conversations: Opportunities to Learn for ESL Students in Mainstream Classrooms." *The Reading Teacher* 54:8 (2001): 750–757.

Blackline Masters

Dear Parent or Guardian,

Our class just finished the sixth unit of the *Making Meaning*® program. During this unit, the students continued to *make inferences* about fiction and nonfiction stories by using clues to figure out things that aren't stated directly in the text. They also practiced asking "why" questions during and after reading to explore causes and effects. Socially, they practiced giving reasons for their opinions and discussing their classmates' opinions respectfully.

You can support your child at home by previewing books together before you read. Read the title and look at the cover illustration, read any information on the back cover, and leaf through the pages. Discuss questions such as:

- (Before reading nonfiction texts, ask:) What do you already know about this topic?

- (Before reading fiction stories, ask:) What do you think might happen in this story? Why do you think that?

- (Before reading fiction stories, ask:) What are you wondering about the story?

You can also help your child understand stories more deeply by stopping every so often while reading fiction aloud to discuss questions such as:

- What do you know so far about this character? What did you read that tells you that?

- How is this character feeling? Why is the character feeling that way?

- What problem or conflict does the main character face? How do you think that problem will be solved?

- What happens at the end of the story? Why does that happen?

I hope you and your child continue to enjoy reading together!

Sincerely,

Apreciado padre de familia o guardián;

Nuestra clase acaba de finalizar la sexta unidad del programa "*Making Meaning.*®" Durante esta unidad los estudiantes continuaron *haciendo deducciones* acerca de las historias de ficción y no ficción al utilizar pistas para poder darse cuenta de cosas que no están directamente descritas en el texto. Los estudiantes también practicaron el hacer la pregunta "por qué", durante y después de la lectura para explorar causas y efectos. Socialmente, ellos practicaron el dar razones por sus opiniones y el hablar respetuosamente acerca de las opiniones de sus compañeros.

En casa usted puede apoyar la lectura de su niño al ver juntos de antemano el libro que van a leer. Lea el título y mire la ilustración de la portada, lea la información en la contra portada si la hay y déle un vistazo a las páginas. Hablen acerca de preguntas como:

- (Antes de leer textos de no ficción haga preguntas como:) ¿Qué sabes del tema?

- (Antes de leer historias de ficción haga preguntas como:) ¿Qué crees que puede pasar en esta historia? ¿Qué te hace pensar eso?

- (Antes de leer historias de ficción pregúntele:) ¿Qué preguntas tienes acerca de la historia?

También, cuando estén leyendo ficción en voz alta, usted le puede ayudar a su niño a entender las historias más a fondo al parar de vez en cuando para hacer preguntas como:

- Hasta ahora, ¿qué sabemos acerca de este personaje? ¿Qué leíste que te deja saber eso?

- ¿Cómo se siente este personaje? ¿Por qué se está sintiendo así?

- ¿Cuál es el problema que enfrenta el personaje principal de la historia? ¿Cómo crees que ese problema se resolverá?

- ¿Qué pasa al final de la historia? ¿Por qué pasa eso?

Espero que continúen disfrutando el tiempo que comparten leyendo juntos.

Sinceramente,

Dear Parent or Guardian,

Our class just finished the seventh unit of the *Making Meaning*® program. During this unit, the students heard and read nonfiction books, articles, and functional texts such as instructions, charts, and maps.

One of the comprehension strategies the students have been learning this year is recognizing how texts are structured. When they read fiction, they discussed the plot and setting of the story. During Unit 7 they discussed how articles and nonfiction books are structured or organized. *Analyzing text structure* or understanding how texts are organized can help readers make sense of what they are reading.

Articles are often organized to inform from one point of view or by discussing the pros and cons of a subject. Nonfiction books often use structures such as compare and contrast or cause and effect to organize information. During Unit 7 the students were introduced to these concepts. They will learn more about how nonfiction is structured as they go through middle school and high school. Right now they are just recognizing that fiction and nonfiction are structured differently.

You can support your child's reading life at home by reading nonfiction articles and books aloud to your child, or by encouraging your child to read independently and then talk about what he or she read.

Before reading nonfiction texts ask your child questions such as:

- What do you think you know about [extreme sports in the Olympics]?

- What questions do you have about [life in the Arctic Circle]?

If your child is reading a nonfiction book, ask your child to look at the table of contents and think about what information readers might learn from the book. If your child is reading an article, discuss what the article might be about, by reading the section headings and skimming the text.

After reading ask your child questions such as:

- What information did you learn about [extreme sports in the Olympics]?

- What information surprised you?

- What do you notice about how the [article] was organized?

I hope you and your child continue to enjoy reading together. Happy reading!

Sincerely,

Apreciado padre de familia o guardián;

Nuestra clase acaba de finalizar la séptima unidad del programa "*Making Meaning.*®" Durante esta unidad los estudiantes escucharon y leyeron libros y artículos del género de no ficción y textos funcionales como mapas y cuadros.

Una de las destrezas de comprensión que los estudiantes han estado aprendiendo este año es el reconocer la estructura que tienen los textos. Cuando los estudiantes leen ficción, ellos hablan acerca de la trama y del ambiente en que se desarrolla la historia. Durante la séptima unidad, ellos hablaron acerca de como los libros y artículos de no ficción están organizados o estructurados. *El analizar la estructura de un texto* o el comprender la organización de un texto puede ayudar a que lo que el lector está leyendo tenga sentido.

Muchas veces los artículos están organizados para informar desde un punto de vista o para discutir los puntos a favor o en contra de un tema. Los libros de no ficción muchas veces utilizan estructuras como la de comparación y contraste o la de causa y efecto para organizar la información. Durante la séptima unidad se le presentaron estos conceptos a los estudiantes. Ellos aprenderán más a fondo como el género de no ficción está estructurado cuando cursen los grados medios y de la secundaria. Ahora ellos están solamente reconociendo que los géneros de ficción y de no ficción tienen distintas estructuras.

Usted puede apoyar a la lectura que su niño hace en la casa al leerle en voz alta libros y artículos del género de no ficción, o al alentar a su niño a que lea por si solo y luego le hable acerca de lo que leyó.

Antes de leer textos de no ficción, hágale preguntas a su niño como:

- ¿Qué piensas acerca de (los deportes extremos en las olimpiadas)?

- ¿Qué preguntas tienes acerca de (la vida en el círculo polar ártico)?

Si su niño está leyendo un libro de no ficción, haga que lea la lista del contenido y que haga conjeturas acerca de la información que un lector pudiera obtener del libro. Si su niño está leyendo un artículo, haga que lo lea por encima y que lea los encabezamientos de las secciones para que le deje saber de que puede tratarse el artículo.

Después de haber leído hágale a su niño preguntas como:

- ¿Qué información aprendiste acerca de (los deportes extremos en las olimpiadas)?

- ¿Qué información te sorprendió?

- ¿Qué notaste acerca de la manera en que (el articulo) estaba organizado?

Espero que continúen disfrutando de la lectura que comparten juntos. ¡Feliz lectura!

Sinceramente,

 Dear Parent or Guardian,

Our class just finished the eighth unit of the *Making Meaning*® program. In this unit, the students explored important ideas in nonfiction. They identified what they felt were the important and supporting ideas in books and supported their opinions with evidence from the text. They also practiced putting important ideas together to build concise summaries. *Determining important ideas* and *summarizing* are both powerful strategies for helping readers understand and communicate what they read. Socially, the students developed the group skills of giving reasons for their opinions, discussing their opinions respectfully, and reaching agreement.

You can support your child's reading life at home. While reading aloud, consider stopping to discuss questions with your child such as:

• What is most important to understand or remember in the part I just read? Why do you think that?

After reading, you can help your child practice summarizing by asking questions such as:

• What are some important ideas that you remember from our reading today?

• If you were to tell someone in a couple of sentences what this book is about, what would you say?

I hope you and your child enjoy your reading conversations!

Sincerely,

Apreciado padre de familia o guardián;

Nuestra clase acaba de finalizar la octava unidad del programa "*Making Meaning.®*" Durante esta unidad los estudiantes exploraron ideas importantes en el género de no ficción. Ellos identificaron lo que creían que eran las ideas importantes de los libros y apoyaron sus opiniones con muestras del texto. Ellos también practicaron el juntar las ideas importantes para crear un resumen conciso. *El determinar ideas importantes* y *el resumir* son estrategias muy poderosas que ayudan al lector a entender y comunicar lo que leyó. Socialmente los estudiantes desarrollaron las destrezas de grupo de poder dar razones del porqué tuvieron una opinión y poder discutir sus opiniones en una manera respetuosa y llegar a un acuerdo.

Mientras le lee en voz alta a su niño, considere parar para hablar acerca de preguntas como:

- ¿Qué es lo más importante de entender o recordar en la parte que te acabo de leer? ¿Por qué crees eso?

Después de leer, usted le puede ayudar a su niño a que practique resumir, al hacer preguntas como:

- ¿Cuáles son algunas de las ideas importantes que recuerdas de la lectura que hicimos hoy?

- Si le fueras a decir a alguien en un par de frases de lo que se trata este libro, ¿qué le dirías?

¡Espero que usted y su niño disfruten de sus conversaciones acerca de la lectura!

Sinceramente,

 Dear Parent or Guardian,

We have come to the end of our school year and the end of the *Making Meaning*® grade 4 reading comprehension program. The children have shown great enthusiasm for the variety of texts we read aloud and the conversations we had about reading. They eagerly explored a number of reading comprehension strategies, including: questioning, recognizing text features, making inferences, determining important ideas, analyzing text structure, and summarizing. The use of these comprehension strategies strengthened the children's reading comprehension skills and should continue to be a source of support for them for years to come.

In the last unit of the *Making Meaning* program, the students used summaries they wrote in the previous unit to help them make summer reading recommendations to their classmates. They reflected on their growth as readers and as members of a reading community and continued to develop the group skills of giving reasons for their opinions and discussing their opinions respectfully.

Summer is a great time for trips to the library and quiet moments curled up with a good book. Your child made a list of books he or she would like to read this summer. Please help your child find the books on the list and encourage him or her to read the books and discuss them with friends. Of course, your child might want to add new books to the list as the summer progresses. Every so often, you might want to read some of the books aloud to your child and discuss their meaning together. Throughout the summer, encourage reading for enjoyment.

Thank you for helping to make the home-school connection successful. Your participation was essential. I hope along the way you and your child enjoyed the reading and the conversations about books.

Have a great summer!

Sincerely,

Apreciado padre de familia o guardián;

Hemos llegado al final del año escolar y al final del programa de comprensión de lectura para el cuarto grado de "*Making Meaning.*®" Los niños han mostrado mucho entusiasmo por la variedad de textos que leímos en voz alta y por las conversaciones que tuvimos acerca de lectura. Ellos exploraron afanosamente un número de estrategias de comprensión de lectura, incluyendo: el visualizar, el hacer preguntas, el explorar los aspectos del texto, el hacer deducciones, el determinar ideas importantes, el analizar la estructura de un texto y el resumir. El uso de estas estrategias de comprensión fortalece las destrezas de comprensión de lectura que los niños tienen y continuará siendo una fuente de apoyo para ellos por muchos años mas.

En la última unidad del programa "*Making Meaning,*" los estudiantes utilizaron los resúmenes que escribieron en la unidad anterior para dar recomendaciones a sus compañeros para la lectura durante el verano. Ellos también se pusieron a reflexionar sobre el desarrollo que han tenido como lectores y como miembros de la comunidad de lectores y continuaron las destrezas de grupo al dar las razones por sus opiniones y al discutir estas opiniones en una manera respetuosa.

El verano es un gran momento para hacer viajes a la biblioteca y para pasar ratos sentado en silencio con un buen libro. Su niño hizo una lista de los libros que le gustaría leer este verano. Por favor ayúdelo a encontrar los libros que tiene en la lista y aliéntelo a que los lea y a que hable acerca de ellos con sus amigos. Claro, es posible que a medida que progrese el verano su niño quiera añadir otros libros a la lista. De vez en cuando, tal vez usted quiera leerle en voz alta algunos de los libros a su niño y hablar acerca del significado. Durante todo el verano, aliente a su niño a que lea para divertirse.

Le agradezco su ayuda en hacer que la conexión de la casa con la escuela fuera un éxito. Su participación fue esencial. Espero que durante el proceso usted y su niño hayan disfrutado de la lectura y las conversaciones acerca de los libros.

¡Espero que tengan un buen verano!

Sinceramente,

Amelia found an old metal box that somebody had tossed into the trash. It was dented and rusty, but Amelia didn't care. That box was the answer to her problem.

She set to work at once, filling it with "Amelia-things." First she put in the hair ribbon her mother had made for her one Christmas; next came the name tag Mrs. Ramos had given her; then a photograph of her whole family taken at her last birthday; and after that the picture she'd drawn in class with the bright red star on it.

Finally, she took out a sheet of paper and drew a map of the accidental road, from the highway to the very old tree. In her best lettering, she wrote *Amelia Road* on the path. Then she folded the map and put it into her box.

When all the apples were finally picked, Amelia's family and the other workers had to get ready to move again. Amelia made one more trip down the accidental road, this time with her treasure box.

continues

She dug a hole near the old tree, and gently placed the box inside and covered it over with dirt. Then she set a rock on top, so nobody would notice the freshly turned ground.

When Amelia finished, she took a step back and looked at the tree. Finally, here was a place where she belonged, a place where she could come back to.

Excerpt from *Amelia's Road* by Linda Jacobs Altman. Text copyright © 1993 by Linda Jacobs Altman. Permission arranged with Lee & Low Books Inc., New York, NY 10016.

Once when Peppe got home, Papa was watching from the window. "You'll belong to the streets!" he shouted.

Peppe sat on the stoop way past his bedtime, then cried himself to sleep when no one would hear. In the morning his shoulders drooped, just a little.

"Hey, Peppe, don't look so sad!" Fat Mary teased, and Peppe tried not to.

But Papa stayed angry. "You'll never amount to anything," he grumbled.

Giulia took Peppe's hand in hers. "Don't worry about it," she told him.

"Peppe, look up when you walk!" Nicolina reminded him as he left for work.

Peppe tried, but when he came home, Papa turned away. "I don't even want to look at you, you make me so ashamed," he said.

"You never play with me anymore, Peppe," said Assunta.

continues

Excerpt from *Peppe the Lamplighter* by Elisa Bartone. Text copyright © 1993 by Elisa Bartone. Illustrations copyright © 1993 by Ted Lewin. Used by permission of HarperCollins Publishers.

Peppe just lowered his eyes and didn't answer. And from then on he rushed through the lighting of the lamps, sometimes forgetting which was which.

"It's a stupid job," he said to himself. And he began to imagine that the people of the neighborhood laughed behind his back.

Soon he would not show his face outside the tenement… and one night, the streets of Little Italy were dark. "Where is Peppe the Lamplighter?" said the people to one another.

Inspectors from the island boarded the ships at anchor to check the passengers. Wealthy passengers traveling first class were usually allowed to leave the ship right away. The inspectors looked for signs of contagious disease among the others. Those who were ill sometimes stayed aboard the ship or were sent to other islands to recover. Those who seemed healthy were taken to Ellis Island.

––––––––––

First, the immigrants were given a quick examination by doctors. Those with health problems were marked with colored chalk. The doctors would examine these persons more closely. Some people were kept on the island for observation. After 1911, Ellis Island had its own hospital to treat the sick.

Sometimes immigrants had permanent health problems that would make it hard for them to work. This often meant that they would be sent back to their native country. But most of the new arrivals passed inspection and moved on to the next step.

continues

Now, the immigrants were asked a long list of questions. Inspectors asked their names, where they were from, and how much money they had. Since most of the immigrants did not speak English, they needed help in understanding and answering the questions. Translators did what they could to help the inspectors and newcomers understand one another.

Even though it was difficult, most managed somehow to answer all the questions. Mothers often spoke for children who might be too little or too scared to speak. The immigrants had to show that they would work hard and stay out of trouble. Usually the ordeal was over within the day. When they received their entry cards, at last, the immigrants could officially enter their new country.

During the years between 1850 and 1860, Harriet worked as a cook, dish washer, and cleaning woman. She used much of the money she earned to make nineteen trips south to lead about three hundred slaves to freedom. Many of them were her own relatives.

Harriet took them from one safe house to the next. Sometimes she led them as far as Canada. She was a "conductor" on the Underground Railroad.

At times Harriet disguised herself as a weak old woman or as a man. She used songs as a secret code. When the runaways were hiding and it was safe to come out, she sang a joyful song, "Hail, oh hail ye happy spirits." The runaway slaves always recognized Harriet's deep, husky voice.

Once slaves began their journey north with Harriet, she wouldn't let them turn back. When slaves were too scared to go on, Harriet pointed a gun at their heads and said, "You'll go on, or you'll die."

Years later Harriet said proudly, "I never ran my train off the track. I never lost a passenger."

continues

Harriet was called "Moses" because she led her people out of slavery. There was a huge reward waiting for anyone who caught her, but no one ever did.

An End to Indecision

Many young people worry about how they look: "Will people judge me by what I'm wearing?" "Is green 'in' or 'out' this season?" Wearing a uniform helps you to feel more confident because everyone else at school will be wearing the same outfit. Nobody will judge you by what clothing you wear.

Because you don't need to decide what to wear, a uniform also helps you to save time in the morning. There is another advantage to wearing a uniform: it will help you to save money, because usually, you'll only need to buy one or two at the start of the year—and there's no pressure to wear costly designer labels to school.

CITY OF LAWRENCE STREET MAP

Index

Reference/Location on Map
Alamo Park C2
Centennial Dr D1–D4
Cherry Tree Ln D1
City Hall A2
City Park B1
Columbus Ave A3
Dayton St............ A4–C4
East Jackson St....... A1–A4
Glenview Dr A2–D2
Harmony Rd C1–C4
Jefferson St A3
Lambert Science Museum D4
Lawrence Elementary D2
Lawrence Shopping Center... C4
Liberty Boulevard........ A1–C4
Mayflower St.......... D3
McCabe Alley D2
North Juniper St C1–C4
Oak Terrace Playground A1
Ohio Rd............. B1–B4
Police Station A3
President Ave A2–D2
Spring Park B3
St. Francis Hospital A4
Texas Ave D4
Washington Pl A1

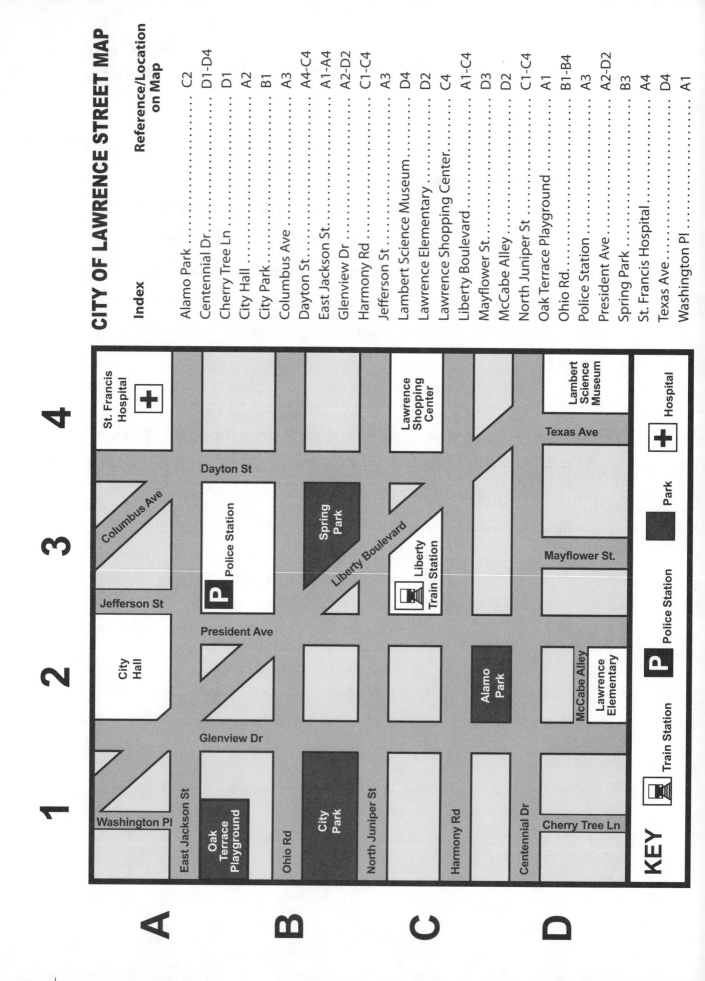

KEY

🚉 Train Station   🅿 Police Station   ⬛ Park   ✚ Hospital

It is 1927, and his name is Charles Lindbergh.

Later they will call him the Lone Eagle.

Later they will call him Lucky Lindy.

But not now.

Now it is May 20, 1927, and he is standing in the still-dark dawn.

He watches rain drizzle down on the airfield. And on his small airplane.

The airplane has a name painted on its side: *Spirit of St. Louis.*

Lindbergh is nearly as tall as the plane itself.

And yet—he is about to attempt what no one has done before:

To fly—without a stop—from New York to Paris, France.

Over 3,600 miles away.

Across the Atlantic Ocean.

Alone.

From above, all Lindbergh sees are many, many small lights.

But now he must concentrate on just one thing: "the sod coming up to meet me."

Closer, closer, closer:

The plane touches the ground.

It bounces, rolls, hugs the solid earth.

It is 10:22, Paris time. The flight has taken thirty-three and a half hours.

Thousands of people are running toward the plane.

For a moment, Lindbergh is dazed.

It seems to him as if he were "drowning in a great sea."

People surround the plane, cheering.

But Lindbergh can hardly hear them.

His ears seem to have been deafened by the hours of roaring engine.

continues

Crowds pull him out of the cockpit.

Men and women are calling his name, over and over.

They carry him on their shoulders.

Others begin to tear pieces of the plane.

More than anything else, Lindbergh wants to save the Spirit of St. Louis.

His first words are a question: "Are there any mechanics here?"

But no one speaks English.

Finally, two French aviators arrive to help him.

Policemen guard the plane.

The aviators take Lindbergh away from the still-cheering crowd.

In the airfield's hangar, he tells the story of his flight to the other pilots:

The cramped cockpit, the aloneness, the long, long night.

continues

Excerpt 2 *(continued)*
from *Flight*

Meanwhile, unknown to Lindbergh, newspaper headlines all over the world are beginning to blazon the news:

AMERICAN HERO SAFE IN PARIS!

In 1937 she planned to fly around the world. When she was told the flight was dangerous, Amelia said, "I've wanted to do this flight for a long time…If I should pop off, it will be doing the thing I've always wanted to do."

On June 1, 1937, Amelia Earhart and her navigator, Fred Noonan, began the trip. They flew from Miami, Florida, to San Juan, Puerto Rico. They flew to South America, then to Africa, India, Burma, Thailand, Singapore, Indonesia, Australia, and New Guinea. They had gone more than three fourths around the world. On July 2 they took off from Lae, New Guinea, for Howland Island, a tiny island in the vast Pacific Ocean.

They never made it.

Amelia Earhart and Fred Noonan disappeared somewhere in the Pacific Ocean. There was an enormous search, but they were never found.

Before she was lost, Amelia wrote to her husband, "I am quite aware of the hazards…I want to do it. Women must try to do things as men have tried. When they fail, their failures must be but a challenge to others."

continues

Amelia Earhart was America's "First Lady of the Air." She was a courageous flyer, a pioneer. She risked her life to prove that in the air, and elsewhere, women were up to the challenge. She certainly was.

Summary
A Picture Book of Amelia Earhart by David A. Adler

This book tells the life story of the famous pilot Amelia Earhart. Amelia was born in Kansas in 1897. She wasn't like other girls. She played sports, made her own roller coaster, and wore pants. Amelia wasn't interested in airplanes when she was little, but that changed when she grew up. In 1920, she went for her first airplane ride and decided she wanted to fly. In 1932, she became the first woman to fly alone across the Atlantic Ocean. Amelia tried to fly around the world in 1937, but her plane disappeared in the Pacific Ocean. She was never found. Today, she is remembered for her courage and for proving that women can meet the same challenges as men.

Excerpt
from *A Picture Book of Rosa Parks* by David A. Adler

Section 1

Twelve years later, on Thursday December 1, 1955, Rosa Parks met James Blake again. Rosa was coming home from her work as a tailor's assistant at a Montgomery department store. She got on the Cleveland Avenue bus and took a seat in the middle section. African Americans were allowed to sit in the back and in the middle section, too, as long as no white passenger was left standing.

Section 2

At the next stop, some white passengers got on, and because the bus was crowded, moved to the middle section, where Rosa was sitting. The driver told the four African American passengers in Rosa's row to get up. Three of them did, but not Rosa Parks. She had paid the same fare as the white passengers. She knew it was the law in Montgomery that she give up her seat, but she also knew the law was unfair. James Blake called the police, and Rosa Parks was arrested.

Excerpt

from *A Picture Book of Rosa Parks* by David A. Adler

Section 3

On Monday, December 5, Rosa went to the local court and was found guilty of breaking the segregation laws. She was fined ten dollars plus court costs. Rosa and her lawyers appealed to a higher court.

Section 4

Beginning on December 5, to protest the arrest of Rosa Parks, African Americans in Montgomery refused to ride on public buses. They found other ways to get to work. Many walked, some as far as twelve miles.

Section 5

The bus boycott was led by Dr. Martin Luther King, Jr., the new minister at the Dexter Avenue Baptist Church. On Monday evening, December 5, he spoke to a large crowd. He explained the reason for the boycott. "There comes a time," he said, "that people get tired. We are here this evening to say to those who have mistreated us so long, that we are tired—tired of being segregated and humiliated, tired of being kicked about by the brutal feet of oppression."

Section 6

The boycott lasted more than a year. During that time almost no African Americans rode a public bus in Montgomery, Alabama.

Rosa Parks, Dr. King, and many others were arrested. Homes of boycott leaders were bombed.

On November 13, 1956, the United States Supreme Court ruled that segregation on public buses was against the law. On December 21, after the court order reached Montgomery, the boycott ended. News reporters came to talk to Rosa and to photograph her sitting on the bus again.

Making Meaning® Reorder Information
SECOND EDITION

Kindergarten

Complete Classroom Package — MM2-CPK

Contents: Teacher's Manual, Orientation Handbook and DVDs, and 27 trade books

Available separately:

Classroom materials without trade books	MM2-TPK
Teacher's Manual	MM2-TMK
Trade book set (27 books)	MM2-TBSK

Grade 1

Complete Classroom Package — MM2-CP1

Contents: Teacher's Manual, Orientation Handbook and DVDs, Assessment Resource Book, and 28 trade books

Available separately:

Classroom materials without trade books	MM2-TP1
Teacher's Manual	MM2-TM1
Assessment Resource Book	MM2-AB1
Trade book set (28 books)	MM2-TBS1

Grade 2

Complete Classroom Package — MM2-CP2

Contents: Teacher's Manual, Orientation Handbook and DVDs, class set (25 Student Response Books, Assessment Resource Book), and 29 trade books

Available separately:

Classroom materials without trade books	MM2-TP2
Teacher's Manual	MM2-TM2
Replacement class set	MM2-RCS2
CD-ROM Grade 2 Reproducible Materials	MM2-CDR2
Trade book set (29 books)	MM2-TBS2

Grade 3

Complete Classroom Package — MM2-CP3

Contents: Teacher's Manual (2 volumes), Orientation Handbook and DVDs, class set (25 Student Response Books, Assessment Resource Book), and 26 trade books

Available separately:

Classroom materials without trade books	MM2-TP3
Teacher's Manual, vol. 1	MM2-TM3-V1
Teacher's Manual, vol. 2	MM2-TM3-V2
Replacement class set	MM2-RCS3
CD-ROM Grade 3 Reproducible Materials	MM2-CDR3
Trade book set (26 books)	MM2-TBS3

Grade 4

Complete Classroom Package — MM2-CP4

Contents: Teacher's Manual (2 volumes), Orientation Handbook and DVDs, class set (30 Student Response Books, Assessment Resource Book), and 24 trade books

Available separately:

Classroom materials without trade books	MM2-TP4
Teacher's Manual, vol. 1	MM2-TM4-V1
Teacher's Manual, vol. 2	MM2-TM4-V2
Replacement class set	MM2-RCS4
CD-ROM Grade 4 Reproducible Materials	MM2-CDR4
Trade book set (24 books)	MM2-TBS4

Grade 5

Complete Classroom Package — MM2-CP5

Contents: Teacher's Manual (2 volumes), Orientation Handbook and DVDs, class set (30 Student Response Books, Assessment Resource Book), and 19 trade books

Available separately:

Classroom materials without trade books	MM2-TP5
Teacher's Manual, vol. 1	MM2-TM5-V1
Teacher's Manual, vol. 2	MM2-TM5-V2
Replacement class set	MM2-RCS5
CD-ROM Grade 5 Reproducible Materials	MM2-CDR5
Trade book set (19 books)	MM2-TBS5

Grade 6

Complete Classroom Package — MM2-CP6

Contents: Teacher's Manual (2 volumes), Orientation Handbook and DVDs, class set (30 Student Response Books, Assessment Resource Book), and 18 trade books

Available separately:

Classroom materials without trade books	MM2-TP6
Teacher's Manual, vol. 1	MM2-TM6-V1
Teacher's Manual, vol. 2	MM2-TM6-V2
Replacement class set	MM2-RCS5
CD-ROM Grade 6 Reproducible Materials	MM2-CDR6
Trade book set (18 books)	MM2-TBS6

Ordering Information:
To order call 800.666.7270 * fax 510.842.0348
log on to devstu.org * e-mail pubs@devstu.org

Or Mail Your Order to:
Developmental Studies Center * Publications Department
2000 Embarcadero, Suite 305 * Oakland, CA 94606-5300

DEVELOPMENTAL STUDIES CENTER™